Healing Hands

The Life Story of Dr. Virendra and Nancy Henry

Medical Mission and Social Change in Tribal Central India

Healing Hands
The Life Story of Dr. Virendra and Nancy Henry

Gregg Brekke

Foreword by Dr. Johnny Oommen

SixView Studios
2016

First Printing: 2016

ISBN 978-1-365-04986-6

SixView Studios
Louisville, Kentucky
U.S.A.
www.sixview.com

Cover design by Mark Thomson

Additional copies available via Amazon.com or chmungeli.org

Contents

Introduction

Giants among humankind.

It's a hyperbole used to describe people of greatness. It is often overused in adoration of politicians, talented athletes, or with esteem for executives or business leaders.

Rarely is it applied to those who eagerly serve the poorest people in one of the most impoverished regions of our world.

The story that follows is a biographical telling of the lives of Dr. V. K. Henry and Nancy (Lott) Henry, who served as Christian medical mission personnel in India from 1960 until their forced retirement by tragic accident in 2009.

Some would call them saints, though they would brush away suggestions of such beautification. Others would call them great humanitarians, though such a label could not contain the scope and breadth of their work. Some would say they were extremely qualified medical professionals. Those who worked with and came to know them would protest that such a designation is only the beginning of their talent.

A Hindu friend of theirs told me he would "worship them as gods" – if only they would allow it.

Throughout this book they will be referred to by their common names – Viru and Nancy – unless referenced in a quote by another name. In our interview process Nancy most often referred to Viru as Papa, and he referred to her as Ma. I've attempted to retain their sense of tenderness toward one another when possible, while modifying references to one another in direct quotes to "Viru" or "Nancy" for the reader's benefit.

The methodology of writing these chapters included the process of transcribing, sorting, and editing over 60 hours of interviews conducted with Viru and Nancy in the Indian towns of Mungeli, Tilda, Khariar, and Bissamcuttack in May and June of 2013. With the exception of Mungeli – where we were able to meet in an air-conditioned room – the other interviews took place while traveling: in car rides to various locations where the Henrys had served, with staff at several hospitals, and on the train to and from Bissamcuttack.

I have, whenever possible, made exact and direct quote of what was recorded on video and transcribed. Still, there are many instances where a long-running response to a question has been combined with other responses, especially where subsequent questions continued the narrative or gave a slightly different version of the story. These extended responses or clarifying statements have been edited into the direct quotes for readability. I have also taken liberties in clarifying sentences where the intent was obviously implied or stated in previous or successive responses.

Due to complications from his stroke on 2 May 2009, Viru's speech was extremely slurred and he was often frustrated in trying to communicate with me. An avid storyteller, Viru's lengthy responses to questions are recorded, but are all too often unintelligible. I readily admit this was a shortcoming of my interview process and a hurdle Nancy and I attempted to work around by having her retell and rephrase many of Viru's responses.

Careful review of the transcripts reveals the places where Nancy interprets what Viru is communicating. In these cases, I have attributed the quote or story to Viru as it was my lack of verbal comprehension that necessitated Nancy's reframing of his response.

In each of these ways I have endeavored to present the direct voice of those quoted and not to alter their responses in any way, other than the above-mentioned combining of clarifying or continuing statements that completed the direct line of questioning.

It was indeed a gift for me to sit with these giants of medical mission. Their vision, innovation, faithfulness, and perseverance cannot be underestimated. As I grew to know them better it became clear that they could have pursued private practice – even in America or Europe – and they would have been wildly successful as a talented surgeon and midwife.

But they chose to stay in India and serve the needs of the rural poor, and to develop education and training opportunities for people who would have never dreamed of such possibilities. Indian through and through, they were missionaries to their own. Viru often bristled at the designation of missionary, but he was no stranger to bringing the Good News, even if that merely meant giving a student from a tribal region in India a "hand up" to pursue education or professional training in medicine.

As I finish this introduction, the Christian season of Lent is coming to a close and it is all too apparent that the Henrys embodied the Easter spirit in their lives and ministry. Over and over again they stepped in to seemingly impossible situations and provided Easter moments when, by human measures, all hope was lost. Were it not for their determination, hope, and faith, the Christian Mission Hospitals in Tilda, Bissamcuttack, Mungeli, and Diptipur might not exist. Were it not for their caring and love, a child born blind and their curious son might not have gone on to such great achievements, accompanied by their spouses.

It was a humbling experience to interview Viru and Nancy for six weeks in 2013, and to have the privilege of telling their story. Viru passed away before this book was completed, so I can only hope his light shines brightly in the pages that follow. He and Nancy have been an amazing gift to medical mission in India, to the thousands of patients they treated, to the hundreds of staff they mentored, to the international medical community, and to me personally.

What follows is a story of love, perseverance, and inspiration that should be shared around the world.

Gregg Brekke
Louisville, Kentucky, USA
March 2016

Acknowledgements

Any author knows the sum total of a book is more than the process of writing in and of itself.

I am foremost indebted to Viru and Nancy Henry for trusting me to share their stories and present them in a way that speaks to the importance of their work, their faithfulness to a calling, and love for the broader community in which they served. Weeks of interviewing, countless questions, laughter, and a few tears accompanied our time together. I am a better person for knowing them and grateful they shared these intimate moments with me.

Nancy was a careful reader of the final manuscript, providing extra details and minor corrections that undoubtedly have made the text that follows more accurate.

Landa Harris Simmons and the Rambo Committee, along with Viru and Nancy's son Anil, got the project off the ground and provided funding for travel, research, and writing. They have shown immense grace and patience throughout the various phases of the project. Their belief in the necessity of telling Nancy and Viru's story, along with their considerable contributions to the production of the book, made the project possible.

As a primary source, historian, documenter, and protégé of the Henrys, I couldn't have asked for a better foreword contributor and manuscript reviewer than Dr. Johnny Oommen. His previously written resources, along with interviews and newly composed materials – including an account of Viru's funeral – provide important insights throughout the book. His adoration for the Henrys is evident. His eagerness and joy as a collaborator has been an inspiration.

The Rev. Kelly Brill and a team from Avon Lake UCC in Ohio, U.S.A., made my first trip to visit the Henrys possible. Accompanied by the Rev. Brill, Nate and Lisa Taylor, Dave Witzigreuter, and the generosity of many church members, we were able to bring greetings upon the 50th anniversary of Nancy's commissioning by the church, seeing the many places she and Viru had ministered, along with a memorable tour of India's historical sites.

Laura Madden, who reported for me on Anil and Teresa Henry's work in Mungeli while I was editor of StillSpeaking Magazine, spent many hours copyediting and pointing out areas of the manuscript that needed clarification. She has been a great friend, critical editor, and encourager in telling this story, sharing a common love for the Henrys and their legacy of mission in India.

Brittany Hesson – master transcriptionist – came to the rescue after nearly all the completed transcripts from interviews with the Henrys were lost in a catastrophic hard drive failure. She delivered typed transcripts from all 60 hours of interviews in just six weeks, accelerating the book's completion by months. I especially appreciate her diligence in attempting to understand Viru's speech patterns and researching Hindi/Oriya name and word spellings.

The hospitality of the staff – doctors, nurses, administrators, and operations personnel – at the hospitals in Mungeli and Bissamcuttack made my stays comfortable and memorable. Being away from home for an extended period to research this book was made easier by their kindness, friendship, story telling, and merry making.

Finally, my wife Lindsay Ross-Hunt has been a full partner in the process of bringing this project to completion. Her encouragement, re-typing, proof reading, and "space-making" made possible the long night and weekend hours needed to work on the book.

Gregg Brekke
Louisville, Kentucky, USA
August 2016

Foreword

Christianity and Mission in India

by Dr. Johnny Oommen

The story of Nancy and Viru Henry begins in the 1930s, when the two main protagonists were born continents apart but with destinies intertwined: in Ohio, U.S.A. and Bilaspur, India.

A reader unfamiliar with the history of Christianity in India might wonder about the context that brought the two together. They may be surprised to know that the church in India is 2000 years old, possibly 1500 years older than Christianity in North America. A brief summary of the origins of Christianity in India from the first century CE – and the story of mission in the Chattisgarh-Orissa area where the Henry story culminates – is included as an Appendix that you may choose to read first if you like.

India is a country today of over 1.2 billion people and a paradox of development. It has both an enviable growing economy and situations of extreme poverty and hunger. According to the Indian government's census of 2011, 79.8 percent – or 966 million people – are of the Hindu religion; 14.23 percent are Muslims; and only 2.3 percent – roughly 28 million people – are Christians.

What role do Christianity and mission play in this context? What is the contribution of this 2.3 percent to the nation and society? Who are they? How did they get there?

The story is believed to begin with St. Thomas – one of the 12 disciples of Jesus – who lived, worked, and died in south India. The story is later narrated through the lives of many missionaries from Europe and America. And today it is an indigenous story of Indian Christians in a space that sometimes feels insecure and shrinking, and yet is part of the fabric of India.

What then is mission in their perspective?

Overseas missionaries to India traditionally pursued the three paths of preaching, teaching, and healing. The face of Christianity in India therefore was churches, schools, and hospitals. For the vast majority of Indians their first and sometimes only contact with a Christian was as a student in a mission school or college or a patient in a mission hospital. The small Christian community of India has made a disproportionately large contribution to health and education in the country.

But the story does not end there. What is less visible and yet palpable is the difference Christianity has made to the status and empowerment of women, and the emancipation and opportunities for the people of the most vulnerable communities in the caste hierarchy of India – the Dalits and the Adivasi peoples.

Disaggregated data shows that a far higher percentage of these most marginalized communities opted for Christianity, given the opportunity it offered for dignity and respect, through a God of love and justice. And while church structures have not always been loving and just or even fair from a caste or gender perspective, there is no denying the positive influence.

Similarly, long before the government or other groups championed the cause of the girl child or access to education for women, the Christian missionaries and schools had opened the door and moved the boundaries.

A fair indicator of this is found in the infant mortality rate, which is seen as a simple proxy indicator for quality of life and development, affected significantly by education of women and the status of the poor. According to the 2014 Sample Registration Survey of the Government of India, 39 out of 1,000 children born did not live to see their first birthday. But when you look at the statistics broken down by state it ranges from 10 to 52 per 1,000 live births. And there is a story hidden in those numbers. The states with the lowest infant mortality, indicating the best chance for a newborn baby, are also the states with significant Christian influence and population. Goa at 10, Manipur at 11, Kerala at 12, and Nagaland at 14 tell this story. And at the other end of the chart is the region where this biography of two brave and dedicated people is played out: Madhya Pradesh at 52,

Odisha at 49, and Chattisgarh at 43. The regions of the greatest health need.

India is changing, as are all societies. A country that was once seen as laid-back, spiritual, and passive is now resurgent, confident, and assertive – seeking a larger space at the table of international power. The change is both external and internal. Some now see expatriate missionaries and charity as irrelevant or even anti-Indian. What does this mean? The church in India is searching for it's own sense of mission; it's role in this changing context.

In 2008, the hospital community at Bissamcuttack in Odisha that Nancy and Viru Henry helped to build and grow found itself in an environment of fear and insecurity, with anti-Christian riots all around. The hospital was untouched; protected by the goodwill of people who had seen the quality of life and selfless, universal service that people like the Henrys had delivered for decades. But on reflection, the Christian Hospital described its position as the "Esther Paradox" – safe in the palace in a time of danger. Who knows, they asked themselves, if we were brought to a position like this for a time like this?

A year later, the Bissamcuttack staff hosted a gathering of Christian health professionals from other such mission hospitals in the state who echoed the Esther chorus. The ideas arrived at from three days of prayer, study, and meditation are worth putting down here:

1. Missio Dei: Mission is God's, not ours. God loves this world and is actively engaged and involved in working out the kingdom of God.
2. Our role is to listen to God's music and to dance to God's tune; to discern what God is doing for the poor, the vulnerable and the marginalized, and join in those efforts.
3. The role model is Jesus himself, who did not consider equality with God something to be grasped, but emptied himself, became a man, took on the nature of a servant, and was obedient even to death on the cross. That is our call: self-emptying, servant-hood, brokenness, Christ-likeness.
4. We are called to the ministry of healing. It is Jesus' ministry and we are co-workers with him. So let us, like Jesus, share the pain of our people. And by his stripes, we are healed.

The group called for a reorientation of the work of our Christian healthcare institutions towards this undergirding philosophy. How did a small, relatively unknown place like Bissamcuttack stumble across such deep theological insight? What was the milieu that enabled such ideas to germinate?

A big part of it is the culture of love and service – of gentle, unabrasive faith, and commitment to the poor – that Nancy and Viru Henry engendered by their personal example and life together.

So let's focus on the real story here. Of Nancy Jane Lott and Virendra Kumar Henry and what God has done through them in a true tale that is sometimes more improbable than fiction. And that is what they would want from this book – that their lives point beyond them, to the needs of people and to God who engineered the script of their lives.

Let us reflect on their story, thoughts and ideas, and yet also on the God behind their story – leading, enabling, sustaining.

May God bless the health work that continues in Mungeli and Tilda and Khariar and Bissamcuttack and other such outposts of the Kingdom of God through frail and fragile people who God chooses to use for a cause that is greater than all of us.

On behalf of all us fans and beneficiaries of the goodness of the Henry family, I want to express our immeasurable gratitude to Gregg Brekke for putting this book together with sensitivity and honesty. God bless!

Bissamcuttack, Odisha, India
August 2016

Chapter 1: A Midwestern Girl Goes to India

Every Christian missionary's story begins with a calling to save or to serve. In many cases, the missionary impulse combines these elements. But more importantly, every calling begins with a family and lifetime of formation that leads the missionary to become immersed in a culture or country to which they feel God has led them.

Nancy Henry was born Nancy Jane Lott on January 27, 1935 to Margaret Edith Lott (nee Greene) and Fred Wilbur Lott at St. Joseph's Hospital in Lorain, Ohio, U.S.A. She was the Lott's eighth child, conceived as a surprise baby for the family. Nancy's delivery was complicated by her breech and posterior positioning in utero – "upside down and backwards," as she says. Yet her 41-year-old mother endured the long labor to deliver Nancy into a family that included brother James Robert, the eldest Lott child who was 20 at the time of Nancy's birth, Fred W. Lott Jr., William (Bill) Howard, Elizabeth Louise (Betty Lou), John (Jack) Oliver, Charles (Chuck) Franklin and Margaret Ann (Peggy Ann, often called Peg) who was five and a half years older than Nancy.[1]

Nancy, the last in line, was to be lovingly called Pumpkin – shortened to Punk – by her parents and siblings.

Nancy's parents met in Urbana, in central Ohio near the state's capital, Columbus. Fred Lott was born in Selma, Ohio, and after he and Margaret married they returned to Fred's hometown for the first part of their marriage. Although Fred farmed, taught school, and was district superintendent of the school district, the income from these several jobs was inadequate to raise a family. Hearing a power company was building an enormous electrical plant in Avon Lake, on the shores of Lake Erie, Fred moved the family north, first working on the construction of the plant, and later in operations.

> "[My father] was a teacher; he was an educated person. He had his degree from Wittenberg College in Dayton, Ohio. He was a twin and his brother was there. They were identical.

1

Other people couldn't tell them apart. They used to fool me when I was a kid. I would go out of the room and they would switch places. I'd come in and run straight to my uncle. That was the big joke. They fooled their girlfriends and would switch them for the fun.

He was born in Selma, Ohio. He went to Dayton for his degree then came back. He was a schoolteacher and got married to my mother in Urbana, Ohio and brought her back. They started having children. There was a bit of a gap between the children. He was farming as well as teaching. He was even made the county superintendent of schools, but he still couldn't make enough money for his family.

He heard they were building the electric illuminating company in Avon Lake and they were looking for people to help build it. They were offering good wages so they left that place and moved to Avon Lake. They found a small cottage to live in and had more kids there. He was one of the laborers, an educated man who couldn't make a living. They made more wages there but more kids kept coming. We had these church people who befriended my family. They moved next to one of them and got a better house next to Mrs. Dunlap. They were very good neighbors and friends until they died of old age. Mrs. Drake, who was from a wealthy family, was also a dear friend.

Anyway, my father helped raise these kids. When the illuminating company was built, they gave him a job. He was a steam operator. It was higher than a laborer so he had some sophistication. They had to train him and gave him a license for that. He spent most of his life doing that and that's how he raised his family. Eventually, we moved into a bigger house on Lake Road. It was the big house on the corner of the road. I was born when they lived in that house and I was child number eight. From there, we moved over to Forest Hill Drive when I was six years old. That was a very good size house. A lot of the boys had gone out so we didn't have too many people in the house. We lived there until my mother died and my father moved out."

- Nancy

The Lott children all completed high school, through the 12th grade, at Avon Lake schools. Nancy's father was committed to community and social causes, serving on the school board and town council and at the Congregational Church in many capacities including volunteer janitor, elder, and moderator of the church council. Nancy's mother had been a nursery school teacher, women's league member, and choir director in her earlier years, and was devoted to her children. The Lott children grew up in, and found their spiritual home at, the Congregational Church on Lake Road in Avon Lake.

> "My father used his educational skills in the community. He was on the school board and became the chairman. He was on the council. He was very much involved in church activities. He and my mother were some of the pillars of the church. She taught the kindergarten in the nursery in the church. She was the choir director also. She was very musical, could play the piano and sing. We grew up in a strong Christian home."

> - Nancy

As Nancy entered grade school, her older brothers enlisted to serve in World War II. The three daughters stayed in the United States while Betty Lou's husband, Dick, also left for the war, leaving behind his wife and two-year-old son. Nancy remembers it as a challenging time as the young men followed the call to service, saying goodbye to their families to enter the war effort. Peg and Nancy remained students at Avon Lake throughout the war.

When Peg graduated, she worked as a dental assistant to Dr. Charvat in Avon Lake. She finished college coursework to become a dental hygienist as Nancy completed high school in 1953. Following secondary studies, the sisters went off to university. Peggy attended the Ohio State University in Columbus, meeting her husband, the Rev. Herbert Muenstermann, a United Church of Christ student pastor serving at the ministry of United Student Fellowship, which included housing for international students.

Nancy studied nursing at St. Luke's School of Nursing at the Methodist Hospital in Cleveland, Ohio. She graduated in 1956.

> "The school was small and they were hoping to make it into a B. Sc. (Registered Nurse equivalent) program. Even when I was there they sent us over to Western Reserve University for all our sciences, both social sciences and physical sciences. We took those courses at the university, with the plan that they were working toward the degree at St Luke's. That all changed. I think there were less patients coming so the hospital wasn't viable, and gradually they closed."
>
> - Nancy

Following undergraduate studies, Nancy completed her nursing degree at the Ohio State University in 1959. That summer, Nancy went with a group of United Student Fellowship members from different colleges in the United States on an educational two-month tour of five European countries to study the history of the Congregational Church and the Evangelical Reformed Church, which had merged in 1957 to form the United Church of Christ.

She says the tour was a wonderful experience – tracing the steps of church forebears in the United Kingdom, the Netherlands, France, Germany, and Switzerland. Nancy specifically remembers viewing movies about the United Nations working among poverty-stricken areas of the world, including India. Her experience also included a detailed background of the religious reforms related to social and political life in these countries.

In addition to the focus on religious and social history, the trip included sightseeing to relevant historical sites, visits to United Nations offices in Paris and Geneva, and stays in the homes of local families in rural and urban contexts. Nancy remembers a short holiday at a snowbound mountain ski resort in the German-Swiss region and a trip to Munich to see the theater where Mozart performed during his childhood. The group participated in annual Kirkentag (National Church Conference), and visited the Ecumenical Centre in Geneva.

To visit West Berlin, the group flew from Bohn to circumvent the post World War II blockade of the city and division of Germany into communist East and democratic West that put Berlin inside East Germany. Nancy remembers Berlin as "a picture of bright lights and prosperity." It was still two years before the Berlin Wall was erected, so with passports in hand foreigners could visit in East Berlin – a contrast of drab, old fashioned buildings, still wearing the appearance of war torn destruction. The group attended Sunday morning church worship, which Nancy remembers as poorly attended by the older generation only. Still, she noted the kind and friendly people "were full of joy to have fellowship with young Christians from the U.S.A." The hospitality was extended as hosts divided the group into pairs and invited them for dinner in their simple homes. They told the visitors they were not allowed to watch the Kirkentag on TV and were eager hear news about the free world.

Nancy returned to America full of enthusiasm from these eight weeks of comprehensive exposure to her church roots in Europe. It wasn't long before she shocked her parents by announcing she wanted to go to India to work as a missionary nurse. She says her parents "stood dumb-founded" at the announcement, their minds torn between the loss of their youngest child and their loyalty to the mission of the church. They confessed that they were proud to see their daughter dedicated to mission half-way around the world, but they were unhappy to see her leaving home as a single person.

By this time, Nancy's brother-in-law Herbert Muenstermann had joined the United Church Board for World Ministries as its personnel secretary and Nancy forwarded her intentions to him. He responded to her request by informing Nancy there was an opening for a nurse in Ghana, West Africa, where he and Peggy had served for six months. But Nancy was emphatic: influenced by her exposure to the church's work in India during her European tour, she was committed to service in India and not interested in other assignments. Though the details of her mission placement were not settled, Nancy was sent to the Missionary Training Center in Stony Point, New York, for a preparation course while she awaited her visa.

> "The board sent me to Stony Point as the first UCC person to give a report of what I got out of the training and if I would recommend it to others.

When I went there, all the other candidates were
Presbyterian. I was the only non-Presbyterian. I had to give a
report to the board and, after that, they started sending their
other missionaries there. It became ecumenical after I left to
go to India. This was a Presbyterian study center and they
had some homes for the missionaries on furlough."

- Nancy

At Stony Point she met Dr. Forrest and Barbara Eggleston, a
Presbyterian surgeon and nurse missionary couple, home on
furlough from their work at Christian Medical College, in Ludhiana,
in the Punjab region of India. They shared many interesting
experiences from their years first in the Himalaya Mountains, at a
rural tuberculosis hospital, and then at the Christian Medical College.
But rumors were already brewing that the Indian government was
changing their policy towards issuing visas to new missionaries.

While waiting for the right assignment in India and a visa, Nancy
took a leap of faith and moved to Philadelphia to live with Herb and
Peg, knowing access to an international airport in New York would
facilitate her travel to India. With a tearful goodbye to her parents,
Fred and Margaret's "baby" left for the east coast of the United States
to stay with her older sister until a visa was granted. During her half-
year wait in Philadelphia, Nancy took a temporary job at a nearby
hospital, and the Muenstermann family welcomed the newborn
Paula. Nancy says the baby's arrival gave "joy and purpose to
everyone involved."

Shortly after Paula's birth, Nancy received a nurse's visa to serve in
mission hospitals in Central India. She was scheduled to depart by
flight from New York on July 3, 1960 with a destination of Bombay
[Mumbai], India, with a two-day stop in Cairo arranged to ease her
transition into the Eastern culture.

> "I was commissioned as a missionary by the United Church
> Board for World Ministries before my visa came. They were
> ceasing to give visas to missionaries in India. The mission
> board had quite a difficult time in getting it. By God's grace,
> in six months, I got it. That was in July 1960 when I left
> America and came to Bombay [Mumbai.]

I think, perhaps, I was the last person in our mission who got a visa. In that transition, I was coming by plane, which was new. They used to send all missionaries by ship – they would spend a month or two having a nice time transitioning on the boat. But here I was, a new generation.

The Rev. Theifield Twenty was the mission board secretary and he asked me to make a stop somewhere, to make the transition. I had some friends of friends at the embassy in Cairo, Egypt. So I stopped in Cairo for several days."

- Nancy

Early in the morning of July 3, 1960, with luggage in the back and the infant Paula in her car seat, Peg and Nancy departed for New York's international airport. When they reached the city two hours later, their car came to a halt in a terrible traffic jam. "Time marched on and it turned into hours of delay," Nancy recalls. There was no way to contact those waiting at the airport as they inched along through small openings in traffic. Nancy understood that missing her flight would mean forfeiting the cost of the international ticket. The Rev. Telfer Mook, mission board India secretary, was scheduled to meet Nancy and Peg at the airport two hours before her departure. Reaching the gate as the departure time came and went, Nancy was stopped in the main entrance and found a smiling Mook. Nancy was confused by his smile and thought, "What is this? Why is he so casual?"

"Relax!" he told her. "There is some technical fault with the plane, so your departure is delayed until tomorrow morning."

"The grace of God was already with me in my journey of faith!" she muses. Nancy departed for Mumbai via Cairo the next morning.

Arriving in India

Nancy recalls the plane descending over Bombay before dawn on a July morning, remembering it was like landing among faint lights shining in the rain. It was monsoon season in India; the relentless rains had been drenching the region for over a month and would not end until late September. When the door of the plane opened, the moist warm air moved in and enveloped the plane cabin. Though busy, Nancy remembers the airport was not as crowded as in New York.

> "From [Cairo] I went to Bombay and it was a good transition. I was in the Middle East, which is also very different. You have to sort out what you're getting into it, quite suddenly. It was only a few days and then I went to Bombay where I was met by my colleague Lela Wasser at the train. She had been in India for 10 years and she was quite adept at what you have to take for an Indian journey on the train and those were earlier days where the trains were different.
>
> There she was, waving over the railing separating the passengers from the public. It took a while to move through the lines to reach Lela who just kept waving. "
>
> - Nancy

Lela Wasser, the first person in the extended missionary family to meet Nancy, headed women's development programs in Khariar, Orissa. Nancy describes her as "an energetic middle aged single lady," who had been working in the mission for over 10 years and was adept at travel within India. Nancy remembers her as a confident and kind person who made people feel welcome, safe, and at home. After receiving the baggage, she guided the way with the luggage trolley out to a taxi that took the pair to the railway station where a train would take them to the western city of Raipur. A porter, known locally as a "coolie," was hired to carry the luggage from the taxi directly to the train headed toward Khariar.

> "We were in a first class compartment and we had coupé that entered right onto the platform. They weren't connected like the trains are now, where you can go from one car to the other. Once you shut that door, you were all alone in that compartment on that train. It's such a different experience than today.

And here was this big cake of ice; it was still quite hot at that time. We didn't have air conditioning in those days. So we used to get a big cake of ice, and it melted slowly and it kept the car cool. You could order it ahead of time and down the line there would be another ice cake for you when that one melted if you had a very long journey.

It was a coupé with two berths, one below and one above, and one little bathroom. It wasn't a full bathroom – it was just a western latrine with a sink, and that's how we got along by ourselves. We stopped at the stations and you could open the door it you wanted to buy something in the station.

It was an interesting journey for me, and Lela later became a very good friend; she's a very fine person. She was not a nurse; she was in women's development. She used to go out, and she had women's groups and it was a lot of spiritual development as well. She was helping them develop in the Christian life, and she worked with the women out in the villages."

- Nancy

As a "secure compartment," after then the train departed a station, the door closed and there was no access to anyone else on the train. Nancy says Lela had packed food and water for the 24-hour journey, so there were "no worries at all." Traveling during daytime, they enjoyed the sights of cities and villages, and fields with cows and goats along the roads. The long journey gave plenty of time for Nancy and Lela to get acquainted. When it was time to sleep, Nancy climbed to the top berth.

Reflecting on her choice of western attire – a dress – Nancy recalls the heat and humidity of the journey:

"It would be better to have the salwar suits of Indian dress for such travel rather than a frock! By the next mid-day the train reached Raipur."

- Nancy

Missionaries in India in 1960

Nancy reached the mission center in Raipur on 7 July 1960. It was a pivotal time in the history of Western mission in India. As has been noted, for several years the Indian government had been slowly reducing the number of visas granted to those classifying themselves as missionaries. Missionaries with specialized skills such as medicine, agriculture, education, and certain engineering fields, continued to be granted entry to work in the mission area to which they felt called. But after gaining independence from British colonial rule in 1947, the country was eager to reclaim its culture, capitalize on the strengths of its own people, and assert self-rule. Unfortunately, the past century of colonization – often conflating British governance with western Christian culture and values – had soured the Indian government against mission activity.

With the knowledge of this relatively recent history, it is important to note that by the time Nancy began her training and service with the United Church Board for World Ministries, the attitude of most major western missionary agencies had also changed dramatically.

Although Indian education and government had been reformed during the British Colonial era, Christian missionaries in the 1960s, by and large, had ceased to act as a colonizing influence in India and more Indian Christians were entering indigenous missionary service to other Indians than foreigners. In this context, western mission organizations were beginning to see themselves as partners in mission, instead of founders of mission and standard bearers.

An ethos of accompaniment had been infused into missionary culture which respected indigenous religions and forms of governance, sought to evangelize by exhibiting Christian values, valued the language and culture of those they lived among, and built partnerships with existing and indigenous institutions.

Nancy Begins Her Indian Journey

The only other nurse at the Evangelical Hospital in Khariar, where Nancy was to assume her first post, was another American missionary named Ruth Hofsteter. She was scheduled to go on mission furlough, traveling back to the U.S.A. for an extended break.

Nancy needed to be trained – hopefully quickly – so she could take Ruth's place. Ruth, also from Ohio, arrived in India in 1947 along with approximately 1,200 other missionaries who traveled to India at the end of World War II. Serving as a nurse and midwife in rural hospitals, Ruth became a nursing supervisor in the central regions of India for more than 36 years, including her time in Khariar.[2]

Ruth's furlough depended on having a reliable replacement, which couldn't happen until Nancy completed language training to proficiently communicate with patients in Oriya. Following her train trip from Delhi, Nancy remembers arriving in Raipur to begin learning the language and culture of those she had come to serve.

> "The train ended its journey in Raipur. At that time, the church in central India was called the Chhattisgarh and Orissa Church Council – it was the name of the church out here. They worked both in Orissa and Chhattisgarh, which was not a state then, it was just an area called Chhattisgarh. It was an area of Madhya Pradesh (MP), which was the largest state in India.
>
> In the year 2000 they cut them in two and created the state of Chhattisgarh. People used the word Chhattisgarh at the time because it was very different from the other part: it was more tribal, it was less developed. Near the Orissa border, there was influence that came from both sides – from Chhattisgarh to Orissa and Orissa to Chhattisgarh.
>
> So there was a Chhattisgarh and Orissa Church Council – it was the body that governed it. They called it the COCC. And my husband has a lot of roots to his grandfather that you'll get later in the story."
>
> - Nancy

Nancy recalls the story of her training, noting the community of missionaries she stayed with and learned from along the way.

> "I was ultimately headed to Khariar in Orissa, though the church center was in what was then called Chhattisgarh, in Raipur. I stayed there for a few days with the senior

missionary, William Baur and his wife Alby. They were like our parents out here. I stayed some days there for an orientation to mission itself and they lived in a huge bungalow, which is still there today. It's now used for Christian weddings. People of the church, and other churches, can rent that for the evening dinner or the relatives can stay there.

My close colleagues at the time were Ruth Hofsteter and Lela Wasser: both have passed on. Though Lela was quite a young woman, she died before Ruth was very old. Ruth was the nurse and the nursing superintendent in Khariar. She oriented me to the hospital because I was to be the next nursing superintendent. She was going to go on furlough so they sent me off to another location for language school – to the German mission in Orissa.

In this regard, I need to mention the Meyers, the Rev. and Mrs. Hulda Meyers. They were very senior missionaries. It's as if they became my parents. They took care of me; they made all my arrangements for travel. The missionaries are wonderful about taking care of one another, and I didn't have anything to worry about.

They were from German backgrounds, from the Evangelical & Reformed Church [branch of the United Church of Christ] – so they knew German and they were very friendly with the German missionaries, which was the nearest mission in Orissa. So that was where they sent me for my language study. Along the way I learned a little German, but I've forgotten it now. It was necessary because I had to learn a little to talk to them.

They sent me to a lady called Ms. Janke who was, I can tell you, a saint. She was a wonderful woman, an older lady who had a boarding school for children [in Kotpad.] It was an ideal place to learn the Oriya language because I could sit and talk to those kids. And there was a retired pastor there who became my tutor.

They call him 'pandit' – he was my pandit. That's the word they use for somebody who instructs you in something. He taught me mostly grammar. We had a little grammar book, and a dictionary. But I learned mostly from the Bible, which gave me quite a good theological vocabulary.

The language [I learned] was Oriya. And by the way, they changed the name of Orissa. It was that for many years, but recently they've changed it to Odisha. So that's the way they say it today. The language, they now call it Odiya.

I studied with them and the rule of our mission was that we had to pass two examinations in the language. The others did Hindi because they were in Raipur and Tilda. But those of us who went to Orissa, we had to learn Oriya. And there was an organized language school for the missionaries – a British Baptist lady named Lilly Quai organized it.

I did my first studies with this pandit, but then I went to the school the missionaries had organized in Oriya and I took the exam and I passed it. I studied from July to until just before Christmas when I went for my first year exam. I had six months of instruction, and then I passed the first exam.

And then I went up to Kodaikanal, in Tamil Nadu where a British lady, Lilly Whey, taught adult literacy. She arranged for some bungalows for us to stay. We tutored there for the second exam. So I had the experience in Kodai and stayed there through he summer. It was a beautiful place – Kodaikanal is a hill station. It's a lovely place to study and to do hiking.

At the end of that course I went down to Cuttack, the largest city in Orissa, and there they had arranged the exam. And I passed it also. So in one year I passed two exams because I was so eager to get to my work.
And I had good exposure to people and the culture. Of course, I could sit and talk to the little girls and they would help me. The Indian languages, the alphabets, are phonetic. So it means you can say what you're reading, without knowing what you are reading. It's a very interesting thing.

I used to go to church, and then those girls – they used to call me Missy Ma – were so excited to come home and say, 'The missy ma just got here and she's already speaking Oriya, she's singing the songs!' The only thing is, I'd just learned the alphabet and how to sound out the words.

But it was a good place to be and I learned fast. In one year, the following July [1961], I went into my work. Ruth went home to furlough and turned her work over to me. And I became the head nurse! I had been nothing more than a staff nurse and to come here and suddenly I was the nursing superintendent!

I didn't know where to begin. It was really quite an experience. But when you have to learn, you learn – the hard way. You make a lot of mistakes, and you learn 'that wasn't right' – and you learn that way.

That was how I arrived in Khariar."

- Nancy

After completing her language training in 1961, Nancy says she was ready to facilitate Ruth's furlough by serving the Indian people as the head of nursing at the Evangelical Hospital in Khariar, and eager to fulfill her call as a missionary of the United Church Board for World Ministries in the United Church of Christ.

She felt assured the call she had first discerned and related to her family was being achieved – the call to deliver healing ministry to the people of India. What Nancy was unsure of at that moment was whether or not this was to be her life's work, or if it would merely be an amazing step of faith on life's journey.

---

[1] Historic outline and source material from Nancy Henry's biographical writings and interviews conducted May-June 2012.
[2] Ruth retired from missionary service in 1983 at the age of 65. She died in Ohio on November 28, 2011 at the age of 93.

Chapter 2: An Indian Boy With Great Promise

Virendra Kumar Henry – known professionally as Dr. V. K. Henry, and to friends as Viru – was born 29 June 1933 in Bilaspur, which was at the time located in the Indian state of Madhya Pradesh, now Chattisgarh. The eldest of four siblings, his birth – not unlike Nancy's – was medically complicated. Diagnosed with obstructive labor, Viru's mother Elwina was advised to abort the child to prevent both of them from dying. "She [the doctor] had not reckoned on the faith and will-power of her patient." She refused permission for the procedure.[1]

Removed from the hospital and now at home, Elwina's mother-in-law, also a physician, was called for help. The child's prospects were poor. She had seen so many obstructive labor cases and was certain of the outcome. Cesarean sections were not yet common, mostly due to a lack of antibiotics to treat patients after the procedure.

> "I was actually not meant to be born alive. I was my mother's first child, and labor was obstructed. The doctor in our place in Chattisgarh advised craniotomy; destroy the baby to save the mother. Thankfully, my mother refused. She shoved her hair into her throat to make herself retch and push, and out I came! So for me, each day is a gift from God."
>
> - Viru

Another biographer of Viru said of the birth, "From the word go, the infant Viru picked up this habit of blasting his way through obstructions that would have stopped ordinary men."

Initially named Ronald Sampson Henri, the infant Viru weighed 10 pounds (4.5 kg), a very large baby for his mother who was only 5 feet (1.5 meters) tall. But Viru's grandfather had wanted his grandchildren to have Indian names, though he'd given his children western names. The grandfather's will won out, and Ronald Sampson was renamed to Virendra Kumar, the "Undefeatable Prince."

The family had refused the craniotomy, in part, due to their Christian values. Viru's grandfather, whom the family called Nana – a common nickname for a maternal grandfather, converted to Christianity over objections from his Brahman family. It was a life altering decision with great social consequences.

"He was a young boy of 12 and lived with his Brahmin parents who were both doctors. Nana was an only child. Some missionaries came to Kanpur and they stayed for a long time. They had revival meetings and would speak to the people to give the good news of Jesus Christ in that area.

My grandfather was so interested in this. Every time they spoke, he was there and he got to know them. The missionaries were foreigners and they were going to travel to Raipur.

He said, 'I want to go with you,' and they replied, 'Well, you have to ask your parents.' They didn't want him to go. He was the only son. For a Hindu family, at a funeral the eldest son does the burning of the body. For days he said he wanted to go with them. His father said, 'you can go with them, but you cannot come back to this home.'

That was a tremendous sacrifice for this father to give to his son. Nana went with them. But his father said, 'Only one condition: if I die, the message will come to you that I have died and you must come and take your mother, as long as she is living.' Nana was in Masamund, but he gave the information of where he was to his parents wherever he went. They were in communication, but he wasn't permitted in the house.

Finally the news came that the father had died. Nana went up and brought the mother back to Masamund. They gave a separate room for her in the house. Hindu women have to do their worship everyday so they need privacy. Her food came from the neighbors who were Brahmans. She couldn't eat the food at her son's house, but she did mix with them. She had a paiti [a tin trunk] and she would open it to check if her things were safe. She had glaucoma and became blind, and she stayed there with my grandfather for the rest of her life."

- Viru

Viru's grandfather took the Christian name Paul and became a pastor, eventually moving to Bilaspur and working with the American missionary, Mr. Schaeffer. Paul married and soon started a family, naming their children after another missionary acquaintance, Henri Jesu Das, or "Henri the Lord's Servant." Paul's youngest daughter, Lena, narrated a series of stories in which she recalled her father's pastoral work and travels.

> "He did a lot of travel through the villages on an oxen cart. He'd have his lantern when they traveled at night and always took a person with him and they'd go through these jungle places to get to the villages.
>
> Thieves came along and they said, 'Give me your watch.' He just took it off and gave it to them. When they were finished, he said, 'I have a gift I want to give to you.' 'What?' they asked. They'd never robbed anyone like this. He was cooperative and gentle. He gave them a Hindi Bible.
>
> 'Please read this Bible. It will change your life,' he said, writing his home address in the Bible. 'This is my address. Come to me anytime and I will help you.' Off these two thieves went.
>
> Some years later, one of them showed up at his home, carrying that Bible. One of them read that Bible and became a Christian.
>
> Nana traveled in this cart all over, for preaching. Many converted in those days. Then he went to follow up with them. Paul was his Christian name. He had his model [in the Apostle Paul] and took the name of Paul.
>
> He came to a place and went over to a lady holding a fussy child. The lady was dead. So he picked the child up and took

17

it home. 'Nani [grandmother], we have another baby in our house.'

By that time his children were older. They had a new baby. He was known to do that. He picked up people who were homeless and brought them home. He must have had a good wife to allow this.

They had a plan for this little girl. They put her in a Christian girls hostel so she would not be too dependent on them. They financed her and educated her. That girl was brought into her full life because of them. He did that many times, even though pastors had very small salaries and he found a way to support them.

Nanajee was a true evangelist."

- Nancy, relaying Lena's storytelling

Viru's father, Albert Henry was Paul's second child and the region's Tahsildar – or revenue inspector – a very high post in the government. The job was transient, and the family relocated with Albert as his job moved them to various areas of Madhya Pradesh. Transferred from school to school, Viru doesn't remember taking exams in his early education.

"They just promoted me because I was the revenue inspector's son. He was a government official. That was the pattern here. After two years, they move you here and there as the government needed.

We called Bilaspur home. My father was transferred near Bilaspur, so I went to Company Garden School. My mother and siblings went to stay with my paternal grandparents; they lived in Bilaspur, so mother decided not to move around. It wasn't good for the kids' schooling.

While we were in Bilaspur, my father got blackwater fever."

- Viru

Tragedy visited the Henry family when Albert, on transfer to Jabalpur in 1938, contracted malaria and quickly died of blackwater fever. This complication of malaria occurs when red blood cells burst, releasing hemoglobin into the bloodstream and into the urine, causing it to flow dark red or black. The impact of these burst red blood cells often overpowers the immune system, adding additional strain on the malaria stricken victim and, in extreme cases, leads to kidney failure.

Albert's sudden passing left Elwina to raise the four children on her own – Viru was just five years old; sisters Vimla and Kamala were four and two; little brother Narendra (Gullu) was six months old. Viru's grandfather Paul was a pastor in Baitalpur, and Elwina was eventually invited there to oversee a mission hostel for the healthy children of leprosy patients.

> "Rev. Schultz was in charge of the leprosy mission. My mother's father was a pastor in Baitalpur where the leprosy mission is located. It was started by our mission, run today by the leprosy mission. There is an organization called The Leprosy Mission. Baitalpur became my hometown; it is very near to [Mungeli.]
>
> My mother was a very young widow, with four children, one being only 6 months old. Rev. Schultz gave my mother the job as the matron of what they call the "healthy girls hostel." They had a way of taking the children away from the parents who had leprosy. Any patient that was admitted into that hospital, the children, the girls, were put in the hostel where my mother was matron. They had [a hostel] for boys also."
>
> - Viru

Though the circumstances that led to the family's arrival in Baitalpur were tragic, the children thrived in the mission and hospital setting and Elwina raised them in an environment of faith and hospitality, and eventually adopted another daughter, Kanchan.

The leprosy hospital was a self-contained unit. Patients were isolated from the general population and not allowed out of the hospital.

Nancy says these patients often had "social problems" that hindered their release and reintegration into society.

These social problems, as described by Nancy, were many for leprosy patients in mid-20th century India. The stigma surrounding those with the disease had not changed – in many cases they were considered social pariah and in need of isolation.
In the beginning of the multi-drug treatment (MDT) era, those with leprosy were receiving medications that reduced symptoms and mitigated the infectiousness of the disease. However, leprosy hospitals operated by Christian mission societies continued to play an important part in the physical and spiritual care of those with the disease.

Policies dating back to the colonial era included the Leprosy Act of 1898, which institutionalized leprosy victims and separated them based on gender to prevent reproduction. These laws mainly affected the poor because those who were self-sufficient were not obligated to be isolated or seek medical treatment. Even when drugs to treat leprosy became available and more knowledge was gained about the disease, the scourge of leprosy remained a persistent and widespread health problem throughout all regions of the country. Leprosy patients were excluded from holding public office, traveling by train, and marrying in the region until at least 2008.[2]

Nancy describes the stigma of leprosy, and the changing response from society and the mission establishment adapting to specialize in its treatment.

> "They were reducing [isolation and stigma.] The leper home was still there, but there were just the old patients that had been there before. The new policy was that you would not isolate them. A lot more education and earlier treatment is possible. They used to go so much without treatment that they were totally deformed.
>
> Even Baitulpur today has become a general hospital so that people will go there and be treated. This hospital was built for lepers and for generations a leprosy hospital. That was started by our mission in Baitulpur: a general hospital and leprosy hospital, both.

There was a time when all of these mission hospitals that had built leprosy hospitals. The tendency was to turn these hospitals over to the leprosy mission. They would raise the money for and recruit the staff. They had their own executives out here and the mission was in Delhi. They could get to be expert on [leprosy] and learn from one place and use what they learned."

- Nancy

Viru remained an outgoing and gregarious child, spending time with the doctors and staff of the leprosy mission. Known for his curiosity and adventurous spirit, Viru laughs when people tell stories of him getting into minor trouble as a child.

"As a kid, he always went off to hostel [for school], but when he was home, he was always looking for things to do. One day, he went over to the general hospital and the doctor stepped out. [Viru] was playing with an exam table that went backwards and the patient slipped off the table.

The reason [Viru] had gone to the hospital was because of a knee injury. He went for a dressing for his knees, which were always kicked up, because he was always doing naughty things. He had a lot of injuries in his young life. He was known to be a naughty kid, always getting in trouble.

My mother-in-law said, 'He was so naughty; I had to tie him to go to the bathroom. I couldn't leave him for a minute.' She tied him to furniture and then would go to the bathroom when he was a little. From the time he was a toddler he had to be controlled. He was an active kid. I think that's where Ajit got that. Ajit was the active, mischievous one."

- Nancy

"Grandma Gas was taken out every evening for a ride in the car. They had a Ford car and every evening, the driver took the grandma out for a ride. She wasn't very mobile and she was happy to go out and see other things every day.

I jumped onto the back of the car. A luggage carrier was back there, an open luggage carrier. You tied the luggage on with a rope, and I jumped on it.

The problem was, they kept going and going. I thought, 'Where are they going? My mommy will be looking for me,' so I jumped off. That's how I got this scar right here [pointing to face.]"

- Viru

Despite his later academic achievement, Viru's grade school education was filled with difficulty. Skipping class so he could spend time outdoors swimming, hunting or fishing, he was known as a tireless prankster by his peers and siblings. Because he was promoted through grades without testing well in his early education, Viru had fallen behind the rest of the class by late elementary school and was required to repeat the sixth grade at the school in Bhatapara.

I failed the English medium and they made me go back a couple of years to catch up. The course had changed – I had to go back and do it in Hindi – and it was very difficult. Had I passed, I'd have gone out of that school, but I was repeating earlier work and was a bit older than the other students at that grade level. They used to call me 'Dada,' which means elder brother. The nickname stuck and they called me 'Dada' everywhere I went, even when I went for my degree later.

- Viru

Once he successfully passed his grade six exams, Viru moved to Raipur to live with an aunt and attend the English medium school, which he finished in 1953.

Previous experience and interest influenced Viru to pursue medicine. As the first grandson in the family, his grandfather Paul wanted him to become a pastor. "Where will you get the money to be a doctor?" he asked Viru. "From the mission, I will get help," Viru assured him.

Upon graduation, the Leprosy Mission arranged an interview for Viru seeking admission as a M.B.B.S. (Bachelor of Medicine, Bachelor of Surgery) student at the Christian Medial College in Vellore. Entrance to the school was dependent upon an in-person interview.

> "My mother forwarded the interview letter. In those days, that would have taken forever. By the time I got the message and arrived for the interview, the selection had finished five days before. I gave up the hope of being a doctor."
>
> - Viru

Although disappointed he was unable to gain admittance to Vellore, Viru entered Ewing Christian College in Allahabad to pursue his B.Sc. in biology, living with his uncle who was only a few years older than him and graduating in 1956.

Following undergraduate studies, Viru taught 11th grade science in Bhatapara for one year. It is during his time as a teacher that Viru became convinced education was the key to self-development in India and he began to formulate ways in which medical mission and education could be combined in service to the people of rural India.

Dr. Lawrence Jiwanmall, the father of one of Viru's science students, Kiran Jiwanmall, was the first Indian doctor in the area and had served at the Christian Hospital in Tilda. Viru met Lawrence in Bhatapara during a mission conference. Though still discouraged about his missed opportunity in Vellore, Dr. Jiwanmall lifted his spirits and offered support.

"If you want to go to medical school, I'll help you in any way I can," he told Viru. Dr. Jiwanmall explained the process of applying for financial assistance and the bond, or years of service, he would be required to work at mission hospitals in exchange for the support.

The first step toward completing this goal was attending medical school, and Viru was accepted to Gandhi Medical College in Bhopal in 1957. Pursuing his M.B.B.S. With the support of the Board of Christian Institutions and the Chhattisgarh-Orissa Church council, he was an active and engaged student. He represented the Ujjain University in field hockey and at inter-university music competitions. Over holiday breaks he went to the Evangelical Hospital in Khariar, Orissa, to work with the German surgeon Dr. J.

Manfred Laun, a towering personality who made a strong impact on the young medical student as a medical mentor, hospital manager and person of faith. While in his fourth year of studies, when Nancy was away from Khariar at language school, Viru did his first major surgery – an amputation of a crushed hand – in Dr. Laun's absence.

In 1962, Viru graduated with his M.B.B.S. degree from Gandhi Medical College and went right to work as a doctor at the Evangelical Hospital. He served from 1962 to 1966 under the supervision of Dr. Laun who trained Viru in most of the surgeries commonly seen.

The work in Khariar was, in part, to satisfy the seven-year service bond Viru agreed to for support of his education in Bhopal. At the time it was common for doctors to commit to a specified term of service in exchange for schooling. The bond system fulfilled a threefold need. First, the Christian Mission Hospital system depended on a steady stream of doctors and nurses to continue operation. By recruiting and training medical professionals dedicated to a term of service within a mission hospital, it ensured those serving were well educated. Second, the bond system distributed medical professionals to locations of greatest need. Many of the mission hospital locations are in isolated rural areas and would not be the first choice for most graduates. Compulsory service guaranteed trained staff would be attending the needs of populations served by the Christian Mission Hospital system. Third, the bond system was a mission in itself, allowing promising students without financial means to pursue a career in medicine and mission service.

Viru arrived at a time when the Indian government's family planning program was, as Nancy says, "going full blast." Population estimates for India, especially rural areas, were projected to grow beyond the level of food sustainability. Demographer R.A. Gopalaswami estimated the population of India in 1951 to be 356 million people. With an expected sustained population growth of 500,000 per year, the demographer projected India's population would rise to 520 million by 1981. He was wrong. In 1981 India's population had risen to over 680 million people.[3]

> "The government used to give men who came in for a vasectomy 10 rupees. I know it sounds horrible. But they

started flocking in for that 10 rupees. Thirty to 40 men came every day. [Viru] used to do his regular surgery schedule. Although he was only an M.B.B.S. doctor at the time, Dr. Laun passed the skills on to him. He'd come out of the door and there's 30-40 guys standing there for a vasectomy. It became too much for our staff to handle."

- Nancy

To speed things along and ensure the doctors and staff had time in the day to accommodate their regular rounds and surgeries, along with this influx of vasectomy seekers, the staff gave each man a razor blade. Patients were instructed to go shave the incision site and then return to stand in line to await their turn for the procedure.

Viru even developed a technique for the procedure to save time, severing and tying both left and right vas deferens through one incision. Although he reported the technique to the medical authorities in Delhi, they didn't recognize it as an innovation. Yet, Khariar Evangelical Hospital received an award for performing the most vasectomies in the district.

"There was a negative side to this – some of the guys would say they were married. Most of them were illiterate people from the village. Some of them really weren't married; they only wanted those 10 rupees. Isn't that terrible? They didn't realize it would end their reproductive lives, although everything was explained to them.

Still, they would give false history and we gradually found that out.

We started a simple screening process: If a guy came and he didn't have a mustache, we refused. He was too young. We had to start looking at them and make our own judgments because we knew some of them were lying.

Some women came as well; they got tubectomies. There were probably many cases where both husband and wife had the procedure. The mother got more money because she had a little bigger operation. It was difficult for us to know. How do you find out? There were masses of people coming from these villages. You gradually find out, through word of mouth, here and there. We had to stop some of them."

- Viru

"See, we kind of wanted the men to have [a vasectomy.] It was such a small operation. They got up and walked home. For the mother it was difficult unless it was after their delivery. But most of them refused. They wanted to think about it, but most of them didn't come back. They had several children. If they did it right after their delivery, it wasn't so difficult, particularly if they had a C-section. To do a tubectomy on a woman is much more difficult than a man. It was good when the men came through, but it was only because of the money. People of status, even though we used to try to convince the man to have the vasectomy, they didn't want the rupees."

- Nancy

Nancy recalls the program being a success, though family planning measures came under scrutiny over a decade later in the mid-1970s, when the government was accused of forced sterilizations, especially in its coercion of poor people.

"Some of the methods they used during the time of Sanjay Gandhi were terrible. He did a lot of unscrupulous things to make it happen more. People were fooled in some ways. He defamed the program and then it had to be cut down. Even after that, it's not been much. Now they're talking about it again [in 2013.] There's some family planning education from the government but it's not as heavy as it should be. This is one of India's main problems: population."

- Nancy

Viru continued to hone his skills as a doctor and, under the supervision of Dr. Laun, discover his passion for surgery, care for his patients, and learn the essentials of hospital administration. Viru eschews the title of missionary, but says it was his early days in

Khariar that convinced him of the importance to work to better the lives of the people served by Christian Mission Hospitals in India, and to strive to create opportunities for Indians who wished to enter into the medical field as doctors, nurses and hospital staff.

Within the regular hum of the Mission Hospital – patients coming and going, surgeries and recoveries, attending to the needs of the community and the staff, maintenance and expansion of the facilities, worship and relaxation – Nancy, the driven and brilliant young American missionary nurse, met Viru, the newly minted doctor from Bilaspur with great promise. Their story is a story of love, a life filled with joys and sorrows, and the transformation of Christian mission medical care in India.

---

[1] Viru's biographical information is collected from a number of sources including "Mission Impossible – Says Who?" by Johnny Oommen and published in CMJI; "The Making of a Legend" published in *To Sir With Love: A Tribute to Dr. V. K. Henry of Bissamcuttack*, September 5, 1998; and interviews conducted May-June, 2013.
[2] Putul, June 23, 2008 - http://southasia.oneworld.net/archive/Article/laws-in-india-criminalise-leprosy
[3] https://www.washingtonpost.com/news/morning-mix/wp/2014/11/14/the-malthusian-roots-of-indias-mass-sterilization-program/

Chapter 3: A Foreigner Took My Heart

Nancy arrived in Khariar in 1961with her newly acquired Oriya language skills, a growing understanding of the people and culture she was going to serve, and ready to jump into work at the Evangelical Hospital. With the added caveat of becoming head nurse as Ruth Hofsteter cycled into a time of furlough back in the United States, Nancy was now tasked with learning the duties of the head nurse and the critical needs served at the hospital and in the surrounding communities.

Along with learning all that would be necessary to assume the role of nursing superintendent, Nancy needed to adapt to her new surroundings at the Evangelical Hospital in Khariar. The acclimation was slow at times, but Nancy's resolve to learn and love India was not spoiled by a few inconveniences and surprises.

> "I had heard so much about malaria. I knew that we were in a jungle area and there could be malaria. I was scared of every mosquito that came near me. When I'd go to bed at night, I couldn't sleep because I'd hear the mosquitoes buzzing around me outside the mosquito net. I kept putting on a [flashlight.] I had my cultural adjustments also.
>
> We were in a place with a lot of snakes – Khariar has a lot of snakes. All of the missionaries had told me stories about the cobra in the bathroom. They'd go in and there was a cobra standing there. When I first got there, we had no lights. In the evening, we had a lantern only. I was looking for snakes in every corner; I really was quite frightened. The other ladies were good and I saw they were confident, so I tried to get it out of my mind. It's not easy to go to another place so different and try to adjust.
>
> The setting is also very simple: a cement floor and a simple bed with a mosquito net. They didn't have running water. They used to fill the tank by hand. The well was here and the men used to dip these cans into the tanks and carry it up the

29

steps. A lot of times, we didn't have any water because it was empty. The water problem was there and electricity was not there at all. Even when we got electricity, it was off more than on. All these things are there and you have to adjust to when you first come. After a while, you learn to cope with it. It's a little challenging."

- Nancy

Although Nancy faced many cultural and environmental challenges in Khariar, the support of the other mission staff kept her going. Even as she initially doubted her choice to come to India, the staying power of those who she joined in the work at the hospital kept her spirits up.

"One thing about the mission, you're never really alone. They don't just send you to an outpost and you're out there all alone. I had two fellow missionaries with me who were very experienced and could solve all the problems. As the nursing superintendent, I had so many problems to solve. There were so many people to help me. The support we got was wonderful. That's how you get through it. By the grace of God, you get through it. You don't think about if I made a mistake coming here. I used to think that, but you get over it after a while."

- Nancy

It was July of 1961, and Nancy became nursing superintendent only a few weeks after arriving in Khariar. Ruth Hofsteter handed over the nursing department to the fresh-faced nurse from America and Nancy began her work in earnest, working with Dr. Laun to take up the responsibilities at the hospital and in providing traveling clinic services to the surrounding area.

"Before my marriage, Dr. Laun was a lone doctor, so I used to drive the huge clinic truck out by myself. There were a lot of things I had to do. He taught me how to pull teeth, give an injection, drain an abscess, stitch a small wound, and differentiate between TB (tuberculosis) and pneumonia. The sound of crinkling paper was the sound of TB. I learned to oscillate the patient [to dislodge mucous obstruction], at my level."

- Nancy

The clinic truck, a rolling field hospital, introduced Nancy to the extended mission of the Christian Mission Hospitals.

"The sides opened and that's where all the medicines were. It was made so there was a wooden railing that kept the medicines from falling over so they got there in good condition."

- Nancy

It was a critical link to serving the poorest populations in India, those who had neither means to pay for treatment nor the ability to transport themselves to the hospital for regular care. Except in dire emergency situations or the occasional large festival, Nancy says most people in the surrounding villages had never been to Khariar. The hospital's ability to provide preventative care – including disease diagnosis, drug administration, emergency dental procedures, treating coughs and minor injuries, identifying and treating malaria, and a host of other tasks – was a lifeline for many in the villages who had no other access to medical care.

Although not compulsory for those receiving care, the traveling clinic also brought Christian evangelism to the villages. Nancy says prayer and teaching about Jesus, the great healer, were an integral component of the village services.

"It was a weekly clinic. [Dr. Laun] went one week and I went the other. He trained me so I could do everything the clinic supported. He could be in the hospital the full week and go out the next week. When he came, we used to go out together. If you had a driver, you took them. If we didn't, I drove. We took a cook also because we had breakfast and lunch out there. We went out quite early so we could see as many people as possible.

We would always have some teaching. We would take charts of Jesus healing people. That's how we started it, with a prayer and a message of why we've come and who Jesus is. By that time, the patients had come. We would go on a market day so we could serve more people. It was a town called Tarbod.

We'd go out there every Thursday. [Patients came] from many villages for the market and they knew this clinic was there. It wasn't very far. You could just walk over to where we were from the main market. We got patients from all villages around there. They'd be waiting to be seen and we'd set up, have our prayer. They would sit on the ground and hear what we said.

Then we had to eat breakfast. They kind of waited while we were eating breakfast, and we had either a male or female nurse to give the medicines while we ate."

- Nancy

Public health needs topped the list of the extended work performed by the traveling clinic. Government-run programs supported immunization and vaccination programs throughout India, which Nancy says was an important part of the hospital's work.

"I remember we used to give TB medicine out there. One thing is if it was something very bad, I couldn't manage. I would try to convince them to go to the hospital with us because the doctors were there. Sometimes they would do it, and sometimes they wouldn't. Then I would tell them the doctor would be there next week. That's how we managed. What I couldn't do or understand, I had to treat it on the spot or urge them to come to the hospital.

We did [vaccinations] in the hospital. The government did a pretty good job in DPT and polio. When we went there, we saw a lot of polio victims. While we lived there, it went down dramatically. The polio vaccination program was quite successful, as was the vaccine for tetanus.

32

When we went to Khariar, it was so common to have neonatal tetanus. Neonatal tetanus, they almost always die. It's transferred during the cord cutting during the delivery. The cord is cut with something dirty and that's the most common way they get it. The midwives in the villages do it."

- Nancy

When Nancy and Viru began their work in Khariar in the early 1960s, polio infections were on the rise. The communicable disease caused partial or complete paralysis in nearly one-third of those infected. Historic records from the early-1950s show a post-polio paralysis rate for first graders of between six to eight children per 1000 in northern India.[1] The immunization program, following the release of the Salk vaccine in 1955, was a lifeline for those served by the Evangelical Hospital in Khariar.

"[Polio] became very rare while we were there. The immunization program was very good. It takes time to see the progress and results, but it was pretty good. We gave immunizations in the hospital. We could easily do it there. We didn't have that much contact with the people out in the clinic. We have records of who they are in their villages, but we can't go and find them in the villages. It's not very effective if they don't get the complete the regimen. In the hospital, if they come, you could follow it up much easier to make sure that they took the whole course of three injections. That was the main reason we didn't do it out in the village."

- Nancy

All the while Nancy was overseeing the nursing program and operating the field clinic, Viru frequently visited Khariar as he completed his M.B.B.S. training in Bhopal. He and Dr. Laun had formed a close bond and Viru worked closely with him and knew the staff of the hospital. Though he visited in 1961 and spend two months in Khariar on a subsequent visit, he didn't arrive as a resident at the hospital until August 1962. During those earlier visits, he'd met Nancy and they had developed a friendship. When Viru arrived in Khariar, he began to accompany Nancy on the mobile clinic rounds, performing whatever surgeries could be done as an outpatient in the hospital.

> "We met under a mango tree when possible. They give very good shade. That's where we'd have the clinic, just under the trees.
>
> We have a lot of clinic stories. Our courtship took place out there. We used to go out to the clinic together. We used to go out to the market and even to some nearby villagers. They'd tell us someone was sick at home and he'd say, 'Okay, I'll go.' If it was light, then we could finish and go to the market also. We had a lot of time together on those clinics.
>
> [Viru] came along as the doctor for our roadside clinics. I remember we ate breakfast and lunch off aluminum plates. He was a good cook. We'd have chicken curry and rice every day. That was our lunch. It was very nice."
>
> - Nancy

Their two-year friendship quickly blossomed into a romantic interest and within the year Viru asked Nancy to marry him. Cultural boundaries, family skepticism, resistance from the mission board in America, and even wonderment about performing an "international marriage" service were at hand. As longtime friend Dr. Johnny Oommen writes:

> What were the thoughts Nancy Jane considered?
> Were there waves of anxiety and guilt, romance and love?
> What were the reactions of the mission authorities, the fellow-missionaries, and the Indian staff?
> This was unheard of in this corner of the world; the missionary marrying the native.
> Even the priest, who had to be cajoled and coaxed into conducting the wedding, said: 'I've never conducted an international marriage before!'
>
> But for Nancy Jane, it was a major choice to be made; a significant decision to be taken. It would be an irrevocable, life-changing decision.

On the one hand,
- She was a missionary; on an assignment.
- In a foreign country.
- Here to serve a while; and then to return home.
- A finite, secure arrangement.
- Well-provided for; looked after.
- Bound by the prim proprieties of a mission compound.
- Dedicated for life to serve God and mankind.
- With the secure identity of an expatriate.
- Option 1: Stick to it; take a furlough; let the emotions die down.

The other choice: Option 2:
- Say yes to this exciting man.
- Follow the heart.
- Cut the strings and take the plunge.
- For wasn't this mission anyway? Incarnational mission?
    - To become part of the people you serve?
    - To allow yourself to dissolve like salt?
    - To become the change you want to bring about?

And she chose Option 2.

In May 1964, Nancy Jane Lott became Mrs. N. J. Henry
Married in the Khariar Church.
A new identity.

She lost her missionary status and salary and security.
She became the spouse of an Indian citizen.
With this so much changed for her.
She has never spoken of all it took.

We have only heard anecdotes; stories that are the tip of the iceberg.
Of how she was disappointed that her husband didn't get a cake for her birthday. But how was he to know?

Or of the evening she had planned a romantic, candlelight dinner; all set and ready for when hubby dear comes home. He thought the electricity had gone. Checked. Put on the lights, and helpfully blew out the candles. And ate dinner!

And her great efforts to be the dutiful, subservient Indian wife.
Taking care to get to know and appreciate all her husband's relatives.
To be the good daughter-in-law.

She even believed her husband when he fooled her into thinking that all Indian wives massage their husband's legs before going to sleep.
And she did it for the next 45 years!

- Johnny Oommen[2]

Most vivid in the memories of their courtship is music. Nancy played the flute. Viru possessed a powerful voice and was skilled at playing the harmonium and drums, among other instruments. He organized a singing group in Khariar that traveled for competition. He was also a skilled songwriter, providing many original songs for the group.

One song he wrote was about finding his lover under the mahua tree (Madhuca Longifolia.) For many, the tree holds mystical meaning and practical value. People use the oil from its seeds in cooking, soap making, and even as a fuel oil. Seed cakes, formed after the extraction of oil, are used as fertilizer. Additionally, the flowers of the mahua tree are used medicinally and, when combined with granulated molasses, fermented to make a mildly alcoholic drink popular in northern India.

Under the Mahua Tree

Under the mahua tree the light of love burns on, my dear, my dear.
Under the mahua tree the light of love burns on, my dear.

From a nearby lake a boat paddler's flute releases a lilting melody.

Today the whole world is charmed by its melody.
My sweetheart, please don't break this bond of love.
This full moonlight scene shall never leave us.

Under the mahua tree the light of love burns on, my dear, my dear.
Under the mahua tree the light of love burns on, my dear.

The heavens above are filled with clouds,
Flame of the forest petals form beautiful red lines on the earth,

As if filling the mang[3] of a wife.
My sweetheart, please don't break this bond of love.
As the mang on the earth is filled in red, so also may your mang be filled.

Under the mahua tree the light of love burns on, my dear, my dear.
Under the mahua tree the light of love burns on, my dear.

-Viru, written in medical school, c. 1957-1961 (Translated from Hindi.)

"We had to sing [this song] wherever we went. Mahua has a lot of meaning to him. It was about meeting your lover under the mahua tree.

After we first met Viru heard I played the flute and asked if I'd like to play a song with him and his choir at a Christian conference. He asked if I knew any Indian songs and I told him I only knew one, something I had heard on the radio and like the melody. I had a transistor radio and had learned to play a popular song, something from the cinema. I don't remember the name of it.

It wasn't common to play a song from the cinema at a Christian conference, but he did it anyway. The lyrics were in Hindi and I didn't understand what he was singing, but the refrain was, 'A foreigner took my heart.'

37

When he sang it, he looked at me, and everyone knew who he was talking about. Someone told me what the lyrics were, but I wasn't sure it was me.

I don't remember if I was embarrassed or not. Probably a little. But also very flattered."

- Nancy

Nancy's father, Fred Lott, visited India December 1963 through January 1964 for the first and only time. Fred hadn't seen his daughter in over three years and Nancy says they were overjoyed to see one another. It was a bittersweet reunion though, as Nancy's mother, Margaret, had died the previous year, in March of 1962. Nancy says Fred fell into depression following the loss of his wife and, hoping to boost his spirits, traveled around the United States staying with his children and grandchildren in the year following her death. Knowing how much Fred wanted to see Nancy, his children collected funds to send him on a worldwide trip that included a long layover in India.

Nancy remembers Fred enjoying his two-month holiday in India. He was most interested in the work Nancy was doing at the hospital, even accompanying her and Viru during field hospital rounds. Viru, a consummate host and entertainer, made sure Fred saw and experienced a variety of Indian essentials, including a hunting trip during which Viru shot a leopard.

"There wasn't much entertainment in Khariar. That was the exciting life, to go hunting. They could get deer – there were all kinds of deer.

[The state] didn't give hunting licenses there at the time. You have to have a license to have a gun in India, but you could hunt game without a license. Viru used to go hunting with all the officials. The raja sahib [regional governor] would go with him. They were great friends. All the rajas in every state did the hunting. It was normal. There were so many tigers in those days, it's not like today. The maharajas, the British, and the missionaries are all gone – and the tigers are almost gone.

But on this hunt [Viru] shot a leopard and had a skin made out of it. He had the head mounted and everything. It's very beautiful. He shot it, when my father was there. A lot happened when my father was there."

- Nancy

But hunting and touring were only part of Fred's experience. He was introduced to, and thoroughly loved, Indian food and culture. A well-read, politically astute, and adventurous person, Fred dug into learning all he could about the people he encountered. The hospital staff threw an elaborate 72nd birthday party for him on January 17, 1694, dressing Fred in a silk kurta [formal, long shirt], and celebrating with traditional food and music. Nancy says it was one of the finest memories of his life.

Another highlight of Fred's experience was the development of his friendship with Viru. Beyond the adventures they undertook, Fred and Viru became quick friends and Viru made Nancy's father aware of their courtship right away and received his blessing to marry her. Nancy says her father saw how happy she was in India, to be doing the work to which she was called. He could also see how happy Viru made her and, although it meant she would remain in India the rest of her life, approved of their relationship.

On 4 May 1964 the church bells of the Evangelical Hospital Khariar rang to announce the marriage between Dr. V. K. Henry and Mrs. Nancy Jane Henry. It was the beginning of a set of new challenges and exploits for the Henrys.

Nancy was committed to being, as she says, "a good Indian wife." Culturally she knew this involved setting the tone for the family – meeting the needs of her husband, children, and the extended family. She was to become, as Dr. Johnny Oommen wrote about Nancy in his article *The Lady Behind the Gentleman*, a "traditional Indian wife."

"For Nancy Henry, it has been a life-long commitment. She came out to India as a missionary, but chose to let go and to immerse herself in the ocean that is India. In marrying Dr. Henry, she made a considered decision to dovetail her individual vision into his mission, to find a joint calling.

39

There would be no furloughs, no mission secretaries to aid her, no backing out if things got tough. She would have to take on a new identity, a new family, a new culture, a new role. The traditional Indian wife is not an easy role to play, but practice she did, until she got it perfect."[4]

- Johnny Oommen

The marriage also brought about an unintended consequence – Nancy was dismissed from her American mission agency. The rules of foreign mission service were clear at the time, she says: once a woman married a "native" of the country she was serving, the mission agency would no longer provide support. But this rule was not applied unilaterally, as male missionaries were allowed to marry women native to the country in which they served.

"I was angry about it at first. Nothing had changed for me – I was still going to be doing the same work they'd sent me to do. The only thing that had changed was I was now married to Dr. Henry.

There were people who wanted me to protest, to write to the mission board and plead my case for them to change the policy. It was the beginning of women's liberation – women's rights in the 1960s – and people in America thought I should fight it. But I didn't. I knew what I was getting into. I knew marrying Dr. Henry could be the end of my mission support. Of course, I hoped they wouldn't do such a thing, but those were the rules and I had made up my mind."

- Nancy

Undeterred, Nancy and Viru never looked back in all their years of service and continued their work at Khariar Evangelical Hospital – serving the medical needs of those in the community and surrounding villages, overseeing the nursing program, teaching others about the good news they had found in Jesus Christ, and growing their commitment to one another and the mission to which they were called.

[1] http://www.ncbi.nlm.nih.gov/pmc/articles/PMC3734678/

[2] Oommen, Johnny, "A Story Untold," collected writings April 2009.

[3] The red mang is a sign of a married woman. It is the part in the wife's hair that is filled with red color. In Indian practice, when a husband was called off to war or danger, he pricked his finger to apply his blood in the part of his wife's hair to give hope of his safe return.

[4] Oommen, Johnny, "The Lady Behind the Gentleman" in *To Sir With Love*, 5 September 1998.

Chapter 4: A Surprise in the Garden

Soon after the Henrys were married, Dr. Laun and his wife went on furlough in Germany and Switzerland, a required break from their work in India. The direction of the hospital was left to Viru who, along with two other junior doctors, were working in Khariar.

> "When Dr. Laun went on furlough, he had to go for one year. The hospital had very few doctors. One was Prem Jiwanmall who is a family friend and his wife was there, she was also a doctor. So they had three doctors, but they were all just fresh out of M.B.B.S. school. They didn't have any specialty. He had to turn over to one of them. The lady, she would never take over the husband, so it was between her husband and [Viru.] It was a very hard thing for Dr. Laun to do.
>
> My husband was elder in age, so it fell to him."
>
> - Nancy

The area around Khariar, the Kalahandi district of Orissa, experienced extreme drought in 1965 and a famine had struck the region. Viru, recalling the lack of winter rains that had left the soil dry and cracked as the summer heat overtook the area, says malnutrition was acute.

> "If they don't get rain in the previous year, the following year is terrible. The crops don't grow and there's no place to go for water or food. That's why there was a famine going on in the area.
>
> Part of the problem was overpopulation. That's why the vasectomy program was deemed necessary by the government. There were just too many people to be supported by the agriculture of the area. Transportation wasn't what it is today – it was harder to move goods from one region to another. You can only imagine how a severe

drought would impact people, especially poor people in the villages.

Bread for the World had a big feeding program going on to assist the people. When Indira Gandhi came to visit we were considered the VIPs of that place, and we got to go greet her at the helicopter when she arrived. She came and saw all the feeding programs in the area. There was a lot going on. It was a very big program."

- Viru

The situation was especially dire for infants and children, the elderly, and pregnant women. Survival in these desperate times often meant sharing all-too-few resources with an entire family. New mothers – often villagers from farming communities, driven to desperation by lack of food and water – began bringing their newborns to the Evangelical Hospital in Khariar to receive foster care, hoping their children would be adopted by other families.

Dr. Laun's wife had begun a nursery for these adoptees, and sometimes abandoned orphans. When the nursery was full, she took them into her own home to provide care or secure permission from the government to assist in placing children in adoptive homes overseas.

"If they wanted to get rid of their children for some reason, if they couldn't support them or the mother died – everyone knew that she would take them.
She took them right in her house. She supervised the care herself, right in her own house. She used to have 8-10 babies all the time.

Later, she was permitted to even take them out of the country. She took many of them to Switzerland, where she was from. She was married to a German, so they came from Germany, but her parents were in Switzerland. She took quite a few over there to be adopted. Some were adopted here. She'd get them all adopted and she'd get more all the time.

We mentioned to you that Dr. Laun went on furlough for one year. So what happens is, the people continued to bring babies while they were not around. We were both in the hospital so I had to keep them in the hospital, which wasn't so successful because they're around sickness and nurses are busy. Although they loved those babies, they couldn't give them the attention they wanted to. We started refusing a few, because I couldn't manage that at home when I was at the hospital. That was known around that the hospital took babies that needed it."

- Nancy

But not all children were delivered to the steps of the hospital. One warm July day in 1965, Viru arrived home to find a special delivery.

"During that famine, my husband came home for lunch from the hospital. She was in a basket, lying in the garden. A closed basket. I can't remember all the details, because he found her."

- Nancy

"It was a cute baby somebody left on our door."

- Viru

Viru and Nancy had been trying to start a family of their own, but Nancy had not yet gotten pregnant. Overcome by the need to provide homes for these orphans, and desiring a child of their own, the Henrys decided to take the child in.

"This one, we wanted to keep her in our house. She was so beautiful with black, curly hair. She was only about a month and a half old, but she already had all this hair. My husband wanted to keep her at home, so I said, 'Okay, because we're not getting good results. We can keep one as our own.'

It was a difficult decision; we actually had someone in mind that really wanted to adopt a child – a Christian person. We

45

said, 'Let us keep her for a while and see if these people would want her.'"

- Nancy

They named the child Anjali (little angel) and cared for her as their own, dividing their time between hospital duties and forming a family. Within a few weeks, they realized something wasn't quite right with Anjali's vision. Though she would move toward sounds and seemed to recognize voices, her eyes moved erratically and she didn't follow objects or people by sight.

"What happened is she didn't fix her eyes. The books say they don't quite see until they're two months anyway and she wasn't quite two months old. Then, Dr. Laun came back from furlough that month, in July 1965. He immediately said, 'Have you had her eyes checked?' We said, 'No, but we've been looking at it and wondering if there's anything. We've been putting torches [flashlights] on this and that. Does she see? Does she follow?'

Looking at her eye, the surface of it didn't look correct. There was some abnormality, some pathology there. Dr. Laun didn't give a diagnosis, but he knew something was wrong. It wasn't normal. The retina wasn't normal and he said to us, 'You'd better watch her.'

She followed the light a bit. At that time, she would look up if you put the light on that one side. I think she could see light from one part of her eye. She definitely followed the light, but she didn't follow us. We were talking to her and moving here and there and she could follow. But if we weren't talking, she didn't recognize our motion.

We decided to take her to Calcutta for examination. The doctor told us she had a condition called chorioretinitis."

- Nancy

Chorioretinitis is an inflammation of the uveal tract, the pigmented middle of the three concentric layers that make up the eye. The inflammation is usually caused by congenital viral, bacterial, or protozoal infections in infants. Contracted in utero, and undiagnosed and untreated in infancy, the inflammation causes partial or complete blindness in a majority of infants affected. The root cause of Anjali's chorioretinitis was unknown, but Nancy and Viru recognized they had received a special assignment to care for their beautiful black-haired gift.

> "We didn't know much about her background. Then we got back from Calcutta and we said, 'Now, we have a girl who's handicapped. We don't want to give her away.'
>
> For some reason, God had brought this girl to us and we decided to keep her. At that time, we were thinking of going to America. Quite a few months went by. We just kept her and she became ours. We wanted to adopt her, but India does not have adoption. You can only adopt your own relative's child. They're trying to get that changed. They are modernizing it. In those days, it was not legally possible. We just kept her as our own, but we decided to find out who left her there. We did find that family. It was a man and the father of the mother said, 'We want to give this baby to you and you can keep her for all her life.'
>
> They had to give that in writing to the courts. That's all we could do. It had to be something in our hand to legally keep her. This all took some months.
>
> She was born in June, but we didn't know her exact birthdate. They told us approximately when in their Hindu calendar it was and we made a birthday for her. We got somebody to tell us about June 3, so we made that her birthday. It was before her first birthday, in April of 1966, when we made this decision."
>
> - Nancy

The Henrys did not leave for America immediately, but kept at their work in the hospital and caring for their infant daughter. Nancy says she was relieved to have Mrs. Laun back in Khariar, especially when it came to the care of the orphans.

"After Mrs. Laun came back, she took the babies back in her house. While they were gone, we had many in the hospital, more than 10 orphans at a time. It became difficult to find somebody. We were very glad when she came back. It ran much better when she was there. She was a housewife that had servants in the house and she needed something to do. She really liked doing that."

- Nancy

By the summer of 1966, plans to visit the United States were in motion. Nancy's sister Peg had visited earlier in the year and gave news that their father was in poor health, having suffered a series of minor strokes. Anjali had turned one year old and Nancy was pregnant. The time seemed right for the journey.

"By the next year (1966), my sister came in April. That's my sister and brother-in-law, Herbert Muenstermann, who encouraged me to go into mission. He was the personnel secretary of our mission. He had originally tried to get me to go to Africa. At that time, he was the personnel secretary of the new board, the United Church Board for World Ministries. He had originally been with the Evangelical and Reformed mission board.

They came with their eight-year-old daughter and spent a few days with us. I was expecting Anil at that time. He was born 7 August. I went to Delhi to meet them. They came to tell me that my father was having small strokes from time to time. When I had come to India, I had lost my mother. I didn't even know she died until one month after it happened. I was totally out of it. They didn't want that to happen this time. They suggested that we come before Christmas.

They said, 'He seems alright and he gets over these things but they are attacks on his brain. We don't know which one will affect his speech or cause him to die.'"

- Nancy

Viru asked permission from the Church of North India Christian Medical Association of India (CMAI) for a break from his service bond to leave for America. Viru remembers it taking a great deal of trust on the part of the church to let them go.

> "They knew we were not going to leave the country, never to return to India. We asked for one year. When [our third child] was on the way, we asked to have his delivery in the United States so that extended our stay a bit. People might have thought Nancy had taken me back to America and run off, but they were very kind and believed us.
>
> Nana [Viru's grandfather, Paul] came to see us off from the train. We all cried. It was very sad. We wondered if we'd ever see him again because he was past 80. He died while we were away."
>
> -   Viru

Due to Anjali's informal adoption status, a legal challenge was in front of the Henrys. Officials refused the family's request for a visa so Anjali could to travel to the United States.

> "We told Peg we'd come in the first week of December. We went to get our passports and visas in Calcutta, but they refused to give one to Anjali. We took the papers we had but they said, 'You can have her here but we cannot give a visa on the basis of this.'
>
> We had to leave Anjali behind. The headmistress of the mission school, a single lady, Grace Solomon – she loved Anjali so much – volunteered to care for Anjali while we were gone. In fact, when we had Anjali baptized, she was the godmother. She'd go on her rounds to the boarding. We had a girls boarding and a boys boarding. We had a school up to middle school and she was in charge of that. She would go on her rounds and be carrying Anjali everywhere."
>
> -   Nancy

Having left Anjali behind, the infant Anil traveled with his parents to the United States, ultimately landing in the New York City area. But the tenacity of friends in India paved the way for Anjali to be reunited with the family within a few months.

> "We had to go without her and Auntie Solomon said, 'I will keep her.' So she kept her. Then Leila Wasser, who was very fond of Anjali, also cared for her. After we'd already been over there for some time, these two ladies worked on getting Anjali a visa.
>
> They went back to the consulate officials. Leila was an American citizen and Auntie Solomon was the caretaker of the girl. They had the papers with them and they finally got a visa, a tourist visa or something like that.
>
> They gave one because they said we wanted to get her eyes examined in America. We wanted to know from the American doctors what we should expect and what we could do for her. They were able to get that visa and she came over all by herself in the spring of 1967.
>
> Regarding her going, of course, they took her and put her on the plane and she went alone. In those days, the airlines were so good. They would make one of the hostesses responsible for this child.
>
> She got so attached to Anjali and it went off very well. The only thing was that Anjali didn't eat anything the whole trip, except for one apple. Everything they offered, she didn't want. I think she was a little frightened, but she was good with them.
>
> My husband got a report from the hostess who carried her out. She told what she did and what she didn't do. She was very good, but she didn't talk much. She didn't eat. She must have been confused. We didn't know how we would manage this. We thought she wouldn't remember us."

- Nancy

After the multi-day flight, Anjali was understandably confused. Also, due to her young age – not yet two at the time of her journey – Nancy and Viru doubted she would have retained much of her English language skills, having spent the previous four months in the care of Hindi-speaking Auntie Solomon. It was decided that Viru would go to the airport to receive Anjali so he could speak with her.

> "I said, 'Anjali, I'm Papa. I'm here to take you. You're in America.' She came right to me, but she spoke only Hindi then."
>
> - Viru

Nancy and Viru brought Anjali home to their apartment in New Jersey. The family of four, including the six-month-old Anil, received Anjali with joy after such a long separation. Nancy says she was worried about how much Anjali would remember of her family, and how she would acclimate to America. To ease her transition, Viru cooked traditional Indian food for her, giving Anjali at least one common frame of reference after her long journey and months of being away from Viru, Nancy, and her baby brother Anil.

> "She was very attached to me, even though she didn't say Mama. She was so taken with her Papa, right from the moment we picked her up we knew she remembered us. He spent the whole evening with her. We had a nice Indian curry ready for her. Viru cooked. He did most of the cooking [in America.]
>
> Curry and rice was ready for her when she came home to the apartment. She ate and ate. She didn't know the things they were offering to her on the plane. Then we thought how she would sleep in a strange place. He just kept talking to her.
>
> Viru said, 'So this is home to us. You've come to America.' Then he lay down on the bed. She was really tired. We gave her a bath and got her ready for bed. He lay down on the bed with her and was talking to her. She went off to sleep just like that. From then on, she was at home.

The only problem was the language. She had forgotten her English. We said we'd have to start speaking English with her. We were speaking Hindi with her so she'd understand. I started speaking English to her right away, because she wouldn't be able to communicate with other people if she didn't learn it."

- Nancy

Anjali's resilience to separation and travel were amazing. Furthermore, Nancy remembers Anjali as an exceptional child, excelling in many ways without regard to her ability to see. Nancy's initial thoughts about Anjali's language ability were how they wanted to teach her English as soon as possible after arriving in America. But she was also aware of her intellect and ability to communicate from a young age. Far from being inhibited by her inability to see, Nancy recounted a few of the ways Anjali's blindness gave everyone an appreciation for her many abilities.

"She was so tiny. It was so interesting. She was so intelligent. She was always speaking with the housekeeper I had in the house.

She would be doing the ironing and Anjali would swing. The two of them would talk. This is a girl who was less than two years old and she's carrying on a conversation. It's amazing how she picked up language, faster than most children.

Another thing we learned about her was this: We had a playpen for her and she'd pull herself up and walk all around the playpen. She never crawled. From that we can see that children see something they want and they crawl to it. She didn't have that, so she just walked, first with help hanging onto to the thing and then she just walked.

I will tell one more interesting thing. I was giving her a bottle of milk at certain times and she'd lie down in her bed and drink it. Then suddenly, I came home, and here's a crashed bottle. We didn't have plastic bottles, so she kept breaking them. She'd throw it out of the crib. Pretty soon, she kept throwing it and I said, 'We had better get this girl on a cup or something. I don't think she wants that bottle anymore.' She kind of rejected the bottle and that's true. She started drinking from a cup right away that she could hold herself.

To raise her was very different from raising a sighted child, in this infant time. It was a very interesting and wonderful experience for us, and later for our children, to have Anjali in the family.

She learned to walk very soon. It didn't take her long. She was ahead in everything. Only her sight was not there. She was advanced in all her other developmental milestones."

- Nancy

With the Henry family reunited in America, there was much learning and work to be done. Visits with family were interspersed with work at a local hospital in New Jersey, raising children, and tasks requested of the New York City-based mission agency. It would be a fruitful and difficult time for the family, and an experience that would influence their work for decades to come.

Chapter 5: Life in America

Viru , Nancy, and Anil arrived in New York in December of 1966; the infant Anil not yet four months old. Daughter Anjali had to remain in India for the next four months awaiting a visa approval before she could travel to the United States. Similar to many working families, life was hectic. Nancy says it was a challenge to juggle work schedules and child care needs, getting used to American cultural and hospital norms, work with the mission board, and fitting in with neighbors and friends.

What had been normal to Nancy about American life merely seven years previously now seemed foreign. To her "very Indian husband," as she recalls, the social norms and pace of life were alien. Yet, ever the consummate professionals, their lives continued with shared appreciation and love. Viru had come to Nancy's homeland, just as she had dedicated her life to be in his. He was going to try his best to fit in and be there when Nancy and her extended family needed their presence the most.

> "We went before Christmas to my sister and brother-in-law, Peg and Herb's place in Leonia New Jersey just across the bridge from New York City where Herb worked as Executive for 'Friends of Vellore' (Christian Medical College Vellore, South India) and Peg had worked as Office Manager for our UCC World Ministries Board. At first we stayed with them because my father was there with them in Leonia. He was so excited to see us, especially his new son-in-law and his new grandson. We could see that he looked pretty good and happy to be there in Leonia. At that time, Peg wasn't working, although she was very active in the community. She was the Municipal Council president, but didn't have an official job then.
>
> Peggy took such wonderful care of Daddy that he liked to stay with her. He used to go visit some of the other homes of our family, but he'd always come back to her home. The added attraction was that young Paula, at 8 years of age loved

to be with 'Grandpa,' so he had extra attention and they became great friends. Peg made a nurse's uniform to fit Paula, including a nurse's cap so she could play nurse and help 'take care of Grandpa.' They also shared their special secrets, for example, due to his diabetes, Peg watched his diet and kept it in control. When she wasn't at home, Grandpa asked Paula if she'd like to go over for a treat at the near-by ice cream parlor and of course that to Paula was a great idea. What fun! On the way back Grandpa said, 'Now Paula, let us just keep this our secret and don't tell your mother.' That sounded like fun too, and so she did.

As Christmas was drawing near, we had an early celebration around the Christmas tree in the Muenstermann home in Leonia which was special to have with Paula in her own home, before taking off for Westerville, Ohio where my elder sister Betty Lou, her husband, Dick and their 6 kids were eagerly awaiting our arrival for Christmas. Herb drove us on the long journey to Ohio. My father also went and took the journey well; he was with us all the time.

He was so pleased to hold Anil on his lap. The proud grandfather held him every chance he could get and Paula always joined him to play with the baby. We had a fabulous Christmas with the Millers. Everybody wanted to hold baby Anil. Everybody else's kids were much bigger by then. He was the star of the show, as everybody passed him around. Viru was also kept busy meeting all these new relatives for the first time, and they loved him immediately.

Peg and Herb had met Viru when they visited India. They were staying with us in Khariar, so they knew him, but the rest of the family hadn't met him. Everywhere we went, we found more relatives and they were anxious to meet him and little Anil. Of course Anjali hadn't arrived in America then. It reminded me of my introduction to Viru's large extended family of 65 first cousins in India."

- Nancy

While Viru's medical certifications were being sorted out he worked for the United Church Mission Board, a position offered by Nancy's brother-in-law, Herb. Viru first worked providing health exams for returning missionaries. Later, he began visiting churches to tell them about the various efforts around the world, encouraging congregations to give financially to the work of the mission board. It was called deputations at that time. Viru traveled extensively in New England and to other parts of the United States, telling stories from India and promoting mission work, while having the opportunity to see the country and interact with American Christians.

"When we first got to America, the first job Viru had was not in a hospital and I was not working at all because Anil was pretty small. I was at home with my sister, but Viru worked in the board office. The mission board office had a section where they did health checkups for the missionaries when they came home. That was in the mission board office in New York City at 475 Riverside Drive, with the National Council of Churches headquarters.

Eventually he began doing deputations in the New England states. That started soon after we reached America and were staying with Peg and Herb. It would have been early in 1967. They asked him to do deputations so he went to tell stories about his experiences as a doctor in the mission hospital. The board tries to grab anybody they can to do these itineraries, which keep the congregation in touch with their mission work. It's something that has to be done a lot. He had interesting experiences in that also.

Somebody in one of his audiences wanted to buy a cobalt machine. It was a revolutionary way to treat cancerous tumors at that time. But it was an impractical unit to send out into the mission field in rural India. It would be too expensive to be maintained, if it could even be serviced in a remote location.

Viru gave an example. My niece, Paula, wanted me to give her a camera, he said, 'I can buy you a camera, but when I'm not here, who will buy the film? 'That will fall on your parents to buy the film and everything it needs. She was too young to have a camera of her own, so he talked her out of it.

It was similar with the donation of the cobalt machine. It might make it to India or Africa, but in those days there would be no one to keep it running, so it would be useless after a while."

- Nancy

The bureaucratic assignment with the board was not to solicit contributions to specific projects, but to support the work of the board in efforts it directed. It was a message Viru heard loud and clear, even as he struggled to understand the complexities of the mission agency's overall work.

"They had a policy where you could not ask for money for your own project when you went on deputations. I was required to have an overall approach of 'it's for the board.' If the board cannot pay salaries to the missionaries, then how can anything go on? You have to support missionary salaries. They were very strong on that and we weren't allowed to ask donations for India.

We were not directly working for the board. We were working for the Evangelical Hospital in Khariar, which was established many years ago by missionaries of the recently merged United Church of Christ. Even then, we stayed very close to the work of the board. If we went to America, we also went to the board office. They could use our services, and I went on several trips to speak with congregations.

I was once on a tiny plane going someplace, maybe New Hampshire. I was the only passenger. I told the crew, 'If this plane goes down, I have to go down alone, and just then turbulence increased and the plane was shaking back and forth while I struggled to reach the back of the plane! I hadn't done any flying at that point other than coming to America. I flew many times after that, but there were so many cultural experiences to understand."

- Viru

Nancy empathizes with the transition and compares the struggles Viru experienced in America to her own cultural adjustments in India.

"He had a lot of cultural matters to deal with there, just as I had in India. But at least we didn't have malaria and snakes to cope with in the U.S."

- Nancy

But Viru wanted to get back to hospital work. Even though the medical board wouldn't accept his medical degree and certification from India. with the help of a family friend, he ultimately found his way to the hospital in Englewood where Nancy already was employed.

"Although working with the mission board was his first job there, he wanted to do something more clinical. We went over to the Englewood hospital and he applied, and got the job. I was in the maternity ward doing permanent night duty and he was an extern there. Englewood is located just over the George Washington Bridge from New York City and next to Leonia where Herb and Peg lived.

The hospital administration settled us in one of their apartments just a block away. We could see the hospital from our apartment window, so it was very convenient. I worked night duty and he worked day duty. That's how we made our schedule, so that we could take turns caring for our children. Every night Viru walked me over to the hospital for night duty. Then quickly he walked back to the apartment to be with the children who were already asleep. In the morning I would rush back to take over the childcare while he dashed over to the hospital for morning rounds. During the day I would feed the children, clean house, wash and iron clothes. We had a nice playpen for Anil and he was happy to be with his toys and watch his favorite TV kiddy programs while I did my housework. . When Anjali came, she also played happily with Anil. By God's grace we were blessed with such obedient children.

We were able to get a red car that Anil could sit in and 'drive' by pushing the pedals and it was his favorite toy. He liked to drive it around in the cemented area with the clotheslines where I hung the wet clothes to dry.

One day when I finished my work, I called out to Anil to take him home, but he was nowhere to be found! I called out loudly in panic and started searching for him. But with my last weeks before delivery tummy, I couldn't run fast and was frantic, not knowing what to do. Our neighbor heard me calling and dashed over to help. She ran out towards the road and found Anil, sitting in his car, waiting for the red light at the crossing along with the halted traffic. She grabbed him just as the light was changing to green. Praise the Lord and thanks be to a kind and caring neighbor!

After lunch we were ready for a nap and that gave me a chance to catch up on my sleep. Viru would return in the afternoon, quietly take the children from their beds and took them out to the park for swings and slides while I slept through until dinner. The children were already in bed for the night when we locked the door and Viru accompanied me to the hospital at 11 PM for duty. Our children were so good as the cycle went on in this unusual routine. However, we could be together with them two days of the week on my nights off. This was life in America. We remembered how we could have household help and an ayeh [nanny] to look after the little ones in India. We were a bit homesick for our Indian life!

I always worked nights in labor and delivery room and we could get good experience at night. There were no doctors staying in the delivery room at night. We nurses had to watch our patients in labor very closely and call the doctor from home and his sleep just at the right time, not too early and not too late. Sometimes we ended up delivering a baby that popped out before the doctor reached! I learned a lot which was useful to my work in India.

We had a friend, Dr. Robbins, and he was instrumental in getting us over to that hospital. He was actually a psychiatrist as well as a neurologist. He kind of mentored Viru, working in the neurology department. He'd go along with Dr. Robbins to learn and also did a lot of things the patient required and was helpful to the team. He was actually doing major operations back in India, so he could handle quite a lot."

- Nancy

"I was doing neurology at Englewood Hospital; it was way different than my [surgical] work in India.

- Viru

"He was just coming from India and he wasn't registered, so he couldn't work independently as a doctor. He worked like an intern; I think they called him an extern. He was a competent qualified doctor from India, but always had someone over him in the U.S.A. He had to be backed up by somebody who could take responsibility. I continued to work at the Englewood Hospital, but he got a better job at Lincoln Hospital in the Bronx where he joined the pathology department."

- Nancy

As these transactions were taking place, Nancy and Viru were expecting another addition to the family while sharing the care of Anjali and Anil, Viru had been offered the job in the Bronx, which meant a longer commute and further negotiating the schedule of the two busy parents caring for two and soon three children.

The trip to the hospital introduced Viru to the new experience of subway travel. Viru tells that he moved casually through the crowd to reach the platform while everyone else was running. He wondered why they were in such a rush. After one or two days missing his connecting train and having to wait for the next one to arrive –

61

ultimately delaying his arrival at the hospital – he realized the cause of the rush. Viru found himself running along with the crowd. It was another step of adjustment in the new life in America.

"I was at home all day with the children. I'd hurry home in the morning after duty and Viru would already be up, had his breakfast and ready to go. I had the joy of spending time with our kids in this cute toddler age. I never saw kids who were so co-operative and fun to be with. In the afternoon when I needed rest, they would happily lie down, take their nap and sleep until their Papa came home to take them out of bed. Viru was in charge of both kids when Anjali came. He'd take them to the park to play outside on the swings and slide, feed them dinner, give them a bath, and put them to bed at night. He was really a special father who could enjoy spending so much time, taking care of his kids and keeping them happy.

That worked out very well because he had no on-call from the Bronx because he lived too far away and did only day duty at the hospital. We couldn't hire anybody to be with our children yet, and we didn't know anyone to do it. We had to manage ourselves and that's how we did it."

- Nancy

"Everybody runs, so I had to run. They didn't want to miss their connection on the other track. In the beginning I'd let them run by me. Then I'd start running. Otherwise I'd miss my connection and be very late. I had three connections to get to the Bronx from Englewood. It was a very long commute and I felt a bit stupid but got used to it and it was good exercise."

- Viru

"There were so many stories about the subway, and Englewood was far from the Bronx. That's when we decided to buy a car. It was a very nice second hand car in excellent condition. We got it through a church that was sponsoring us. The mission board used to have churches sponsor people working in the missions. I was not a missionary and he was not a missionary, but we were serving in a mission hospital. I went on doing the same work I was doing, even though I wasn't officially a missionary. When I got married, I made that decision to go on doing that same work for which I had been commissioned.

They connected us with a church in Michigan City, Indiana. Rev. Frankenfeld was the wonderful pastor there. We went there twice, I believe; and we were continually in contact with them. We mentioned to him that we need to buy a car somehow, to our delight, he replied, 'You know, somebody is selling a good car in our congregation.'"

- Nancy

"It was a beautiful blue Chevrolet Impala sedan. Rev. Frankenfeld said that it would be inexpensive and it had been well taken care of. We paid for it, but didn't pay much. It worked out that Herb went there to get it for us. It was much easier for him to drive the car out on the freeway to New Jersey. It also gave Herb a chance to meet Pastor Frankenfeld, an old friend from their seminary days in St. Louis."

- Viru

"We were about to welcome Ajit into the world at that time. So we hired a high school girl to come and help in the house. I had to have a C-section so; it would take time for recovery. Then this girl would be home with Anjali, three years old and Anil, two years old, while I was in the hospital. We thought it best to bring her ahead of time so she would be used to the house and routines. She didn't know the Hindi language, so Anjali started to speak English with her.

When I came home from the hospital with my beautiful 10 pound baby boy, Anjali was speaking to me and to him in English! It didn't take long for her to pick it up, once she had to do it. She and Anil were full of excitement to meet their new brother, Ajit. He looked like a doll and they wanted to touch him and give him a kiss. They had been left every day in the care of Nani while my husband was at work. It seems that they were quite attached to Nani.

That was our life in America."

- Nancy

Nancy recalls the differences she felt in returning to America. She had become accustomed to life in India, and to the hospital system there. Nancy particularly was disturbed by the medical system's reliance on doctors to do all the medical tasks in the hospital. With her training and field experience in Indian hospitals, she felt ready to do much more hands on work than American hospitals would allow a nurse to do.

"I didn't like the system in America, I'm sorry to say. The nurses don't know how to deliver a baby under normal circumstances and if there is no doctor around, they have to just catch it, which could cause complications. In America where I was working as a nurse in labor and delivery room, there were no doctors on duty for labor and delivery at night. Our job was to get the doctor there. We nurses were trained to monitor a mother in labor, but only doctors conducted deliveries. We had to call the doctor just on time – not too early and certainly not too late! Where, if you go to countries with trained midwives, you'll find that the infant mortality is less, like the U.K. and Sweden. These countries have the lowest infant mortality rate in the world. The U.K. midwives are trained so well, the doctors come only when called for any emergency or abnormality. The midwives are giving complete prenatal care of a normal pregnancy. They know how to recognize complications and when to refer to doctors. They are trained so well in a 2 or 3-year course, and give appropriate health education and support to the pregnant mother who enjoys rapport with her midwife.

In India also, the trained midwives are generally very good. I always found that I was lacking in this field and thought the least I could do was to request work in that department, labor and delivery at Englewood Hospital. I am an American trained nurse and studied obstetrical nursing in our course, but not how to diagnose and treat the patient. So I decided that when I went back to India, I must take the midwifery course.

In India, all nurses are trained midwives, and they conduct normal deliveries in a safe and accepted manner. In 1978 I completed the midwifery course at Christian Medical College, Vellore to become a registered midwife in order to start an auxiliary nursing-midwifery school which was approved by the Christian Board of Nursing (Mid-India Board of Education of the Christian Medical Association of India) and The Indian Nursing Council of India (the government agency)."

- Nancy

Viru was happy to be working in a clinical setting, gaining experience in pathology at a large institution. But he was confused by some American social norms; none so striking to him as people's behavior at a funeral. Following Fred Lott's death in March, 1967, the Henrys were surprised by the jovial attitude of those attending the funeral. In addition to the sense of communal mourning that accompanies Indian funerals, Viru was especially disturbed because of the great affection he felt for Fred and the relationship they had developed since their first meeting in India in 1963.

"Funerals were most different. According to Viru, all they worried about was eating and drinking coffee. I have pictures from my father's funeral, and many of the family were talking, eating, and laughing. It is a much more serious occasion in India. This he didn't like at all. He was quite upset and went outside. He had gotten so acquainted with my father. They really clicked. He was so fond of him, and as Daddy got more incapacitated, my husband took special care of him. He gave him a bath, shave, and dressed him every day at my brother, Charles' apartment in Avon Lake. He gave him his food and whatever help he required including walking him about in the apartment. He didn't like it that everyone was laughing and talking. He just didn't feel that way. It was a kind of culture shock for him. Viru lost his own father when he was only five years old and never had the joy of growing up with a father-son relationship. It is natural that he enjoyed being with my father as a father who loved him.

One thing is, so many of my brothers and sisters hadn't seen each other in many years. They brought their families so, of course, they had to talk to each other and catch up. It is actually a kindness that the ladies of the congregation prepare a fine meal, which is generally served near the kitchen in the church. This custom is an act of Christian love and much appreciated by the family.

It is very different in India, much more sober. The Indian Christians have another custom. The mourning family doesn't take interest in food, so turn by turn friends and neighbors prepare a very simple meal of rice, dal [a thick lentil sauce], and a cooked vegetable. They carry the meal to the family home and serve the food to those in mourning, encouraging them to eat. This goes on for 2-3 days. It is just another act of Christian love in another setting."

- Nancy

Although described as very charming and romantic, one story of Viru's misunderstanding of American culture made for a lifelong running joke in the Henry family.

Early in their married life Nancy had prepared for a romantic dinner with candles and a beautiful table, Viru came home and asked Nancy, "Are the lights not on? The lights are on in the hospital. Are there no lights here?" He pushed the power switch and said, "Look, the lights are on. Why are you wasting the candles?"

"I never said anything. I was a new bride so I was just quiet. He didn't know about it until much later. In rural India the electrical supply is frequently going off and for that candles were kept in the house."

- Nancy

The story would come around again just prior to Fred's demise, at the 75th birthday party for Nancy's father and his twin brother,

Frank Lott, held in mid January at the Aquamarine Restaurant in Avon Lake, Ohio.

> "My whole family was there so it was a big group. It was all in candlelight. Viru asked Herb, 'Why do they have all this candlelight here?'
>
> 'To make a romantic atmosphere,' Herb replied. Then he remembered the Khariar incident and they both laughed. I had to adjust to this culture so I shouldn't do that anymore.
>
> By the way, in Khariar, India, my father celebrated his 72nd birthday on 17 January, 1963. We have pictures of him wearing typical Indian dress (white pajama kurta). He really was enjoying his visit.
>
> Every morning children came running to the bungalow because he was handing out wrapped sweets every day to the kids. The crowd got bigger every day. He was very fond of children. We had Christmas there."
>
> - Nancy

In addition to coming to America to attend to the needs of Nancy's father, the Henry family also sought further diagnosis and possible treatment for Anjali's chorioretinitis. Through his hospital, he found doctors who recommended resources that would lead to the best diagnosis for eye diseases. They knew treatment or healing of Anjali's eyes was a long shot, but they had to try.

> "Once she was in the United States, she had an eye examination at Mount Sinai, the big Jewish hospital in New York. We took her and they examined her eyes under anesthesia. They took photographs of them. We sent the photos of her retinas and inner eyes to the Retina Foundation.
>
> There at Mt. Sinai, the doctors said that the optic nerve was affected and it was more than just the retina. They suggested we send the photos and see what they say. The Retina Foundation is famous in Boston. They wrote back to us,

'Right now, we have no solution for this. Research is going on. You keep in touch with the developments,'

The interesting thing is, now that Anjali is grown up, she knows what's going on. She's sent me articles and things that she had hoped something would be done. Her problem became too complicated. Because she was blind, she had painful eyes that had to be removed, one by one. It was a sad thing for us, but remarkable because the prosthesis that were implanted are connected with the muscles, so that the new eye which is lovely can also move.

I don't know if they have anything today or not. It was hard for her because she'd have some hope and it wouldn't work out.

They said, 'We don't have any information for you because science is changing so fast. You never know what's going to be. Right now, we don't see anything in the near future that can be done for her.'

As medical professionals, it was disappointing to us. We had hoped that in America there would be something that would help her. It didn't work out that way.

But she's had a lot of positive things happen to her. God has blessed her in many ways. If she had been left in an Indian village, she'd have been only a beggar. They have nothing in those villages for blind people, particularly untreated ones. If they have cataracts, there are camps they can go to have their cataracts done. But not for her particular disease.

Even as I know she's blessed to have come into our home, we have received much more blessing having her as our daughter."

- Nancy

Ajit, the third and final Henry child, was born in June at Englewood Hospital where Nancy worked in labor and delivery. She had hoped

Viru could perform the Caesarian section, but as she'd discovered in other instances, it wasn't the American way.

"I was working in labor and delivery room; I was right in my own department. I could choose the best doctor to do the operation. They wouldn't let my doctor husband – who had plenty of experience in performing Caesarian sections – come in and do it. There are good reasons for this and this is keeping with medical ethics.

But they wouldn't even allow him to come inside to see it – not like in India where we allow a relative to witness surgery. Still, I had an excellent specialist who was so nice and very competent, and the delivery of Ajit went so smoothly. Viru got the news outside and was delighted to have a healthy baby boy weighing in at almost 10 pounds, just as Viru himself was at birth."

- Nancy

Following Fred Lott's death in March and the birth of Ajit on 17 June 1968, the Henry family began to feel the pull of India, calling them back home. Thankful for the experience they'd had in America, almost two years to the day from when they left India, they returned in December 1968. Dr. Henry published a simple remembrance of this transitional time:

"In 1966 we went for a two-year visit to the U.S.A. to visit family and for experience. We already had two children in Khariar and our third was born in the U.S.A. Our love for India and a desire to serve in my own country brought me and my family back to India in 1968."

- Viru

Chapter 6: A Time in Tilda

The Henrys arrived home to India in December 1968. Their two-year stay in America over, they returned to work with the Church of North India's Medical Wing. There was a need for a medical director and nursing superintendent at the mission hospital in Tilda, a small town on the rail line between Mumbai and Calcutta. Even though it was an isolated location, its proximity is within 40km of Raipur, an important city in the state of Madhya Pradesh. However, in the year 2000 Raipur became the capital of the new state of Chattisgarh and that made it an important stop on the route between the coasts.

> "We came back to Tilda and celebrated Christmas there in 1968. At that time, Tilda was a 110-bed hospital started by missionaries sent out by the Evangelical and Reformed Church Board of International Missions. An early pioneer doctor and Medical Superintendent was Dr. Whitcomb. A school of nursing was also added through the initiative of Sister Minnie Gadt, a Deaconess and early missionary of the Evangelical and Reformed tradition of the United Church of Christ. Of course it was started long before the Evangelical and Reformed Church merged with the Congregational Christian Church to form the UCC [in 1957.]"

> - Nancy

> "We arrived at Mission Hospital, Tilda, District Raipur, M.P., and took up responsibilities, myself as Director of the hospital and my wife as Nursing Superintendent. This was a busy 110-bed general hospital with medical, surgical, and obstetrical services."

> - Viru

Nancy and Viru were already familiar with Tilda, described by Viru as a "sister hospital" to Khariar. Although 200km separated the two facilities, they were part of the association of Christian mission hospitals operated by the Church of North India, with roots in the

71

United Church of Christ and Disciples of Christ mission agencies from America. The Henrys were selected for their experience and skill at running a hospital, as was demonstrated when Dr. Laun took his furlough from the Khariar facility.

The Doctors (Mr. and Mrs. Deshmukh), in charge of the Evangelical Hospital in Tilda were leaving to pursue further education so Viru and Nancy were requested to assume the vacated posts.

> "The medical superintendent and his wife were planning to go for their post-graduate studies. They asked us to go over to Tilda. Communication is very good there. Basically, it's a village set-up. Even Tilda was hardly even a town in those days. It's grown up a lot, but it was hardly even a town.
>
> It was a general hospital with about 3 or 4 doctors, of which two, Dr. Mr. and Dr. (Mrs. Louisa) Deshmukh, wanted to go for their post-graduate degrees. They were both M.B.B.S. doctors at that point. They had not done their Masters. They did come back to that hospital later. After we left, they came back.
>
> We call that their "postgraduate studies." This is India, where you do a degree in your specialty. They don't have that in America. You have a basic degree and you build on that. It's a kind of a fellowship thing. In India one gets additional letters behind their name.
>
> You've got to do postgraduate here for a specialty. Its similar, but not exactly the same, as becoming an M.D. in the United States."
>
> - Nancy

The Deshmukhs had arrived in Tilda in 1962. Dr. Madhu V. Deshmukh graduated from Christian Medical College in Vellore in 1958 and served at Mure Memorial Hospital in Nagpur prior to Tilda. The hospital was in ill repair and, according to a biographical sketch, "on the brink of closing down," when the doctors Deshmukh assumed their roles in Tilda, having been encouraged to take the post by the former principal of CMC Vellore, Dr. J.C. David. According to his biography, when the Evangelical Hospital in Tilda was turned over to the Henrys it had made a comeback. "The Hospital has blossomed into a community health hospital catering to the poor and needy of the community. It also has an A grade School of Nursing."[1]

The couple departed for CMC Vellore for postgraduate studies, he in general surgery and she in gynecological-obstetrics, and the Henrys assumed leadership of the hospital.[2]

> "When we went to Tilda, Ruth Hoffsteader was in Khariar. She had been the nursing superintendent in Tilda. There wasn't any nursing superintendent [in Tilda] when I went. There was Ruby Merkel – she was basically the principal of the School of Nursing – and she was doing both jobs. They're supposed to be separate, but she had to do both because there was not a full-time nursing superintendent there. [Ruby] left six months after we got there to return to the U.S.A. I had to also be the principal as well as the nursing superintendent."
>
> - Nancy

Though the conditions in Tilda had greatly improved under the guidance of the Deshmukhs, Viru found "there was not proper discipline" among the staff and he set out, as he says, to "put things in order."

> "When someone did something which was not acceptable and I talked to them about it, immediately they would say, 'If you don't like my work, then you can just fire me.' That was the typical answer, instead of 'Yes, I will do better in the future.' This was the reply-- a very arrogant type of reply. They knew we needed them. They played it hard instead of trying to cooperate with the things that have to be done.
>
> It wasn't doctors. It was other staff. All levels of staff did it. We don't know why. There wasn't much overlap or turnover. They left very soon after we got there. There wasn't much of a turnover. You just took over and they left. They were waiting for us to come so they could go, but I knew that we had to

straighten up the discipline of the staff."

- Viru

Ever the diplomat and strategist, Viru set out to find a solution to the discipline problem. He sought the advice of Dr. Lawrence Jiwanmall, the first Indian Christian doctor and chairman of the Tilda medical committee.

"Dr. Jiwanmall was the father of my peers. He was there as the chairman. He was the first Indian doctor. They had only missionaries before him. He was the first Indian doctor to work in Tilda, and he worked quite a few years faithfully there.

When his children got bigger, he decided he wanted to be more independent and earn more money. The mission paid very low when Dr. Jiwanmall was there. He said, 'I've got a family. I've got to educate them.' He went and settled at a place called Bhatapara, a half-hour train ride away. He started his private medical hospital there. It's doing good work in that place even today."

- Viru

"That's right, he was on their medical board. Everybody respected him. He was a very good person and had a lot of good sense. He also liked my husband very much. Actually my husband worked in Bhatapara as a teacher for a while. It was Dr. Jiwanmall who said, 'You go after medicine. You want to be a doctor, you go after medicine.' He really encouraged him. He was a very nice person, but a very strong person also.

Viru went to him as a mentor and asked, 'What shall I do? This is the response I'm getting. I'm not getting cooperation from the staff.'"

- Nancy

"He told me, 'When a dissent like that happens, you just suspend the person, and we will see in the medical community about it.' Suspension means you get half-pay, but you will not work. You're suspended for a certain period of time. In the meantime, it will go to a higher medical committee for an inquiry and making a decision about it, whether they're going to be kicked out or they're going to be kept."

- Viru

"Along came somebody who did something serious – he wasn't showing up for duty regularly -- so I took the advice and suspended him.

That straightened everybody up. That habit stopped. They stopped saying, 'Well, fire me.' They were not expecting me to do that so they were trying anything to get out of work.

Everything was better after that and no one else did it. There were much better relations with the staff."

- Viru

It was a major leadership test for the new Medical Superintendent, and one he passed with the help of a trusted colleague and elder. But the work of the hospital in the community, the nurture of the staff, and training of new medical personnel was most important to the Henrys.

"He has this talent. You have fun together and then you can work together. We had picnics and parties and he used to tease them. It was casual then. Once they got to know him, the way he was, everything turned out fine.

We had four doctors and a staff of 75. It was important that the relationships be strong and trusting.

There was a nursing school at that time already. A missionary from the Evangelical and Reformed Church mission had started it. She was a deaconess from St. Louis, from

75

Deaconess Hospital. Her name was Sister Minnie Gadt. It's the German spelling."

- Nancy

Minnie Gadt had originally served a hospital in Baitalpur and came to Tilda in 1929. She started the School of Nursing in 1934, which originally trained only male nurses. In 1941 the first female students were admitted to the School of Nursing in Tilda and it was operated as a co-ed institution since that time.

> "Finances were limited, but the school managed to grow to more than 50 students as many mission hospitals looked for training opportunities for their sponsored male students. With a large group of male students, we were able to take part in football and other sports.
>
> Devoted volunteer services were also appreciated of Mrs. Joyce Baur, who set up the nursing school library in a systematic way. From her, Mrs. Ratna Jiwanmall took over the library and also taught English to the students."

- Nancy

Viru's love of and talent for music, with which he'd wooed Nancy in Khariar, was also on display in Tilda. In addition to his duties as Medical Superintendent, he organized a choir that performed locally and traveled to competitions.

> "He built up a choir there with some very good singers. We had one male nurse who played the tabla drums very well. He did a lot with music there because he had a lot of good musicians. They performed various places including the Christian Mele [a large festival] on a river island near Baitalpur."

- Nancy

> "The Christian Mele at Madhughat was a joy to attend. And every year I prepared our hospital choir for the competition and we won first prize thee years. We cannot forget Mrs.

Nelson's lilting voice and Barkat Koushal's tabla beat to keep us together. Even our little four-year-old Anjali sang a song and bagged a prize.

The different Christian institutions send their choirs. Nancy would play the flute and I'd sing and play the harmonium. All the denominations participate in that Mele. It's inter-denominational-- even the Mennonites. Disciples. Church of Christ.

They bring a very good Christian speaker from outside. Our mission has a leprosy hospital there. We also had schools there in Baitalpur. The schools are still there, but the mission has given them up. The government runs them now."

- Viru

The hospital continued to grow as the Henrys provided leadership and reformed the inner-workings of the staff. Soon, they began to outgrow their facilities and a building project was commissioned to add labor and delivery space along with space for outpatient surgical services.

"We were getting more and more delivery patients.

But [the labor and delivery area] was very, very tiny – one room. It was a labor room and then there was a little ward there to keep post-partum patients in. Viru wanted to build a new maternity unit there and the board had sent money for this – 50,000 rupees.

[Viru] had to go out and raise the rest of the money and he got more than he needed. Even more than the amount the board gave, he got in donations. He used to go out and meet all the people he knew. By that time, they knew him also. He'd been there a while. Beyond that, the rest was a matching grant.

Amazingly, he earned enough from these donations that he could also make a new ODP (Out Patient Department,) that was also new."

- Nancy

The new facility would be much larger and include two stories in the building; a nursery and delivery ward downstairs and private rooms upstairs. A separate building would house the nurse's dining room. As Viru and Nancy recall, the paid "private room" concept was just starting to take hold in Indian mission hospitals. It had become an important concept in sustainability for the mission hospitals that had become more independent of American and European financial resources in the post-colonial period. Outside of charging for surgeries and private rooms, Viru says the services of the mission hospitals were "pretty much charity." So with diminished outside funding, the mission hospitals needed to cultivate new revenue sources.

Ever the entrepreneur, and not always the best at following rules, Viru pushed the project ahead although final approval by the mission agency hadn't been granted. Bhanu Ram, a, engineering friend of the Henrys in Tilda, offered his services and a local contractor agreed to oversee the work.

> "The normal procedure was that it was sanctioned you could do it. They had a building committee of the board. They were to come there, inspect the project, advise, and approve the plans. Then you start building. They didn't come and they didn't come. He was too much in a hurry so he just went ahead. Such a strong will. He just went ahead and started the work. By the time they finally reached us, the building was already up to the first floor roof.
>
> They were very surprised but they didn't scold him because they approved what had been done."

- Nancy

While in Tilda, the Henry children grew and explored. At age five, realizing she would not receive the education she needed for adaptation from local schools, the Henrys sent Anjali to the boarding school for the blind in Dehra Dun. It was a sad time for the family, though they knew it would prepare Anjali to function well and thrive in the world as a blind person.

Anil and Ajit were doing all the things young boys do, sometimes to humorous or accidental ends.

> "At about age two and a half Ajit fell up to his chest into the tank of waste water collected for garden use. He hung onto the grass and started shouting. Luckily those working in the hostel kitchen spotted him and rescued him.
>
> Nancy reached home to find Rahel Bai (our faithful ayeh) working hard to wash off the layers of black dirt while [Ajit] happily played in the water as if nothing happened!
>
> When Anil was five years old and had not yet started school we decided to try out the village school, which he found fun. But when Rahel Bai reported that he was calling out 'galli, (dirty swearing words in Hindi language). His father made it clear that he was not to speak these dirty. It so happened that he got the mumps. He recovered from the mumps, but never asked why he was not going back to the school again.
>
> We will never forget the time when both the boys were bitten by our own dog. It was only when the dog got away and bit one of the male nursing students who was playing football that we realized it was a case of rabies. Ouch! Those 21 days of injections really hurt, but we were relieved to have the protection!"
>
> - Viru

A new well and a pump were donated by the Dau family of Neora, which solved the water shortage problem and eliminated the use of wastewater in the garden. It was one of a number of physical improvements to the facilities in Tilda overseen during the Henrys' tenure.

One example of the critical need for a mission hospital that could provide free care in Tilda included the story of a very poor woman experiencing a difficult labor. The baby's delivery was obstructed and she required a C-section, but had no money to pay for the surgery.

> "A patient came and she had already had six children. She needed a C-section quickly. The family said, 'Okay, we have to go and sell some land to give you money for that.' I said, 'Don't do that. You can pay gradually.'
>
> She also needed blood. The family didn't have anybody to give blood, so I gave the blood. It was a very strange feeling. Here I am, operating on a patient and my blood is running into her.
>
> They never did sell the land. They proposed that, but I said, 'No, don't do that.' They were poor people. If they sold their land, they would have nothing. It wouldn't have been much land, and they would have lost everything. This was why it was important to maintain the Christian Mission Hospitals – we cared for everyone, even if they couldn't pay."
>
> - Viru

As the building project was underway the Deshmukhs were planning to return to Tilda. They were finishing up their studies in the spring of 1972 and planning to come back to Tilda if the post was available.

> "At the same time, Viru applied for post graduate M.S. studies in surgery at the Christian Medical College in Ludhiana. He'd received word they were willing to give him the seat. They had an open spot for him to study if he wanted. He wrote back saying, 'I'm in the mission hospital and I'm in charge. My relievers have to come. On top of that, I have to finish a building I am building. Then I will come. You can put me in next year's batch.'
>
> They said, 'No, when the Deshmukhs return, you can come.'
>
> To anybody in India, they won't believe it. If you don't take that seat immediately, it's given to someone else. There's more to the story, because Dr. Eggleston who taught in

Ludhiana already knew us. He knew me because I'd met him during my missionary studies in Stony Point, at the ecumenical training center. I was the first non-Presbyterian to go there as I've mentioned.

We went over to meet him, Dr. Forrest Eggleston, and his family. He was an experienced surgeon. His wife was also a nurse. They had been working in CMC Ludhiana, and was a professor of surgery there, and the Head of the Dept. of Surgery.

It helps to know somebody else. You know you can count on this person to really come through. They're working in a mission hospital themselves and that sort of thing. He had a heart for the mission. He trained so many people who were in a mission. He had the value for that, that he was committed to the mission."

- Nancy

Dr. Eggleston convinced Viru to begin studies in Ludhiana as soon as possible. But entrance to Ludhiana would have to wait a year, allowing time for the Deshmukhs to finish their program and make arrangements to return to Tilda.

"Ludhiana is a medical college [and] hospital. They also have nursing students. It's the same as Christian Medical College Vellore in the south. Ludhiana is in the north.

Anyway, since we knew him previously he was sure it was good to save [Viru's] seat, and he did. Other people can't believe it was saved because it is so hard to get those seats. It's so hard. The Department was willing to save it for him, so it was quite an event."

- Nancy

When the time came for Viru to enter class in Ludhiana in 1972, the Deshmukhs had not yet returned to Tilda. The hospital came under the care of Dr. Kiran Jiwanmall, the younger son of Dr. Lawrence Jiwanmall. Kiran had received his M.B.B.S. and knew the operations of the hospital in Tilda well. He would be able to take over leadership until the Deshmukhs arrived.

"There's one other story that you didn't tell about Viru in Tilda. You have to remember that he was only a basic doctor at that time, but he was doing all these operations advanced. He was taught by Dr. Laun to do so many internal operations. He was able to manage that and he had a lot of confidence.

A patient came in and the senior doctor had suggested that she was too sick. She was trying to deliver a baby and needed a C-section, and she had very low blood pressure. She was in shock. She also had all these little kids around. The father, her husband, was there with all these kids.

Viru was advised by the other doctors, 'It's a very poor risk. Don't take it. She'll probably die on the table.' But he saw those children and said, 'Okay, is it better for her to die trying or to just die like that? May I go ahead and do it?'

He did the surgery with just local anesthesia. He didn't want to put her out. It was too much of a risk. He got that baby out fast and the baby lived. The mother got better and went home with her children.

That was a very important thing that happened there. He had the courage to do what he felt he must try. Our son Anil who is now a surgeon himself, is the same way. He will rather try than say it's not possible. When the alternative is that a patient is going to die, why shouldn't we try? That is the same, so make the attempt. Explain it to the relatives. It's a very high risk, and then go ahead, after prayer to the Almighty God!"

- Nancy

With the building projects complete and the hospital in the capable hands of Dr. Kiran Jiwanmall, the Henrys began the next chapter in life's adventure together – surgical training for Viru, and nursing supervision and community health work for Nancy.

"So it was that in April 1972 we packed a few belongings into the International Harvester van and headed for Ludhiana. Three and one-half years had rushed by without our realizing it, and we tearfully said farewell to our faithful staff and students, passing the torch of the hospital leadership on to Dr. Kiran Jiwanmall and, in nursing, to Miss Sushila Hanifulla."

- Viru

In 1974, The Deshmukhs returned to the Evangelical Mission Hospital in Tilda. Louisa was appointed Medical Superintendent and Madhu became the Director of the hospital. They led the medical mission in Tilda for another 22 years, retiring in 1996.[3]

---

[1] http://cmcvellorealumni.org/sites/default/files/1993-3%20pdf.pdf
[2]Hilsley, Brian C., "Miss Marion Conacher, MBE – Wardie Mission Partner 1981-1993", http://www.wardie.org.uk/wp-content/uploads/2014/03/TILDA.pdf
[3]Hilsley.

Chapter 7: Ludhiana Preparations

The Henrys' eight-cylinder International Harvester van – donated from the United States to the hospital – was loaded with clothing and the few possessions they could take with them on their trip to Ludhiana. Full of enthusiasm, the Henry family made the long journey north to begin the next phase of education and preparations for the medical mission work ahead of them.

> "In 1972 we left for Christian Medical College, Ludhiana, Punjab. There I was fortunate to join the Surgical Department under the leadership of Dr. F.C. Eggleston, a renowned American surgeon who spent many years serving at Christian Medical College Ludhiana."
>
> - Viru

> "We didn't even bring a refrigerator. We bought a small one [in Ludhiana] and sold it when we came back to Orissa. We took very limited things with us and they provided furniture there. We left everything else in Tilda.
>
> We left our furniture. We took our main belongings when we went. We rode in that van and had all the things we were taking in the vehicle."
>
> - Nancy

Anjali, now seven years old, continued on at the boarding school for the blind in Dehra Dun. Anil and Ajit moved with their parents to Ludhiana and would begin primary school while their father was completing his postgraduate education.

The timing of the family's arrival in Ludhiana was also advantageous for Nancy. A position had recently opened up with the health services department for the staff and families at the medical college.

"There was a nursing superintendent there from the U.K. I applied for the position and went to see her. She said, 'We'd like to use you for some special projects around here. We're looking for someone to do them, and you've arrived.'

The first thing they gave me to do was to help build up the staff and student health services. They had so many tuberculosis cases among their students and staff, even doctors. A very high percentage of them were getting TB. They had a medical department and Dr. Cowen herself was a missionary from the U.K. who oversaw the health program for staff.

I started working with Dr. Cowen, trying to organize certain things. I got involved with the immunization program. We used to do small x-rays of all the staff. The staff and students totaled 1,500. We were taking care of them in health services. I was provided with two types of guns. One was to do testing for the antibodies of TB. Then, accordingly, we gave the BCG (Bacillus Calmette Guerin) vaccine. There were various steps in the immunization program – testing, reading the results, and then you have to immunize.

We were also doing some other immunizations with another gun I had.
I found that many of students and staff were not coming in voluntarily. I had to find a way to catch them. I made friends with the anatomy professor, Dr. Finch. He told me, 'You can come during their dissection time. Then they can't run away from you.' So I did that.

I also went early in the morning to the boys' hostel and the girls' hostel and would wait as they came down the steps. They'd come running down the steps and they'd see me there with my immunization gun. I did what I had to do to them. It became a big joke.

My husband used to go hunting now and then even though he didn't have much time. He was a surgical resident and they were busy seven days a week – day and night. Once in a while, he was able to go hunting with a group and they used to joke, 'Mr. Henry roams in the night with his gun and Mrs. Henry roams in the day with her gun. Look out for her. She's after you.'

It was a lot of joking and fun that we had."

- Nancy

Incidents of tuberculosis were reduced dramatically through the immunization and monitoring program begun by Nancy. Though she says the program was not able to reach 100 percent of the staff, students, and families at the medical college, the monitoring program allowed them to identify new cases of TB much more quickly so they could provide early and more effective treatment.

Along with being a student, Viru was the hospital's surgical registrar, keeping track of scheduling and materials needs in the surgical ward. His stipend for this work was 4,000 rupees per month, a meager sum for a doctor. Housing was provided, in what was called the staff colony where the Henrys and other families stayed. The houses were small, flat roofed, and connected in rows "right out in the sun, they were hot," Nancy recalls. Although the family had to live simply on the funds they received, the convenience of being only a 10-15 minute walk from the hospital, along with the camaraderie of the other staff, made the situation more workable.

With the immunization program running smoothly, Nancy was soon recruited to another set of tasks, gaining skills she would carry with her to other hospitals.

> "The second job I had was when the hospital was constructing private wings. They had to be outfitted, so I went and got all the equipment. In those days, they boiled everything in the ward: the instruments, the dressings. Everything was done in the ward. I had to provide all the wards with the equipment, set up the nurses' stations, and things like that.
>
> When this job was finished, the nursing superintendent called and said, 'You know, we'd like to start CSSD' (central sterile surgical department.) That means they provide all the sterile

equipment you need. We created this department. It was not there at the time. We couldn't believe that such a big medical college didn't have it so we needed to set it up immediately.

We started with the [surgical] theater and we sterilized their equipment: preparing the linen packs and all that, in the evenings. We had another staff that came and did all their linens and the instruments for the theater. They did the major instruments there, and they sent them over for autoclaving. All the autoclaving was done in this department. A group came from America to set up the new autoclaves and get them going. They came from an organization called CHOSEN, attached to a Christian Hospital. They were volunteers from Erie, Pennsylvania.

The American Sterilizer Company was there and men that retired from the company got together and started CHOSEN so they could send out equipment used for sterilizing medical instruments. These men came and helped. Some of the equipment was refurbished. They had to get some new things also. It wasn't very available in India. There was one company that we could get autoclaves from and most of the equipment came from America that had been refurbished by them."

- Nancy

Aside from acquiring the sterilization equipment and putting it in place, an entire departmental workflow had to be designed so instruments would make their way through the autoclaving process and cleanly be delivered to surgery theaters and procedure rooms. The Medical College continued to use, and teach, Nancy's pioneering work in the years to come.

"We had to set up a hot-air oven for dry sterilization. We had to design the department, how we're going to have one non-sterile area, where they bring the items for processing. Then it gets packed in the middle, sterilized, and then to another unit. It had a wall in-between so it wouldn't mix back and forth. Then it would be issued from another window.

I had already supplied these wards with this equipment so now I had to rotate it so there would always be fresh supplies in each ward. For one ward, we could supply everything they needed sterilized. We supplied it to them and took their used equipment away. Then we processed that for the next ward. That's how we did it: one ward at a time until the whole hospital was done.

When a team came to a procedure room, [the equipment] was already packed and ready for them. We had some back-up equipment that we could exchange in case of emergencies. I had to do a lot of equipment buying for those wards, especially when we set up the CSSD. I had never done anything like that. It was a very interesting project for me. That's the main thing I did in Ludhiana."

- Nancy

Ever the optimist, Nancy pursued new assignments as learning opportunities. She says her training as a nurse was an important part of learning to adapt, improvise, and be entrepreneurial when needed. The missionary impulse to find solutions that meet peoples' needs was a continued trait throughout Nancy's life and one she shared with Viru, also known for his innovation, sometimes brash, pursuit of projects that bettered the lives of his patients, the staff, and the communities surrounding the hospitals in which they served.

"Everything I've done in India, I came in cold. In Khariar, I was suddenly a nursing superintendent. I had never been anything but a staff nurse in America. You have to learn quite a bit. It helped prepare me. That's why I say God prepares us always for the next step. [Viru] was prepared to be a surgeon when he was only a doctor. Where they sent him next, he had to take over and do the surgery and run the hospital. We were all put in these positions. Step by step, somehow we were always prepared to do the next step. I think that's the hand of God taking you through all these things."

- Nancy

Viru thrived under the tutelage of Dr. Eggleston, the skilled surgeon and Presbyterian missionary Nancy met years earlier while at orientation in Stony Point, New York. Much more than a professor to his surgical students, Dr. Eggleston and his wife created a family atmosphere for those studying with him at Ludhiana.

> "I had a wonderful experience there because Dr. Eggleston turned out to be an excellent teacher. He loved to teach and he was a missionary for the Presbyterians. He always wore white pants and a white shirt. He used to come to the hospital on a bicycle and he would be there within minutes when he was called. It was a step through bicycle. It was probably his wife's. But he would be right there to support his students.
>
> I remember we had parties at his house. He used to get out the golf clubs and we would play in the yard. He allowed a wet party. They could have spiked punch. He was a Presbyterian. He was a little liberal, like us."
>
> - Viru

Nancy remembers the kindness and welcome the Egglestons showed the students, each hand picked by Dr. Eggleston to study with him, especially as the importance of having surgeons in mission hospitals began to grow.

> "They used to make homemade ice cream for us. Their house was always open to his students.
>
> Before Viru's time, [Dr. Eggleston] never really tried to get the mission guys there to do their surgery training. Whoever applied – they didn't have to take an entrance exam in those days – had to pass Dr. Eggleston's test. He made the decision who he took. He had many non-Christians as well. It wasn't that he didn't have any students from the mission hospitals, but it was from their initiative, not his. He just made the selection."
>
> - Nancy

As Viru had seen during his experiences in Khariar and Tilda, having surgical capabilities was a great asset to a mission hospital. It was possible to perform many more skilled operations with a trained surgeon than was capable with an M.B.B.S. doctor. Viru believed having surgeons at mission hospitals would save lives and minimized the need for often-treacherous transportation to larger hospitals. But he had also seen the financial potential of surgical services, charging for procedures that had previously been outsourced to state hospitals, thereby providing a revenue stream for the mission hospital.

"It was actually my husband who opened up this idea. There are so many M.B.B.S. doctors out there and he saw that a mission hospital couldn't run without a surgeon.

If we could have more surgeons coming to Ludhiana for training, he said you'd be doing a great job for the mission hospitals. So many of their doctors can't get seats for their surgical studies. Viru changed so much of the thinking around the need for surgeons in mission hospitals. I don't think he was aware of the impact he had on the program at that time.

Meanwhile, the Deshmukhs had come back to Tilda and Dr. Kiran Jiwanmall himself wanted to come and be trained in General Surgery.

Dr. Eggleston was called 'Boss,' and Viru said, 'Boss, there's this doctor that took charge from me. He's a Christian doctor, but he's trained in Vellore.'

When Dr. Eggleston went to America for his furlough, another doctor was put in charge of the department. Viru went to him and told him all about Kiran, and he was accepted. Kiran was the first Vellore-trained doctor to come study in Ludhiana and Viru's influence gained him a seat.

There was another doctor working in Khariar who wanted to come. His wife was from Ludhiana. Viru went to speak up for him also, and then for Dr. Ajit Singh and Pushpa who are still in Khariar.

In Ludhiana, they called Viru 'Dada' because he was older and had a lot more experience than the others. He was a mentor to the other students. There's another 'Dada' nickname he got in Bissamcuttack, that one means grandfather.

Having trained surgeons was a way to support the mission hospitals. It just happened that all these people were working in the north. All the people we've named worked in a mission located in north India. Some were Ludhiana graduates so they got in because that was the preference."

- Nancy

Beyond location and alumni preference, the Christian Medical Colleges in Ludhiana and Vellore were separated by language. Those who had studied and worked in the north were versed in the Oriya language; those stationed in the south spoke Tamil. Although language was not an insurmountable difference that would have prohibited doctors from pursuing their M.S. at either institution, there was still a preference for keeping doctors in a geographic area because of their familiarization.

"It was a big problem to get the mission doctors into graduate studies because it was all merit-based. The highest marks get in. There were people who could do the course but they hadn't gotten the highest marks in previous programs. That's what the sponsorship program was for. The Church of North India sponsored all these people. It made sense to make their selections from north India because of language. Vellore still today selects most of its candidates from the south which is sad as the need is more in North India.

We were from Bissamcuttack so we were in the middle, neither north nor south. But we worked to have doctors trained and stay in the north while I was at Ludhiana."

- Viru

The three-year program went by quickly and Viru and Nancy were soon thinking of the next stop on their vocation and ministry journey. As Viru's graduation approached, the answer came during a surprise visit.

> "In 1975, I obtained my Master's Degree in General Surgery (M.S.) at the Christian Medical College in Ludhiana.
>
> It was my aim and ambition to serve in rural India where there was no surgeon. It happened that at the same time a Danish doctor, Dr. Elizabeth Madsen, founder of the Christian Hospital in Bissamcuttack, Koraput District, Orissa, reached Ludhiana and met Professor Eggleston, searching for a surgeon to take over this hospital in rural Orissa."
>
> - Viru

> "Dr. Elizabeth Madsen just walked into Dr. Eggleston's office in Ludhiana one day. She was very unique. She said, 'Dr. Eggleston, I need a surgeon.'
>
> The mission board was still providing nearly 100 percent of the support to that hospital. She used to give free treatment and even the bus fare for patients to get home. She would say, 'I've come to serve the poor people. How can I charge them?'
>
> Slowly, the Danish mission society told her, 'We can't go on like this, giving you 100 percent of the money you need. You've got to find a way to start making that hospital self-supporting.'
>
> She knew that without a surgeon she could not get the amount of income they would need. She went to his boss, Dr. Eggleston, and said she needed a surgeon.
>
> Dr. Eggleston said, 'You know, surgeons don't grow on trees.'"
>
> - Nancy

Viru had completed both his service bond and education by the spring of 1975 and had no obligation remaining to the Church of North India. He had done all and more of the seven years of service that he has promised the Church of North India in lieu of his support and help to get through his medical course. Although he could have pursued a lucrative career in private practice, Viru wanted to serve the rural poor people of India and deploy his nascent vision for sustainable mission hospitals in a setting that was ripe for innovation and transformation. Dr. Eggleston told Dr. Madsen, "We have one doctor who has worked in Orissa. He is free of obligations. You can talk to him."

Dr. Madsen told the Henrys the Danish mission secretary was soon coming to India to visit with missionaries, though he was only available for meetings in Delhi. Both parties agreed to interview with the mission secretary, ready to explore the possibilities in Bissamcuttack. Dr. Madsen traveled from Orissa and Viru and Nancy came from Ludhiana for the meeting.

> "She was a cigar-smoking Danish lady. She brought some cigars for me.
>
> I'd already tried cigars with Nancy's father. But I said, 'No, I can't take that one.' She sat with her cigar and we talked about Bissamcuttack during the interview.
>
> The timing was incredible. I was finished with my M.S. in surgery and she needed a surgeon. I'd been in Orissa and knew the language some."
>
> - Viru

Dr. Madsen had been in Bissamcuttack for 22 years by the time she met with Viru and Nancy in 1975. In the mid-1950s, Madsen was in her 40s and leading a very successful private practice in Arhus, Denmark, when she felt God's call to take her medical skills out into the mission field. She contacted the Danish Mission Society and asked if they needed doctors.

Dr. Madsen's first assignment came in 1953, when she worked at the Rainy Hospital in Madras, India, for six months. After she had acclimated to the country, language, and treatment needs of the people, she moved on to serve mission stations established in Rayagada, Gunupur, and Bissamcuttack.

"She was such an interesting person. When she was sent to the Bissamcuttack area there was no hospital at all, but she really wanted to work in the villages. It was her dream that she would be a village doctor, helping all those people in the village that didn't have a doctor.

When she started going out to the village, she realized that there were some people that had to have a hospital. There was no hospital nearby at all, so she found it very difficult to give them full care without a base hospital. She had to leave village work and start a hospital."

- Nancy

Dr. Madsen began her work in Bissamcuttack on the veranda of the Bissamcuttack Church in 1954.[1] Purchasing land north of town, the foundation stone was laid for a dispensary on 16 April 1954. Bissamcuttack was the largest town in a hilly landscape dotted with remote villages. She trained local people to take on administrative tasks at the clinic and delivered critical care to villagers via a makeshift ambulance when possible, and on foot when needed. Regular rounds included taking her mobile clinic to Buduni, Kodugulami, M. Patraguda, Muniguda, and Dangsorada.

The patient load increased and the need for a more stable space soon compelled Madsen to move services to her one-room home, which became the hospital's outpatient area. Joined by Mr. Prabhunda Nag, Christian Hospital Bissamcuttack's "right hand man" – a lab technician, substitute doctor, accountant, nurse, driver, and business manager for the next 35 years – Madsen expanded the capacity of the hospital bit by bit.

The first ward was constructed in 1956 with 10 beds, six for men and four for women. Dr. Madsen experienced serious illnesses in 1959 and 1971, forcing her to return to Denmark for a year of recuperation each time. Yet, by 1975 the hospital had grown to 40 beds and a total budget of 400,000 rupees, 300,000 of which came from the Danish Mission Society. After two decades of service, "Dr. Ma" as she was affectionately known, was aging and running out of energy at the same time the Danish mission society was running out of money to support the mission.

Options were few. Dr. Madsen felt closing the hospital would be disastrous to the region, jeopardizing the wellbeing of those served and reversing the gains she had seen in public health accomplished through the hospital. But finding someone to take over the hospital – especially a doctor who had ideas of how the institution could become self-sufficient – was going to take a leap of faith.

Viru and Nancy were intrigued by Dr. Madsen's story and the promise held by the hospital in Bissamcuttack. Still, many preparations had to be made before the Henrys could make the move back to Orissa.

> "We had to arrange for our children's schooling. We said, 'If God finds a place for our children, that'll be our signal that we are supposed to go there.' Both the boys were in local English medium school in Ludhiana, near the hospital.
>
> Before we went to see the hospital in Bissamcuttack we started writing to different schools and asked people what were some good schools not far from Vishakhapatnam, which is not far from Bissamcuttack.
>
> They gave us suggestions. We wrote here and there, but nothing seemed to be working out. We wrote to a place that [Kiran] Jiwanmall's mother told us about. Lovedale is in Ooty, a hill station in the South India, in the State of Tamil Nadu. You have to stay in a hostel to go there. It's a residential school.
>
> I wrote to the Lovedale School about the boys. I told them everything about our situation. We got a postcard back from them. It said, 'Dear Dr. and Mrs. Henry, I'm sorry to say that for admission into Lovedale, you must register your child before they're born.'
>
> We laughed and laughed. I guess they have so many applications that the pregnant mother has to register the child before they're born. So that one went off the list.
>
> I had known a school started by our mission. I had been there one summer for my language studies. I knew the school was

very expensive. I wrote to them. They wrote back stating their fees, saying, 'Your children are welcome to study here.' But we didn't apply because the fees were too high for us.

Lo and behold, they wrote back to us. They said, 'We'd like to have your children in school.' They offered a full scholarship to both children, including boarding fees, food, and school fees. All we had to supply was their clothes and travel. We said, 'That tells us something. That seems like a sign.'

The school is Kodaikanal International School, one that we as a family have now been associated for two generations as our grand children too graduated from that school and my son has been heading their board for over twelve years as a gratitude for what he received."

- Nancy

With their children successfully admitted to a boarding school, about 1000 miles away from Bissamcuttack, the final step in the Henrys' transition to Bissamcuttack was their assessment of the hospital, the work, and its potential.

"We went on a train from Raipur. It was an old coal-fired engine. We got off at the Bissamcuttack station. Today, we don't stop there because it's a local station. That was a local train. It stopped at every station. It was quite a ride out there, very slow."

- Nancy

"We finally got there after a long train ride. They came in the jeep to pick us up. They had one jeep [Dr. Madsen] had gotten secondhand. We spent a few days there seeing the place. It's a beautiful area, greenery all around. It doesn't take long to fall in love with this place. We said, 'This is a beautiful place and this hospital is going to close if we don't come.'"

- Viru

Their previous experiences had laid a foundation for the work ahead of the Henrys. Yet, Bissamcuttack was an entirely new experience for the couple.

> "We had been in village hospitals before. Both Khariar and Tilda are village hospitals. This was even more village-y than Tilda, definitely. There were a lot of trees around. It was so clean and neat; whatever was there was beautiful. It was simple and small. That impressed me so much. Dr. Ma took us all around the hospital. She was staying where the missionaries had lived before. The theological people there had all left by that time. She stayed upstairs and put us in a room downstairs.
>
> That house is still there today. It's been given over to the pastor. They use part of it to board boys who come over from the village to attend school there.
>
> We were very impressed that God would send a place to us like this. Then the admission letter from the school came.
>
> That was it."
>
> - Nancy

The Henrys' visit to Bissamcuttack and letter from the school occurred in the spring of 1975. They soon gave Dr. Madsen their final approval of the offer and returned to Ludhiana to prepare for their move. Anil and Ajit left for boarding school in July, not to see their parents until the family celebrated its first Christmas in Bissamcuttack.

Viru and Nancy arrived in Bissamcuttack in late November. Preparing for the transition, Dr. Madsen had already included the Henrys in the civic roles she and others from the mission played in the community. It was the beginning of a relationship with the community – ever aware of its peoples' needs – that would last for the next 35 years.

"I remember that we had just reached Bissamcuttack and Dr. Madsen had received an invitation from the IMFA, the Indian Metal Feral Alloy plant.

They made thin steel for airplanes – mainly their fuselage and similar things. It wasn't a very big plant, but they used to have Founders' Day in honor of the father of the man who was running the plant. They always invited the hospital representatives. We had very good relations with them.

We were brand new and Dr. Ma handed this invitation to me. We went, had a lovely time, and met so many people. We started our community relationships with them, going to that event. We hadn't even settled in when we were whisked off to this affair.

That's how our life was. We were always invited to community events. There was a paper mill a little farther away and they always invited us to celebrate with them. We became part of the community.

That was our beginning there."

- Viru

----

[1] Christian Hospital Bissamcuttack, *Golden Jubilee Souvenir* publication, (1954-2004), pg 11.

Image Collection

Dr. Henry receives the Lifetime Achievement Award for his work in medical mission, 1994.

Patient arrives at the hospital by "village ambulance."

A view of the Christian Hospital Bissamcuttack campus, circa 1980's.

The Henry family attends elder son Anil's medical college graduation, 1989.

Viru at work preparing one of his famous barbeque dinners.

Viru sings *Mahua Perda Tale* at a fellowship dinner at Christian Medical College Ludhiana, for Professor and Mrs. Eggleston, 1995.

Dr. Johnny Oommen with Dr. V. K. Henry, circa 1995.

A villager arrives at the hospital wounded from falling into a pit designed for catching wild boar.

Proud grandfather holds
the long awaited twin boys,
Abhijeet and Abhishek,
1998.

Younger son Ajit with his
beloved dogs, Reena and
Tipu, circa 1988.

Baby Anjali, circa 1966.

Dr. V. K. Henry graduates
from medical college, 1963.

Most beloved maternal
uncle and aunt (mamu and
mami), circa 1980s.

The Fred Lott family of
eight children, Nancy at
three years of age, 1938.

Wedding bells for Viru and Nancy, May 4, 1964.

The Rev. Kelly Brill of Avon Lake UCC with her daughter, the Henrys, and Mrs. Windsor, the church photographer.

The Henry's visit and speak at Avon Lake United Church of Christ, Nancy's home church, circa 1980's.

Granddaughter Ankita gets special ride home from the village, circa 1995.

The Lott family attends Nancy's commissioning service at Avon Lake United Church of Christ, 1960.

Nancy and her parents along with the ministers of the commissioning service; brother-in-law Herb Muensterman on far left, 1960.

Viru, his mother, and
Nancy in their garden.

Ajit Henry with parents
and sister, Anjali, at his
graduation from
Woodstock School,
Mussoorie, circa 1987.

Doctors gather to conduct
night report after morning
prayers including Dr.
Padmashree Sahu, Dr.
Henry, Dr. Johnny
Oommen, and Dr. Hema
Mahanti.

Peg Muensterman, sister to
Nancy, the last two living
children of the Lott family.

The Henry family in Tilda, 1972.

Nancy and Viru leaving for the United States, 1998.

Kamini sister and Madhu sister sit on either side of Dr. Liz Madsen, founder of Christian Hospital Bissamcuttack, 1988.

Wedding bells for Anil and
Teresa, October 15, 1990.

Inauguration of the
maternity unit and OPD
extension at Tilda, 1972,
attended by the secretary of
the mission board, the
chairman of the mission
board, the Rev. Gurbachan
Singh, and Dr. Lawrence
Jiwanmall.

Anjali receives the first
prize at a song competition
at Indore.

Nancy in her beloved
Bissamcuttack garden.

The Elwina Henry
extended family, 1988.

Fred Lott enjoys a dhooly
ride during his visit to
India, 1962.

Ajit at 4 and Anil at 6 years, 1972.

Dr. Henry's choir at a song competition at Madhughat Christian Festival.

Viru with his jungle prize, along with Fred Lott, Markus and Mickey Laun as children, admirers of Uncle Viru, circa 1965.

The Henrys en route to their Darjeeling honeymoon, 1964.

Viru and Nancy at a missionary conference, 1967.

On the way to church, six days after marriage, 1964.

Indian missionary group at the Henry wedding, May 4, 1964.

Viru's extended family at the Henry wedding, May 4, 1964.

Dr. Manfred Laun (left) greets Nancy (back to camera) as she arrives at the Evangelical Hospital in Khariar, July 7, 1960.

Leela Wasser rides in a bullock cart with Dr. Laun to make village health visits in areas surrounding Khariar, circa 1961.

Johnny and Mercy Oommen in Bissamcuttack, circa 1995.

Nancy is blessed for missionary service with the
"laying on of hands" during her commissioning at
Avon Lake United Church of Christ, 1960. Her
father, Fred Lott, is in the light suit.

Chapter 8: Bissamcuttack Beginnings
1975-1977

The historic timeline of the Christian Hospital Bissamcuttack contains the following entry, dated November 1975: "The Henrys arrived in Bissamcuttack to take on a vital hospital that was facing impending closure."[1]

To those involved in the mission at the hospital these seemingly oppositional statements, "vital" and "facing impending closure," were not conflicting sentiments, though the hospital's continuation was in jeopardy. The vital work was the extensive list of medical services and support the hospital provided in the area, against insurmountable odds. A highly motivated but minimal staff kept pace with the needs of the hospital, but just barely.

"Facing impending closure" was a financial reality for the hospital. The facility had grown from its beginnings as a dispensary to a 40-bed hospital under Dr. Madsen's care. Still dependent on the Danish Mission Society for 75 percent of its 400,000-rupee budget, the hospital was given an ultimatum: become self-sufficient or close. The mission society would begin phasing out its support for the hospital's budget over the next four years.

> "The money was to be reduced month by month. They made a sliding scale and wanted to see how we'd manage the budget with less money."

> - Viru

Facility upkeep and expansion, along with staff development and retention, were major concerns as the hospital approached its fiscal slope. Construction of the "A" and "B" wards, a maternity ward, and an operating theater had occurred from 1969-1972. The Danish Mission Society contributed a majority of the funding, but Dr. Madsen, using personal finances, and DANIDA (Danish International Development Agency) had funded the completion of these sections.

The Christian Hospital Bissamcuttack had grown substantially from its early days, yet the growth and sustainability was dependent on foreign funding sources. As the goals and purposes of American and European mission organizations shifted to partnering with established in-country organizations it was evident that the hospital couldn't continue as it historically had. The hospital could no longer operate with the majority of its operating funds arriving from overseas.

> "[Dr. Madsen] was a medical doctor and she didn't try to do many surgeries. The man, Dr. Petersen, who had gone home with his wife, was called there to do the surgery, but he didn't stay very long."
>
> - Nancy

Dr. Kai Petersen had joined Christian Hospital Bissamcuttack in 1968. The Danish doctor was recruited to establish and grow the surgical capabilities at the hospital and to strengthen collaboration between Bissamcuttack and Danish medical schools through the Elective Students Program, which afforded Danish doctors the experience of training in a foreign country. Pedersen added a research component to the health work at the hospital and took personal responsibility for the education of a group of local children, even finding sponsors for each of them and following up on their progress over decades.

When Petersen returned to Denmark in 1973, his absence was immediately felt. Dr. Madsen, with no one to lead the expansion of surgical efforts as a revenue source for the hospital, began looking for options to replace these vital components of the hospital's services. The need for these areas to be managed and maintained, as well as Dr. Madsen's desire to return to village clinic work, were driving factors in the search that led to Viru and Nancy's arrival in Bissamcuttack.

Even with the capabilities Dr. Petersen had established, the hospital had work to do when the Henrys arrived, modernizing and enhancing all areas of the hospital's operations.

"They had a small surgical theater. That's where Dr. Petersen started. There was no x-ray when we arrived, which is pretty hard for a doctor. He managed with very simple facilities.

[Viru] was without x-ray capabilities for one year. He got it from REAP, a radiological group in America that refurbished x-ray machines for missionary hospitals. We found out about it and he started corresponding with them. It took about one year for it to arrive. If a patient really needed an x-ray, they had to go an hour away by bus to get the x-ray and then come back.

There was only one autoclave up in the lab for equipment sterilization and it was not very big. She used to go up and look at the slides because that's a malaria area. It's a sickle cell area. She needed her lab. She had a separate building for it, only about two rooms. It is still there. She built good buildings."

- Nancy

Good buildings aside, the hospital compound at Bissamcuttack was still quite simple when the Henrys arrived. A senior staff house and a hostel for nurses accompanied the recently completed wards. Nancy describes the area as "rugged," still on the Indian frontier between urban, rural and primitive places in 1975. The installation of electric streetlights and telephones were some of the first modernizations to follow the Henrys' arrival.

"One problem was there wasn't a single streetlight on the compound at night. There was a place where we had wild animals. Our place had no fence on it and it was next to a big hill. There were bears, hyenas, and leopards roaming around our house at night. The bears used to come down to eat the food from the garbage cans at night.

We had the missionary house. Actually, no one had ever lived in it. They had a Danish missionary [Dr. Petersen] but his wife became sick and he suddenly went back to Denmark. The house was there and built for them, but they never occupied it. We were the first to live there.

There was also a hostel. They had a problem getting enough nurses so I was part of the team that started the nursing school. We had to house the single nurses and the main building was there. Viru made two or three extensions to it. It's all there. What [Dr. Madsen] made was well made. She had put in five rooms for students so she was already thinking about that. She was a lady of vision. There's no doubt about it. She looked forward to the day when someone would come take over the hospital so she could do the village work.

The streetlights were a big problem. They had to go on-call at night and there were no lights at all. So that was one of the first things Viru did. They needed streetlights around the hospital.

The town of Bissamcuttack had no streetlights either. They got so many of their improvements watching the mission hospital get them. They were getting along without these things but when they saw them, they got them.

We also brought telephones to the town. Nobody had a telephone before we arrived."

- Nancy

"The postmaster said we could get phone service if we could guarantee the installation of seven phones. Not seven phone customers, mind you, just seven phones. It could be the same person having two phones. The hospital had two phones: we had one in our house and there was one in the hospital.

Then five others got phones and we had telephone service in Bissamcuttack. I knew the tribal minister and he had become the central government minister for communication. I went to see him and he told me, 'You have to give us telephone service too. We can't do without it.' And so we arranged it. All these other places around didn't have phone service, but we did.

The hospital wanted facilities. Before that, everybody was satisfied with what was there. There were no streetlights when we went. It was absolutely dark at night. We put streetlights into our compound and pretty soon the town wanted to have streetlights too. It's funny how the town just grew with this hospital. They saw things going on. We got television and then they got television. Before that, they never thought about having it.

The community benefitted from the role model of the hospital, of what could improve the quality of life."

- Viru

Lacking a dependable public power grid for these modern amenities, the hospital relied on generators to augment the electrical needs of the facility. The members of Avon Lake United Church of Christ, the American congregation from which Nancy was commissioned as a missionary in 1960, purchased the first generator shortly after the Henrys arrived in Bissamcuttack.

"The generator provided a vital link to creating a culture of reliability and readiness for the hospital staff and community.

The first time we went to see [the hospital], there wasn't a generator. It was installed shortly after we got there. The power was so irregular, it used to go off at all times and we didn't have a generator. That was one of the early projects. Avon Lake [United Church of Christ] bought the first generator and the provided funds to build the generator house."

- Nancy

"We added more generators after that. As the hospital grew larger we needed bigger generators. We kept the Avon Lake generator for a long time as a standby so that part of the hospital would have light."

- Viru

Unlike hospitals in the United States and Europe, family members generally provide meal preparation and basic housekeeping for patients. Not only does this greatly reduce the cost of providing care, but it also keeps families together. Private rooms, meals and housekeeping are available to those who can afford it, but the majority of patients arriving in Bissamcuttack, in 1975 and today, opt to have family members provide these services.

Nancy specifically remembers families who arrived via bullock cart, oxen-drawn two wheel carts. Without access to automobiles, many of the rural and tribal residents of the area had no other means of transportation – especially if they were to bring provisions for an extended hospital stay.

> "[The hospital complex] was all in the open. People brought in their bullock carts to carry everything they needed, and you'd see them cooking everywhere.
>
> There's a tamarind tree there, near the patient wards. They used to sit out under it and cook. We have some photos of that.
>
> Then we built a dharamshala[2], a place for them to stay. It means a holy shelter. We had a separate cookhouse and a separate sleeping place. That was the first building in the outpatient area.
>
> The original outpatient ward was an old building they had to tear down to make the maternity unit. It was in one building where the offices, outpatient, drug department, and the storeroom were there. The operating room was also there. There was one ward up above and the old maternity was there, which is still there. We had to tear down the main building because the maternity went in that place."
>
> - Nancy

As the work of the hospital grew with expanded facilities, electricity for expanded operating hours, and better staff training and infrastructure, the hospital swelled with patients. Building projects were soon underway to meet these demands.

"[Dr. Madsen] had consulted with people in Denmark on building projects. DANIDA gave mission hospitals support and we called on their expertise as the hospital grew. Their architects would draw up plans and would come see the completed building sometimes. They were also working in Africa. The early buildings were designed and built by them. The architect was so good that we kept using him. He was Danish but lived in America.

They made good buildings, but it was very expensive to have them do the building. Their charges were very high. I found we could get good help in India. The same architect who'd been working with Dr. Madsen agreed to work with our builder in Bissamcuttack. He could make the buildings less expensively."

- Viru

"The building projects took years. I think the next thing that was built was the new outpatient, and a theater was already there.

The outpatient department was built right in the front just off the main road, with another entrance into the operating theater. It had x-ray in it also, with three rooms for the lab.

We were even able to fit the dental clinic in that building. We wanted to have a dentist. There were consultation rooms and waiting space. There was an eye department and place for ultrasound. These were all the things that gradually went into that building.

As the order of building went, the outpatient facility was the first thing that was built. The dharamshala was not the first thing built there, but came soon after.

We didn't have the basic things to do his work, so he needed to have these facilities and equipment first."

- Nancy

Along with getting facilities and equipment in order so the hospital could begin serving patients and generating a profit, the financial management of the institution needed to be scrutinized. The Henrys instituted a number that included "blocking the loopholes through which money was being lost" and entrusting financial oversight to a key administrator whom Dr. Madsen had been working with for over 20 years.

> "Mr. Prabhundan Nag, joined the staff in 1955 and he was like an adopted son to Dr. Madsen. He used to call her 'Ma' (Mother). His house was there across the street and he was what we called the business manager. Now they use the term administrative assistant. He was Dr. Ma's right hand: a lab technician, nurse, driver, substitute doctor, accountant, manager – everything. He served the Christian Hospital Bissamcuttack for 35 years.
>
> The administrator, Dr. Ma first and then Viru, was the head doctor.
>
> When Mr. Nag retired, Solomon had been his right-hand man. He's a self-made man. He's picked up everything and is very good at figures. He's done a very good job.
>
> At first, the outpatient department and x-ray were very essential things we needed to have. We turned the old outpatient department into an administrative building so the pharmacy could have more space. I didn't have an office as a nursing superintendent so they found me an old patient room."
>
> - Nancy
>
> "We needed more space for patients and couldn't immediately build more rooms. There was an old ward that was used in the old days for tuberculosis patients. He asked a friend of his to finance the renovations there so we could put patients over there. We made that into some private rooms, we needed those private rooms. There were only about five of them. On the other end, they made a little office for Nancy. At that time, they needed the room she was in for the patients.

They kicked her out of there and she moved to end of that ward. That building was lying empty when we got there, but we soon made use of it.

[The transition] happened quickly and there's a plaque on the wall with the date on it. The ward is named after the man who gave money to build it – the Barasia Ward."

- Viru

The financial development and sustainability of the hospital, especially with the looming decrease in funding from the Danish mission society, was at the forefront of the effort both to increase revenue and reduce costs and waste. Dr. Henry is often cited for employing the "Robin Hood principle." Taking from the rich – in the form of at-cost surgical procedures, private rooms and care services – to care for the needs of the poor who relied on the open and public general wards, their families, and good will to receive needed medical care.

"He had a sliding scale for payment at the hospital; one scale for the private patients and another for the general patients. Even then, we had to give concessions for the very poor. No one was turned away."

- Nancy

"Now they have started a national program where they give the low poverty line people a smart card. They didn't have that in our day. Our son Anil can tell you more about the program, but that's a very new program.

If you wanted free care in the 1970s you had to go to a government hospital. They used to take bribes from patients to get things done, so really, it wasn't free. They also had to buy all the supplies and some of the medicines to get their treatment. So the cost could be more than what they pay at a mission hospital for little or no medical care. Then they had to go to a mission hospital for care. They got better care and we didn't have a bribery system."

- Viru

An integral part of life at the Christian Hospital Bissamcuttack was daily devotions. Staff was expected to attend and, regardless of their religious affiliation, expected to imbibe the ethos of its leaders. The mission hospital was there to serve the needs of the community, especially to freely serve the needs of the poor and those without other options. Deviation from these principles was not tolerated.

> "Well, we did have one or two cases [of staff bribery] but we were able to terminate them. They knew we were strict on those things. I don't think most of our lower income staff members came [to the hospital] with an idea of service. Maybe they developed it after they got there. We had morning prayers every day and it was a big topic of how we ran the hospital, that we were there to care for everyone.
>
> It was an interfaith effort. We didn't discriminate based on religion. There were hardly any Muslims around there. As far as I know, they're not there today. There were one or two people but it was very rare. It was Hindus and Christians. It was largely Hindu in the community. There were very few Christians there. The hospital staff was mostly Christian, but the people in town were mostly Hindu."

> - Nancy

Cost control became a major effort at the hospital and Nancy was in charge of making sure loopholes were closed. Tighter supply management and expense oversight were the first tasks in ensuring the financial accountability needed to meet the goal of being fiscally independent from outside funding within five years.

> "How you manage the finances to get out of the 5-year sliding scale – where you had to be on your own? Well, the story of the laundry is part of it.
>
> When we went there, Dr. Madsen, she was managing the laundry herself. She managed it out of a little wooden house

that wasn't very big, and there were some lines outside. That was all there was to the laundry.

We had an open fire with a big pot on it. They boiled the clothes in it. She wanted everything absolutely clean. If it wasn't clean at the end of the cycle, she'd say, 'Here, have some more soap powder.' So she'd hand over more soap powder until that guy was getting so much soap powder. That was more soap powder than that job needed, it could have been more efficient.

That was the thing I took from her charge: the laundry. As the nursing superintendent, we had to see everything was in order. I said, 'We've got to do something.' And my husband said, 'You had better stop the hole in the bucket. The powder was going out of the hole. You couldn't possibly use that much.'

Gradually, we got that amount down. I gave out the supplies myself. I started giving all the hospital supplies because I knew what they really needed. I put the laundry soap in a bucket of water so we could give them more.

So we managed to cut down a lot of expenses, and the laundry soap is only one of those instances. We found ways to save on other things, too.

I was dispensing the drugs. I was ordering the drugs. All supplies for the hospital, I ordered and gave out myself. Of course, I was out in the wards and I knew what was needed. [The hospital] still wasn't that big. We had maybe 60 patients or so at a time. I could still get around all the patients every day; know who they were and what they needed. I could do my nursing administration as well as look after all these things."

- Nancy

As the hospital's administrative tasks and patient load grew, Nancy realized she needed help so that she could focus on nursing superintendent tasks. Moving from a two-person administrative staff of Viru and Nancy, to a larger distributed staff provided significant challenges. Yet it also allowed new leadership to develop and face the needs of the ever-expanding facility.

> "Later, we kept getting more and more patients and more and more staff. As we got more nursing staff and more patients, then I had to train somebody to do these things. I found an honest and good person, Ruth Oskar, and she took over the supplies. I also taught her how to give the prescriptions.
>
> The nurse who handed out the medicines, she would take the medicines from her. The ward would come and take their medicines from her. I trained her how to do all of that. She had been working with Leila Wasser in the women's program in Khariar so she had some experience working, keeping records, that sort of thing. She did a good job with that until she had a stroke.
>
> Then I trained another young man who was a clerk and he's still doing it today. He was just a boy then, well he's older now. He was a clerk in the accounts office. He was working doing the clerical work, typing, looking after the mail. He was very efficient. He knew English well and I asked my husband if he thought it was the right thing to do. Ruth had a sudden stroke so I went back to doing these tasks for a while. And I asked, 'Can I train Banay?'"
>
> - Nancy

Management of supplies and the pharmacy became more important as the patient load increased. Binay continued in the role, augmented by a licensed pharmacist and, as the team grew, more help to manage the supplies and medical needs of the hospital.

> "He's still doing it today. He's doing a very good job. He's learned a lot about drugs and the pharmacy. Now it's many more types of drugs, and he's learning it very well.
>
> We have a young pharmacist with him now. He's working in that area and they have an assistant with them as well. It's so big now. He took over the supplies. He's a very honest man

and he was careful to make sure that not too much went out without being accounted for.

We had an exchange system. [Nurses and attendants] have to bring the empty bottle. If they needed another bottle of disinfectant, they had to bring the other bottle back. Even in the drugs, if a vial of injection finished, then you brought back the vial and that gets exchanged. It keeps it static, it keeps things on the ward, and it also keeps it honest because it's an exchange system. That's still running today.

Bissamcuttack now has 200 patients. It's grown so much. They have a new pharmacy and everything has changed a lot. In those days, somehow, God provided us the people we needed to get the things done at the time."

- Nancy

Additional needs, such as cataract camps, came to occupy the time of doctors and surgeons in Bissamcuttack in the early years after the Henrys' arrival. Never a facility to back away from patient needs, the staff became familiar with the treatment of cataracts, relying on the team of doctors in the compound to meet the unique needs of the thousands of people in their area with degenerative sight problems.

"Dr. Dean, who was in Mungeli, as the head of the eye hospital, was an excellent surgeon. There were many, many cataract camps all over. We found so many older people coming in with eye problems, particularly cataracts. I think India has more cataracts than any place in the world. Many eye doctors from abroad come here for the experience of diagnosing and treating them

Cataracts are primarily caused by the sun. It's a strain on the eyes. As far as I know, it's the sun. There are Vitamin A deficiency diseases too. There are plenty of those in India as well. I wrote to Dr. Dean and asked if he could please have an eye camp. He agreed and brought his team with him because we had nothing in place to care for eyes.

We had nurses trained to do the injection and the anesthesia. They give an injection in the nerve to anesthetize. A nurse was trained to do that and take care of the patient afterwards. He stayed for five days or so and did more than 100 cataract surgeries.

It was a very big camp. There was a community house, open with a roof, and we put straw all over the floor. The patients slept on that. We had them over in the hospital as well. It was very large because he had his team and I think they had another doctor with them as well.

He taught me to operate on cataracts, so that when the team couldn't come, we could at least do some. There were a lot of old people who would come and they were totally blind, cataracts in both eyes. In those days, it was a simple surgery where the cataract was removed from the eye and the cornea sutured back. There were no intra ocular lenses. These came many decades later. So patients wore thick glasses after the surgery for the rest of their lives.

But you never do two eyes at once. We'd do one eye and then when that gets better, you could think about doing the other eye. If anything happens to one eye, then you have the other eye. An infection may pass onto the other. Some of them were happy with that one eye and never came back. Some came back and did the other eye.

Then they were given special cataract, thick glasses, that they wear. The lenses are removed from the eye, and then the glasses take over the focus. That's how they can see.

The patients would come for their dressing everyday, all in a line, holding hands. It's so sweet to see. The one who can see a little bit will be in the front, guiding all the others. They would all be holding hands, sharing in their eye recovery experience."

- Viru

With the bulk of the physical facilities established in Bissamcuttack by 1977, the Henrys were ready to embark on the next phase of their mission, including training, education, and expanded services to remote villages.

The Danish Mission Society was still on its arc toward ever decreased funding for the Christian Hospital in Bissamcuttack. But Viru and Nancy were well on their way to establishing the facility as a role model of self-sustaining mission hospitals in India.

---

[1] Christian Hospital Bissamcuttack, *Golden Jubilee Souvenir* publication, (1954-2004), pg 13.

[2] In Hindi, Dharma means religion, and shala means sanctuary, thus a dharamshala is best described as a 'religious sanctuary' or rest house, either created for religious pilgrims or as a religious endowment for those in need.

Chapter 9: Bissamcuttack Growth
1977-1996

Only two years into their tenure at the Christian Hospital Bissamcuttack, the Henrys were well on their way toward building the infrastructure of a modernized and sustainable hospital. New facilities were being designed and built as quickly as possible, staff was being trained, and equipment installed to handle the increased patient load as the hospital grew.

By 1977, nearly halfway through the phased reduction in financial backing from the Danish Mission Society (DMS), the Henrys had started to generate revenue to support much of the hospital's work. Yet, they knew a continued relationship with the DMS would be a benefit to both the hospital and to those who had cared for the mission in India for many years.

> "At first, the Danish Mission Society was subsidizing our salary also. It wasn't very much. By about 1977 we were getting our salary from the hospital, but they wanted to continue paying the chaplain salary. That was a very small amount.
>
> Viru told them, 'We can cover that. Let us say we are financially independent from the mission board.' They had a country secretary, the one who interviewed us in Delhi. When he left the board they hired another one and they came to visit us when they arrived in India. If they could make it for our board meetings, they would sometimes attend that.
>
> At one of the DMS meetings the secretary proposed that Viru should come to Denmark every other year. They financed for us to come the first time. They were eager for us to come meet everyone and their board members who were so interested in the hospital. For the first one, they called us and paid our way."
>
> - Nancy

"We met all the board members. They spoke to us in English, but their meeting was conducted in Danish. We sat there and went through quite a bit of it. In the breaks, we could interact with the members.

I had some strong talks with them. They were not supporting us at all by this time. I wanted to know where they stood and if they'd be open to doing any capital grants or other funding options like that, especially for non-recurring items, for a particular need like a building or vehicle. They were open to it and they did continue to support us in some things.

I think they gave us a vehicle first. We only had an old jeep. I think they gave us our first vehicle, if I remember correctly. We had an old red, secondhand 4-cylinder petro station wagon.

We used that red car for some years. Even Anil drove it. He used to fill it with mangoes to take to the family when he had to go to Raipur to bring things for the hospital. That was a good mango area. We got them cheaply. Anil learned to drive very early."

- Viru

The regular exchange between the Danish Mission Board and the hospital board introduced Viru to other mission agencies throughout Europe. Not only were these agencies willing to help fund capital projects in Bissamcuttack, but they were also eager to send doctors for training in tropical medicine and acute care specialties particular to India.

"Most of the time, Viru went alone on the trips to Denmark. I went with him at least three times. Mostly, we stopped in Denmark first for the board meetings and then we went to America. It was nice. We met a lot of people every time, even attended a Christian Medical Society meeting over there."

- Nancy

"I've been to Denmark, Germany, and Switzerland for various mission agency meetings. The partner out here was the chairman. I used to always go to meet the German mission. It's not far from the Danish border. It's in Hamburg.

We became friends and they wanted to share in the work here, so they started financing projects also. The Germans financed the rebuilding of the local church. The secretary of the German mission also visited Bissamcuttack. The German mission agency hadn't been involved with us and when I met the secretary, I said, 'Don't you think you should make a visit to Bissamcuttack also?'

He said, 'Definitely.' From then on, he always came to visit us and see the work at the hospital. Although they changed the secretary three times while we were in Bissamcuttack, the Germans always kept their relationship with us. They would come and spend a couple days of fellowship with us also."

- Viru

Given a deadline of 1980 for the end of subsidies, the Henrys worked diligently to exceed their goal and achieved financial independence in 1979. An entry in the Christian Hospital Bissamcuttack 50th jubilee book says, "1979: CHB reached the point where income expense balanced. From this point until today, the hospital is run on a no profit-no loss basis, recovering the cost of operations through user fees, self sufficient for running expenses."[1]

"It was a sliding scale and he stuck to it. We were [financially] independent earlier than they had required.

[The Danish Mission Society] wanted to maintain the relationship with us, and we with them. They no longer provide any oversight so they stopped coming to our board meetings, but when we visited Copenhagen they always gave us a guest room in their center. We always went to the secretary's office. It was a long-term relationship and they continued to be involved, but we were no longer dependent.

Later, we had other Danish friends and they started inviting us. Gradually, we stayed with our friends."

- Nancy

Although the hospital had achieved the goal of funding day-to-day operating expenses, it continued the vision of serving the poor Dr. Madsen had established.

"You'd treat all the patients, no matter what.

No one would go without treatment. If they really didn't have money, they were given a concession, part or whole. They don't have to put down a lot of money. If you go to some other private hospitals, you put down money and then they work. Here, you don't have to put down money. If they come with an emergency, they don't have that money to begin with. You have to start treating them. Sometimes you get your money back and sometimes you don't.

That was a principle Dr. Madsen had. She only treated poor people. She even gave them bus fare for the way back. We didn't do that.

And we treated more and more people every year, expanded the hospital, hired more staff, and still God always provided."

- Nancy

Income generation was only half of the financial equation that allowed the hospital to sustainably function. Cost reduction, recycling, repurposing, and partnerships were necessary components of the hospital's success. The Henrys and their staff became experts at cost-saving measures that were the difference between fulfilling the mission of the hospital – to serve the poor of their area without cost – and financial failure.

"Viru always called it the Robin Hood approach. He charged more for the rich so we could afford to charge less or give free to the poor. We also were very careful. We didn't waste things and re-autoclaved syringes as long as their life was good. We started getting gifts from REAP, a medical supply mission in Michigan (U.S.A.)

Anil took on the task of making the orders through Harold Hanson, a personal friend I met at Stony Point. Harold and his wife are both pediatricians that worked in Thailand. When their children got older, they went back to California, but they kept in touch. He volunteered and headed an organization called Medical Ministries International which would collect donated supplies, furniture and equipment from US hospitals and send them overseas.

Harold would go around and collect unwanted medical items. The things they were throwing away in America, I couldn't imagine. It was horrible: rubber gloves, syringes, disposable things that hadn't been opened.

The request came one time on a long list of things you could order. I was so busy at that time, and Anil said, 'Aren't you going to order this?' He was always so interested in what was going to happen. He asked, 'Do you want me to order these things? You can tell me what you need.' So he made the order.

Five truckloads came with this stuff in 1980. I don't know how many containers. Anil got it through CASA [Church's Auxillary Service Agency which had an Indo-US agreement through Church World Service to bring in containers customs-free] and he sat in the truck and came back with it. He came up from Madras with all this stuff.

All the staff came together because it was a huge amount. We had to organize everything to store it. Anyone who was not working came and helped. The men came over and lifted an x-ray machine. It was so heavy.

It was like a party for everybody. By that time, we had built a new laundry and we had two big storerooms so we had room for all this new equipment. I was directing them where to go with the things, but it was a big project."

- Nancy

The supplies were a boon for the hospital, saving it hundreds of thousands of dollars by reusing equipment that was being discarded by hospitals in the United States. It also enhanced the capabilities of the Christian Hospital Bissamcuttack by modernizing and updating much of its infrastructure. While some modifications were needed to adapt equipment to Indian power requirements, much of the equipment received in these shipments is still in use to this day.

"We received so much. Trolleys, these stainless steel carts on wheels. They sent so many. I could put two in every ward. The nurses were so happy. They had to carry everything on a tray and it would fall off. They could take their things down to central supply to exchange things. Our hospital is on a hill so you had to go down that ramp. Those trolleys were great.

We also got patient gurneys, one or two tables, and operation lights. Those operation lights and a lot of the tables came from another organization named Chosen, but they were American [running on 110 Volts.] Our electrician changed the lights over to Indian bulbs and to our current [240 Volts.] We were originally importing those bulbs for I don't know how long. He switched them over and it's still like that today. He re-wired and changed the socket so we didn't have to order bulbs from America.

We got several loads like that. It was such a big help. We got so much use of those things. It was a lot of work. We'd have to dig in these boxes, but we had a list of things. You'd look at the list and find the things.

There were all kinds of things. We might have had only one of a certain piece of equipment in a ward, but now we had multiples. The nurses were so happy to have all that stuff. We didn't waste it. We were very careful in taking it out and cataloging our inventory. We released a minimum amount at a time. There was so much we didn't have to buy because of those shipments."

- Nancy

"We got most of the beds from abroad; Harold sent them. We put them in the new recovery room, in the casualty. They were special beds for that sort of thing. We had adjustable Fowler's beds in all our private rooms. We had more than one shipment, and it's still going on."

- Viru

By 1984, a three-phase master plan for building and expansion had been drawn up with the help of the German mission agency, EZE. They supported phase one and began phase two while the Danish group Danchurchaid joined the effort to finish phase two and complete phase three. The effort resulted in the construction of additional wards, operating theaters, an outpatient department and staff quarters, among other facilities. Dr. Johnny Oommen, head of the community health department, recalls the rapid pace of development.

> "In the infrastructure development of the hospital, when they came in '75, the first few years were survival years.
>
> The hospital was costing 400,000 rupees: 300,000 external and 100,000 from here. It had to become self-sufficient. By '79, we were self-sufficient.
>
> The 80s were the building years. Dr. Henry was saying that he was thinking about a building here and a building there. A doctor from the CMAI [Christian Medical Association of India] told him not to make piecemeal plans. You need to break this down into phases.
>
> An overall plan was made and broken into phases one, two, and three. Four and five were additional phases. Then these plans were put to people to support. Phase one and half of phase two was German money. Halfway through phase two and phase three it was Danish money.

This is how all these different buildings came up through the 80s. By the end of phase three, the major developments were already done.

The church was built in 1984. Phase four was the early 90s, the English-medium school. I came in 1987. The nursing school was being built. Phase four and five were additions. Phase five, we did with our own money, mostly.

Until phase four, we had mass funding, then had to pick up phase five on our own. There was no more continuous flow of money. This goes on until '98, then there was no building for some time."

- Johnny Oommen

As the Christian Hospital Bissamcuttack grew so did the need for increased financial management and investment strategies. Officially declared a charitable organization in 1966, it no longer paid taxes and could receive tax-exempt contributions. It also meant the hospital had to be careful not to show a profit, no matter how successful it was at collecting fees and increasing efficiency.

"We put money we earned in a trust with the CNI [Church of North India.] It was initially 100 Lakhs."[2]

- Viru

"He put it in a CNI trust so we got interest from that. He saved it.

The hospital was doing very well. We were declared as a charity hospital so we didn't have to pay taxes. But you have to show a deficit in your accounts. If you have too much money, you lose your charity status.

It's allowed to put money in a trust for the security of the organization. Then you can show your deficit. This was in 1985.

You get interest and the principal remains there. He always said to think about what would happen to the hospital if something happened to him. He wanted them to have a source of money beyond patient fees."

- Nancy

Surgeries had become the largest source of income for the hospital. In 1976, the first full year the Henrys were in Bissamcuttack, the hospital performed 726 surgeries. By 1983 that number had grown to 1,790. A decade later, in 1993, the hospital performed 2,422 surgeries. A statistical overview of the hospital's procedures shows its staggering growth.[3]

Procedure	1976	1983	1993	2003
Outpatient consultations	15,423	29,572	36,764	48,448
Consultations per day	*49*	*94*	*119*	*158*
Inpatient admissions	2,030	3,194	4,691	6,750
Hospital bed capacity	*75*	*80*	*150*	*150*
Childbirth / Deliveries	NA	247	458	1,042
Total surgeries	726	1,790	2,422	2,574
Lab investigations	0	42,423	76,669	98,224
X-Rays	0	225	3,054	6,349

The influence of the hospital grew with Dr. Henry as its charismatic leader. In addition to foreign mission agencies continuing their relationship with the hospital, local and regional leaders began to see the Christian Hospital Bissamcuttack as a community resource and a top-tier facility due to the transformations accomplished by the Henrys.

Clashes between Hindu and Christians were not common, but also not unheard of, in Orissa, even Bissamcuttack. Some saw Christian mission efforts as colonization, westernization, and exploitation of land and labor. Others saw it as a threat to Hinduism and tradition since conversions to Christianity primarily occurred among Dalit (low caste) and tribal (non caste) peoples.

The 1967 Orissa Freedom of Religion Act states that no person may "convert or attempt to convert, either directly or otherwise, any person from one religious faith to another by the use of force or by inducement or by any fraudulent means."[4] It was a law and principle the Henrys ensured was upheld.

"Certainly, conversions weren't being done in the hospital. Our approach: 'faith in action.' People could see the difference between a Christian hospital and other places. They came there for that: the love, the affection, the ethos around the mission hospital is different. They came for that.

We had good relations with the community. It's not like [the violence] that happened later. It's not too far from Bissamcuttack. It had reverberations. Just because they were angry with those people, it spread all over Orissa at that time. That's a long story. Many Christians were killed, mistreated, and raped.

When we went, the Hindus and the Christians lived peacefully together. There were no problems.

The town's leader, the tahsildar as they call him, was a friend to my husband. He was the mayor of the town. He was always in good contact with those guys."

- Nancy

"I had many friends in the town. We had good relations. They are still my friends, such good friends that they come to see us sometimes. They keep in contact by phone. Anything I need help with, they are there. That's the kind of lifelong friends we made.

Before we came there, Dr. Madsen was a little aloof from the community. She did her work and took care of poor people. What could they find wrong?"

- Viru

"That was something [Dr. Madsen] told us about. She said she refused some of the richer people because she only had

140

time to take care of the poor. That's an interesting thing. My husband never did that. Whoever came was taken care of.

I don't think she had any retribution against her. The thing is everybody wants to rush to a foreign doctor. She told us that she just didn't have time for them. She was a lone doctor. She had one or two junior doctors with her, but she was the main person."

- Nancy

Acclaim for the hospital grew as its reputation for providing excellent care to people of all castes and socio-economic groups grew. The Henrys remember one particularly difficult case that became part of the glue bonding the community to the work of the hospital. Treating all who came, and serving them with compassion and excellence, was a value the Henrys ensured applied to every patient.

"My brother, Herb, was visiting the hospital and we were sitting outside one evening when about 20 men brought a patient in who was seriously ill. They were driving a jeep and he was in the back.

In the forest, the men build pits where they put these wooden stakes with a point on the end at the bottom. Then they cover it with leaves. It's on the path of wild boar so they just fall in and are impaled. Well, this fellow had fallen in."

- Nancy

"The stake went right through his abdomen. It went through the anterior part. He came in holding the stick. He was a thin guy. He didn't have much fat. It's a miracle it didn't hit his liver or spleen. He's so sensible that he came to the hospital.

From hole to hole, front to back, I had to make an incision. The liver was bleeding.

Every time I'd go to stitch, it would start bleeding more. We couldn't get ahead of the bleeding. We were giving blood and everything. So I took a big gauze lap pad that was for soaking up blood and soaked it in saline.

I stuffed it inside him and took it out gradually. Every day, I'd pull a little bit more out. I had to explain why I was leaving it inside him; they were worried I wouldn't remove it. The bleeding didn't stop for 10 days. When the pad was finally out, the bleeding had stopped and I stitched him up."

- Viru

"That fellow was about to be married soon. It was a miracle he lived.

The family was so thankful they made a beautiful display out of decorative things. They made it themselves. I don't remember the message on it, but it was a tribute to [Viru] for saving his life. That's still in his consultation room there. He said, 'You have to come to my marriage.' And Viru did.

Viru was very active in the community. He had a lot of friends in the town. That's how he was, even with the staff. That's how he spent every Sunday. He would go and visit the staff in their homes. He would take off after breakfast and I wouldn't see him until late lunch. He would go to the hospital also and make a round. He used to go every week to a few houses of the staff and keep track of what's going on with them to have a close relationship with them as well as the family.

He just went to say hello and catch up, particularly if there had been an event in the family. They probably gave him a cold drink or something. It was just a friendly call. He was always available to them. They used to come to him with their problems.

There weren't many staff in the beginning. We only had about 40 staff and 40 patients. Now they have about 150 staff. That's including community health and the school. We've branched out in a lot of ways over the years."

- Nancy

"Dada," the nickname Viru received while in school at Ludhiana due to his being older than the other students, took on a new meaning in Bissamcuttack. No longer seen as "elder brother," his role as caretaker of and counsel to the staff earned him their respect and they honored him with the title once again.

> "Dada also can mean grandfather, or paternal grandfather in Hindi. They called Nancy 'Dadi,' grandmother. There's a park outside the crèche [the daycare and preschool] with those names on the gate.
>
> When our children were young, they started calling us by our first name. They heard other people use those names, so they started. We started calling each other 'Mama' and 'Papa.' It got shortened to Mom and Dad, but we stayed with Mama and Papa."
>
> - Viru

> "It's nice for me to have another name for him because in Indian culture, the wife does not use the first name of the husband. Terry [Anil's wife] says, 'Anil,' but that's a modern generation. I was there in a generation where they won't take it. They will say 'the eldest male child's father.' They don't say their husband's name. I needed another name for him also.
>
> I could have called him 'Anil's father,' but that seemed rather odd. I like just one word. So when he suggested we call each other Mama and Papa, I thought it was a good idea. Otherwise, you just avoid saying it, because it wouldn't be polite to use his first name. If I'm talking to Americans, I say Viru."
>
> - Nancy

Viru's visits to staff homes and his genuine care for the families that served Christian Hospital Bissamcuttack earned him great respect. He could be decisive and authoritative. His temper sometimes got the best of him. He was resourceful and innovative. He listened to the people he trusted, and he trusted them to follow through on their plans. Some senior staff even called him "Boss" because of these traits. But always, these same staff members say, he led and mentored with care and compassion, keenly aware of the needs of the people the hospital served and of those who served the hospital.

> "If someone on the staff had a problem, if their roof was falling down, if there was some problem in the house, they would tell him, and he'd get it fixed. That was hospital quarters.
>
> Even if they had personal differences in the family, he would help settle that also.
>
> If there was a death in the family, he would prepare food. He talked about the shock of being at a funeral in America, where they have a dinner and everybody's laughing.
>
> It's different if somebody dies in your community in India. First of all, we go and meet them. Then we find out what is the food arrangement. Turn by turn, every meal will be served. We will go there and serve it to them. Very simple food. We don't just send the food over. We would prepare it, take it down to them, and serve it. It's a support. We were part of that also. Somebody in the family would be telling who would bring each meal.
>
> [In Bissamcuttack], they don't like to eat if someone has died. The wife won't eat if the husband has died. You go and personally invite them, and then they would start eating. The women will stop eating if they lose a close relative. That's part of the Indian culture in showing grief.
>
> In Christian families, it's so different from Hindu. When a Hindu's relative dies, everybody starts shouting and crying and beating their chests. It's so depressing to see. Christians will cry and do more quiet things. The religious difference is

there. We have hope for our relatives. We're going to miss them. Hindus believe in reincarnation. It makes a big difference in the response."

- Nancy

Hard work and dedication from the staff was well rewarded, as the Henrys established a fund for staff recreation, which meant picnics and outings to the lush hills around Bissamcuttack.

> "So many people wanted to give me money. That's the system here. Offer a little money to the doctor and you get better treatment. But I never accepted it. I told them we had a picnic fund for our staff they could contribute to.
>
> There's something called a dharmpeti in Hindi, a 'holy box,' or literally a 'holy tummy.' It's a religious donation for the poor. I told people we take care of the poor and we didn't need a special fund. But we started a dharmpeti that went through the accounts as official donations. We never took the money directly.
>
> I told them, 'Go to the office, give your name, make a donation, and get a charity receipt.' That way it was on record and not a bribe, but a contribution to the hospital staff fund."

- Viru

> "The staff picnics are just like Anil does now in Mungeli. Bissamcuttack was a beautiful place. There are a lot of places you can go for nice picnics in that area.
>
> There's a waterfall not far from the hospital. It's changed a lot because they've dammed it up to send water to the fields. But in those days, it was beautiful and flowing. The kids would slide down the rocks. It was slippery because there was always water. They'd stitch leather patches on their pants and slide down. They loved it.

Even in Tilda, Viru had the picnic fund. Whenever we had enough money, we had a picnic. We also had many staff dinners in front of our house.

Anil grew up with those things, so naturally he feels they should be done here in Mungeli too.

It brings fellowship and it's very important. We're saving lives and you can't always joke and you have to be strict. There are situations where we have to be strict. You need another time where [hospital leaders] go and sit with the others and have a good time. It kind of compensates for those other times. The boss should have fun with the staff. It's the staff fellowship he was always interested in, as is Anil."

- Nancy

Viru was also well known for his sense of humor. Along with being the "boss" who took care of patients and his staff, he was quick to play practical jokes and play along with cases of mistaken identity.

"He'd take the jeep out and, many times, he'd go out and get the patient.

There was one time in Bissamcuttack, he went to get a patient but there wasn't any driver available. They got a call for the ambulance to go to a particular place and they'd go in the jeep to show where the patient is.

They thought he was a driver. He never said he was a doctor.

So they talked smart to him, saying 'Driver, pull over. We want to have a cup of tea.'

'Yes, sir,' he replied.

He sat in the car, enjoying the whole thing. He waited while they were drinking their tea. When they got to the hospital, he helped remove the patient and got him into the room where he was to be examined.

Viru put on the stethoscope and started examining the patient. These fellows had such huge eyes looking at him. 'Who is this guy? He's not a driver. He's the doctor.' It was a shock to them.

He was enjoying playing the role. He was quiet about the whole thing and we had a great laugh about it."

- Nancy

An increased demand for the hospital's services, accompanied by large and growing staff and their families, necessitated additional building projects. Continuing the 1984 master plan, phases four and five of the hospital's expansion was again supported by Danchurchaid between 1993 and 1996. The hospital added ultrasonography, endoscopy, casualty services, intensive care, and additional housing to the compound.

But hospital services were only part of the overall goal the Henrys had for the Christian Hospital Bissamcuttack. As Viru had realized during his year teaching 11th grade science in Bhatapara, education was the key to self-development in India.

"Health For All [an Indian government campaign] was a stupid idea," he famously said. "They should have aimed for Education For All, and health would have happened automatically."

On its own, the growth and stability of the Christian Hospital Bissamcuttack would be an amazing feat. Literally pulling the institution from the brink of closure as Dr. Madsen departed took superhuman effort. Growing the facility from a 10-bed clinic to a profitable 150-bed modernized hospital complex in under 20 years was equally tremendous.

What is truly remarkable, however, is that while this growth was happening, the Henrys were developing robust education, training, and community outreach programs in Bissamcuttack. In Viru's mind, the mission of the hospital had to be extended to provide education and employment opportunities to those in the community. It also needed to be a world-class training facility capable of shepherding the next generation of Indian medical professionals.

147

With uncommon perseverance, ingenuity, and passion, Viru –
always accompanied by Nancy's support and entrepreneurial spirit –
not only transformed the landscape of health services in
Bissamcuttack, but they created an entirely new paradigm for
education, service, and employment in the region.

---

[1] Christian Hospital Bissamcuttack, *Golden Jubilee Souvenir* publication, (1954-2004),
pg 14.
[2] 100 Lakhs is 10 million Rupees (INR). In 1985 the sum was equivalent to
approximately $800,000 USD. The devaluation of the Rupee has continued since
Indian independence in 1947. The same 100 Lakhs is valued at approximately
$145,000 USD in 2016.
[3] *Golden Jubilee Souvenir,* pg 17.
[4] Retrieved 18 March 2016 -
http://www.lawsofindia.org/pdf/orissa/1968/1968OR2.pdf

Chapter 10: An Acclaimed Training Ground
1978 - 1998

The Henrys firmly believed education was the path to better health and alleviating poverty in India. New educational initiatives accompanied every turn of the hospital's development in Bissamcuttack. Not only did the Henrys have the conviction that education was a means of betterment for the people of India, but they realized mission hospitals were in need of qualified doctors, nurses and staff members. They also felt mission hospitals had a unique capability and responsibility to provide educational opportunities in their communities. Over the Henrys' tenure, the Christian Hospital Bissamcuttack became a model for the development of an education framework capable of serving its own needs as well as the needs of the community.

The School of Nursing Begins

A nursing school was first among the many educational milestones in Bissamcuttack. Nancy had become principal of the School of Nursing in Tilda when Ruby Merkel returned to the United States. And so once again, Nancy assumed the dual role of nursing superintendent and principal when she initiated a School of Nursing in Bissamcuttack in 1978.

> "There were very few nurses [in Bissamcuttack] when we came. Unless one nurse knew someone they could get to come, that was it. It was not very organized. Whoever came and asked for a job, we hired basically. The nearest nursing school was Berhampur, which is near the ocean. They had a Christian nursing school there."

> At first, we got nurses from there. We asked them to send some and they did. It was a British Baptist hospital. That hospital is part of the same board as Tilda and Khariar. Those Baptists joined the Church of North India later. There was even a British Baptist doctor there. It was a lady doctor. There

were various British nurses and missionaries. They weren't new missionaries, but the old ones were there.

We arrived in Bissamcuttack in 1975 and the first nursing class came in July 1978. In January [1978], I went to Vellore to study midwifery because we had to teach it. Nurses learn general nursing and midwifery.

At that time, midwifery was a six-month course. I could just go off for six months from January to June. In July, we opened the school. In fact, the student selection was done by Ruth Hofsteter [nursing superintendent in Khariar] for me. She came from Khariar and half of the girls were from Khariar."

- Nancy

This running joke, that Ruth would have selected student candidates from the Khariar region rather than Bissamcuttack, was based in fact. Limited resources, combined with an exciting new program at an expanding hospital, meant the competition for entry to the School of Nursing was fierce.

"The first class had seven students. I think my husband always liked the number seven or it was just how many candidates they had.

We started very small. It was an ANM [Auxiliary Nurse Midwife] level, a two-year course. There were not many girls who had the qualifications. Up to 10th pass, we can take for the ANM course. Up to 12th pass, we can take for the GNM [General Nurse Midwife] course. There weren't many girls who could have qualified for entry to GNM.

They became registered midwives in our two-year course. General nursing was in Berhampur at the time. We decided that our impact would be on Orissa. The Kerala girls used to go out to Delhi when they graduated, and everywhere else. They weren't helping Orissa."

- Nancy

Retention of trained nurses and doctors to serve in Orissa, and specifically to serve in mission hospitals, was a key long-term goal of the Henrys' education initiatives. Still, the lure of private or government hospitals in larger cities was always a factor for some of the students, but many who were trained at Bissamcuttack stayed. Others sought out the experience of training there and were drawn to the mission and vision the Henrys displayed.

> "We had a certain aim and objective to help the health of that underdeveloped state. To this day, it's still that way. Our nurses are in all places. They've made a big impact. They're ANMs. They stay around. The GNMs we started in 1996 are leaving. They were staying while we were still there.
>
> The bird kind of flies away when they see something they want. We couldn't hire all the ones we graduated. We didn't even have that many posts. Today is a different thing. They want to go where they can make money."
>
> - Nancy

Prior to the construction of the two story nursing school in 1987, the School of Nursing met in a two-room home adapted for training. Nancy also arranged for certification and oversight of the school so the program's credentials would be universally recognized if and when nurses transferred to other hospitals in other regions of India.

> "We started the school in an old building. We have staff living in that house now. The building was lying vacant when we came so we made it into a school. We had two small rooms. There was the tutor's office with a few shelves of books as a library. The final room had a bed for practicum things and cabinets for materials for their demonstrations. We called it a demonstration room. These are requirements.
>
> When we were planning for this school, we went to Bhubaneshwar. We went to meet the head of the nursing department and she told me, 'We already have so many ANMs. There's no need for you to start another school.'

I had asked her to come inspect our place for ANM. She said, 'There's so many we've trained that are sitting at home doing nothing.' We had hired a few of those and we realized we didn't want them. They couldn't take a temperature properly. Their training was minimum. We would have to re-train them so we might as well train them from the beginning.

I think it's more difficult to re-train a person than it is to train them the right way from the beginning. We immediately lost interest in that. Our education center would have been far away from us in making dealings with diplomas and all that stuff. We realized that was not an option for us.

So we went to the Christian Medical Association of India (CMAI). They have nursing medical boards: a North India board and a South India board. They also have the Mid-India Board of Nursing Education.

We went to see the secretary. She said, 'You can apply to join us.' She gave us what was required to be recognized. The Indian Nursing Council recognized their work.

In those days, they never came to inspect. They do today. In those days, they depended on this board to do everything. They gave the examinations. In fact, it was originally called the Mid-India Board of Nursing Examinations. They changed it to education. It's more than just the education. It's the whole monitoring of the education and setting up the standards.

I went to a meeting there a year before I went to Vellore. They had their board meeting there in November of 1977. I went there and talked to them. They authorized me to start the school. I think she'd already inspected by that time. They said, 'You go ahead and plan to start next year.' I have a feeling that inspection was done before that. I had been in contact with her, they came and inspected, and then I sat in a meeting and it was approved that the next year."

- Nancy

The authorization and certification of CMAI was the first step in opening the School of Nursing. Staffing it with qualified trainers was another matter. As the school began operations, Nancy recruited Dr. Madsen, Viru and a family relative to teach courses in the first years.

"This board, they just tell you what to do and you do it. There are steps. You have to have certain equipment, certain staff, and certain rooms. They were very kind in letting me start with the first year. I didn't even have one tutor when I started it. We had sent somebody for training. It was [Viru's] cousin's sister, Kamini, who was our staff nurse. We had sent her off to the MIBE graduate school where they train tutors. They got diplomas in teaching, public health, or administration. They had three areas they could train in. She was sent for education to become a qualified tutor. That was only a one-year course. She had gone off for that so they allowed us to start. The doctors helped me in her absence. My husband taught anatomy. I was also the nursing superintendent.

Kamini was [Viru's] maternal uncle's daughter. She was a trained nurse. She did the three-year training in Tilda. In the beginning, we could get our relatives to come. That was one way to get nurses. She was working for us as a staff nurse and she helped me teach practical procedures and supervised them. Then we sent her to tutor training. When she went off, I got a retired Tilda tutor to come help me. It was only a one-year contract while Kamini went for her training.

Then we also needed a community health person. We had a doctor sent for community health. In the beginning, Dr. Madsen taught the nurses community health. Viru taught them anatomy, she taught community health, and I taught the nursing subjects. We covered all the subjects. By the next year, I had a retired tutor from Tilda join me. That was very helpful while Kamini was out.

The next year, students have two classes. That's a midwifery year. It's a community. That's very important in the ANM. They're trained to work under GNMs in the hospital. In the village, they can be independent. They were trained more in community than in hospital care. Dr. Madsen left about that time and started her community work. By that time, Viru had trained a new community health doctor. We sent him to the school of public health in Calcutta. It's a government institution. He came back and he taught it."

- Nancy

Community Health Extension

As the school acquired full staffing, Dr. Madsen was able to return to the work she loved: community health in the villages. After handing over charge of the hospital to Dr. Henry in April of 1976 and working with Nancy to institute and instruct the first class at the School of Nursing, she was free to go. She built a home in 1978 in Bandhaguda village, about 7km (4.3 miles) from Bissamcuttack, and established a community clinic among the tribal people of central Orissa who often lived very primitively.

> "Freed of the burden of running a hospital [Dr. Madsen] developed an innovative community program of the next ten years, that covered 99 villages in four gram panchayats[1] – Hatamuniguda, Dukum, Piskaponga, and Daklguda. She pioneered strategies in community health, with village health workers, village clinics, mass programs, etc. Soon she realized that the key to sustained good health was actually education.

> So in 1979, she began the first night schools in the region, introducing kerosene lanterns in villages that had never had one before. She, assisted by Madhabo Rona and Balakrishna Himirika, designed education primers in the Kuvi language. Before she knew it, she was also doing roads, wells, and check dams… You name it, she did it. In all this she had the backup of the Christian Hospital Bissamcuttack behind her, and external support from Oxfam and Danida."[2]

To give nurses real-world experience, the community health program opened several centers in nearby villages. The first was in cooperation with Dr. Madsen in Bandhaguda. The efforts were well supported by community leaders and by 1980 nurses began regular rotation in the village. It was not a glamorous assignment, but Nancy and her nurses enjoyed the challenge and the opportunity to serve those who would have had little to no access to healthcare without their presence.

"The first clinic was purely run by nurses. No doctors went there at all. The community gave us a building. It wasn't much but a mud hut with a grass roof. Our nurses stayed there and I went, too. We started that in 1980 and it was required for the program. All the nurses had to go and live there.

The first place is called Daklguda. We started at another site, not really near Dr. Madsen's house. She lived near the main road and we went to the interior. I think the whole area is called that. Johnny [Oommen] did a survey of that area and the area where he was opening a site. There was less infant and maternal mortality, and much better statistics.

All we had were nurses out there. We realized what nurses alone could do out in the village level. They were doing health teaching. They were doing home visits. They were treating malaria immediately instead of letting them get to the brain malaria.

All the health statistics were improved. They were given prenatal care. They did deliveries and they recognized if they couldn't manage it they would send somebody on a bicycle to the hospital. It was only an hour or so to the hospital and they would send the ambulance out. We may get somebody nearby with a jeep, but there weren't many of those. The nurse was willing to the take the patient if they could find somebody. They had to wait for the ambulance otherwise.

I spent a lot of time in the villages at that time. I had the girls out there so I wanted to know what was going on. I spent at least one or two days out a week in the village.

Once I went out in the monsoon rains. We had to go through a river to get to the village. I waded across in water up to my knees. We walked out to all the villages. I went out with the nurses for this village visit. We did a lot of health teaching

155

and treated sick people. It was a nice visit. All of a sudden, it just started pouring rain. It just came from nowhere. We had umbrellas since it was rainy season. The rain came right through the umbrella. We had to walk all the way back to the center.

The jeep left us and we waded across and went back. There was a fixed time they would pick us up. It was a lot of fun, to be honest. We got back and made some tea. We said, 'The jeep must have come by now. We better go. They'll be waiting for us.' The nurse and the lady that worked there walked us down and the river was overflowing. It had filled up and it was fast.

I waved to the driver who was on the other side. The nurse got some men to hold onto me and they walked me across. The water was not over my head but it was fast. Alone, I wouldn't have gone off with it. They're used to crossing in this horrible torrent. Somebody else carried my bag and they got me over and I got in the jeep to go back. We waved goodbye and we went."

- Nancy

The river crossing became an annual issue, as monsoon rains predictably swelled the waterways fed by mountain streams.

"There was another time, at that same place. We had two British medical students that came to Bissamcuttack from Wales.

They reached on Monday. On Tuesday, the nurses go out to the village and they said they wanted to go to the village to stay out there. They had just arrived from England, but they were eager to go. We told them what to take with them. Food, they get from a market over there. Our nurse would get it and feed them there.

They took their belongings and went out. That time, they walked with very little water across. They were planning to stay several days and it kept raining. They got stuck over

156

there and could not cross back. We knew they were okay but we thought they might get scared. We used to drive out to see them across the river . It was a fixed time and we'd meet them to reassure and check on them. Finally, the water went down a bit so they could cross back.

Viru is an excellent swimmer. He could swim across the width of a wide river. He had done that in his college days. He had the courage to say he could get them through it. Even a good swimmer can get caught up in that water. He got across and brought them back one by one. We were so worried about them. There are hills all around and the river can fill up so fast. The streams are moving in and it goes up so quickly with flash floods that you could get swept away easily.

They were happy but mainly glad to be back. They'd only spent one day in Bissamcuttack and the jeep was going out. They were very courageous girls. They smiled when they came back."

- Nancy

Living in the village was a rustic affair. A simple home was shared by two nurses. They were responsible for a routine of visits to nearby villages and taking care of their daily chores such as cooking and cleaning. Nancy ensured the connection was maintained to the hospital in Bissamcuttack and their peers.

"The house was very simple. It had a little latrine in the back. We built a pit that was their latrine. It wasn't a septic tank. They have a kind of latrine in the villages. You cover stuff up with it, fill that up, and then make a new one. They did have a place for taking a bath, behind their house. Before we had that, they went down to the river to take their baths. We thought we should give them more facilities.

We had one main nurse, Ms. Premamani Palo in the beginning. She had only one helper, Mrs. Somwari Das, known to all as Somwari-Ma.

She was there for quite a long time. Later, when [the main nurse] left for a government job, we started getting two nurses so they would have peer group company. We'd choose girls that were good in community health. They'd go out there because they liked community health. We'd bring them in for special functions and parties at the hospital so they didn't get totally isolated.

Nurses did their service in the village for two years. We'd place a senior one and a junior one together so we'd change one every year. Now we call it a service agreement. It's a promise to go and serve in an area."

- Nancy

Community health and village outreach are "looked down on," according to Johnny Oommen. But from its origin, beginning with Dr. Madsen, Christian Hospital Bissamcuttack had an active and integral community heath and development program. Nancy, and subsequently Oommen himself, would continue to prioritize these programs as necessary and essential parts of the hospital's mission.

"As a doctor, I've been asked, 'You look intelligent. What went wrong?'

Community health is less glamorous in some circles, but in other circles, public health is quite paying. Normally, nurses go into community health and their parents ask them why they're being sent on punishment. We very often have to deal with that.

It's something Mrs. Henry did. She was very keen on community health so she prioritized it. Every year, when a new batch of students came out, community health always got the first choice on which nurses we wanted. That tradition has continued. They needed to be able to make decisions on their own and manage independently so you needed more capable ones. We have developed a system slightly differently.

What I have done over the years is asked all the nurses in the department to vote on who they think would be the best person from the next batch. Each person gets three votes and I collect those together to get a ranking list of who we think will be best. I also ask the school of nursing tutors and principals. They give the academic view.

Our girls are looking at if they gelled with the community when they were students. Now we get a priority list of who we're looking for. Then we talk to those girls and ask if they'd be interested to come to community health. If the first one says no, then we go with the second. Then we go over this list with the nursing superintendents and almost always, we get the ones we've asked for.

The tradition of giving us the first choice is something Mrs. Henry instituted. This process is a participative decision because these girls are going to have to live together. I would rather have them say whether they can live together than to deal with subsequent fights.

As a result, these nurses are better prepared for hospital jobs. At the end of a year or two with us, they have skills that the others don't have, especially analytical skills. The ability to think logically, to question, to make decisions, all this is different."

- Johnny Oommen

The School of Nursing Growth

Commitment to Bissamcuttack extended to the selection process for nursing school candidates. Nancy was determined to train local students and to give them opportunities to stay in the community and serve throughout their careers. One challenge for these students was that much of the required instruction was in Hindi. Most of the students were raised speaking Oriya and had learned English in school, but Hindi is – in comparison to Oriya – as different as French is from Spanish.

"The enrollment at the School of Nursing went down the second year. We were determined to have students only from Orissa. When we started under this MIBE, the language becomes Hindi. I wanted to go into the government because the language is Oriya. My fear was if the Oriya girls would be able to do either in Hindi or English. We decided to give them English books. Some of them didn't pass their 12th year. We had to give them English books because we couldn't get Oriya books for them. The exams are given in English and Hindi.

I always had this fear in my mind of how would our girls would do in the board exam. Even, the practical exam, you have to speak English or Hindi. The examiners are coming from all different places. They don't even know Oriya. It's either Hindi or English. I say God just blessed us. We had one girl who was from the Hindi side but she was working in our hospital as a nurse aide. Her husband was the chokidar [caretaker] in the bungalow where we stayed. It worked out fine. She had two children but her mother-in-law was there to take care of them. She came first in the whole MIBE in the final exam. One girl failed and had to retake the exam. If they fail the board exam, they have to repeat. Out of seven, six of our girls passed.

My husband was always a big teaser. He gave the results. He called out the girl's name and said, "Oh, I'm so sorry." The girl almost fainted. She passed very well. They learned not to believe anything he said. I'll never forget that. The girl fell over. They caught her. She was a very good student and worked very hard. He was a real character. I wasn't so happy with it because my poor girl had such a shock. Everyone else laughed about it and she was a good sport about it. I told him to never do that again.

In the next nursing class, we only had six students. We had more candidates but they weren't fit to enter yet. We give them a written test and an interview. Rather than taking everyone to fill up the class, we wanted to make sure they could do it. I think it's worse to be selected and then to fail.

The one who failed the board exam that year, did pass the next year. She is a nurse who still works at the hospital."

- Nancy

Commitment to the Christian Hospital Bissamcuttack and loyalty to the Henrys by staff have been contributing factors in the growth and stability of the hospital. This extended to students from the School of Nursing, especially those who had been hand selected and marked as promising candidates by Nancy. Her trust in them fostered decades-long service by these nurses.

"Shudarshini [a 1980 graduate from the first class] is still there, in charge of maternity. She was very good in her practical and I made her in charge of maternity. We used our service years to do duties. We had a service year doing night duty alone in the premature infant and incubators. That's what they're doing right now with these students. They have to take more responsibility because they don't have staff nurses.

She stayed there. She was the first one I had in charge and is still in charge today. She's from our first batch. She can make a diagnosis so quickly.

She's a charge nurse. The MIBE allowed us to keep her there because of her experience. We have another one there from the second batch who is still the charge nurse in the medical ward. They're doing such a good job. Why should we kick them out? The doctors are totally satisfied with them. They have learned so much in their experience, even though they don't have their GNM letters. The board allowed them to stay on as charge nurses.

Down in the surgical ward, we could get one girl to stay on. She married a local fellow and she became the charge nurse. We have a GNM charge nurse in the surgical ward and all the other wards now. They're all GNMs that are made charge nurses. Because these girls are from the first and second batch, they had done it all these years. I don't think anyone could do it better than them.

Some of these girls did not pass their 12th grade exams. You had to have 12th pass to enter the GNM course. The ANM course was only a 10th pass. It's a pass qualification, not a fail qualification. Quite frankly, I taught them how to take charge duty. In those days, I was one-to-one with them, teaching. They just picked it up. They were young; they would have probably been between 18-20 when they started."

- Nancy

Dr. Johnny Oommen joined the staff of Christian Hospital Bissamcuttack in 1987 as head of its community health programs. His recollection of the time is also one of rapid growth. He also remembers the frustration the staff felt as doctors came for training in Bissamcuttack only to leave once their service bond had been fulfilled.

"These are two sets of stories. One is a set of people who are still here. They came in like Mrs. Henry said, you spot a person with capability and you give them responsibility to help them grow in that process.

Another list altogether is people who came here, especially as surgeons. Dr. Henry would get very upset if they left. 'Anyone I bring in, they just run away.' That is another set, people who cut their teeth here."

- Johnny Oommen

Education and Excellence in Care

Heavy patient loads, approaching 300 outpatient consultations on the heaviest of days, and the expansion of the hospital to 150 beds by the late 1980s necessitated a new model of leadership and hospital maintenance. Moving toward a distributed leadership model and working to decrease the number of days patients stayed in the hospital post-operation was a key to maintaining the efficiencies Viru had created.

Still, there was no reduction in service or turning away patients as these heavy patient days became more common.

"The load is very heavy now. I don't know how they did the OPD [outpatient department] today because the numbers were looking huge. There must have been about 250-300 today, on a Monday. Monday's a heavy day.

Dr. Henry always felt that a mission hospital with less than 150 beds has a corporate personality. The minute you cross 150, you're a different kind of hospital. You don't know everybody by name, the kind of bacteria you have are different. His argument was, up to 150 patients, you could have a one-leader model. Though we officially call ourselves 200 [in 2012], it's more around 240. There are days when we have 240 patients admitted. In reality, we've long crossed that. We've tried hard to decrease it, but it's just not possible.

The number of patients you have, in community health, we have a formula. P is equal to I into D. Prevalence is equal to incidents into duration.

You cannot decrease the number of people coming to you. The only thing you can decrease is the duration of stays. Earlier, we used to keep all our patients 10 days after surgery. Now, by using dissolving sutures, you can decrease that to maybe seven. If you decrease the duration of stay on the same number of beds, you can increase the number of patients. The only way we can move forward is to decrease the duration of stay. Right now, our average is six to seven days.

The labor and delivery patients are only two days so that's a huge transit number, except for the C-sections. The normal deliveries are all going out at two days.

The other thing we've talked about is [outpatient] surgeries, where you can come in and be operated on and then go home. These are ways to decrease the duration of stay so we don't have to increase the number of beds. It's killing us. We don't have the staff. I would love to go back to 150 beds. If you can decrease the duration of stay from seven to four, then we can go back to 150 beds. The bed occupancy rate was 95 percent last time we did our survey. "

- Johnny Oommen

"75 percent is good, so 95 percent is crowded."

- Nancy

But for all the growing pains, Johnny and Nancy attribute Viru's personality and reputation as an excellent doctor and administrator for the attraction to and retention of doctors at the hospital. Although many trainees passed through the doors of Christian Hospital Bissamcuttack, all recall their time as formative and adding further inspiration to their careers and mission.

"Every Founder's Day, 5 September, we do a meditation in the morning. I think that's the only time we sit down and think together.

One year, I described the life of the hospital as a train journey. We asked people what year they got on and off the train. It worked out beautifully.

You're never the same person. You got on the train one person and you got off changed, sometimes negatively changed, but almost always, positively changed and having grown and moved forward. We fight over the train seat as if it is only my seat. It is only my seat when I get on to when I get off. It is our responsibility to treat that seat well and leave it better than when we got on. We must pass it on to the next person when they get on."

- Johnny Oommen

"Dr. Henry, his way of dealing with the doctors was so special."

- Nancy

"Can you think of any doctor that left because he didn't like working with the boss [Viru]? I can't think of one. They all left happily.

Young doctors come to work for us for their two-year bond. Then they opt for higher studies. How many of them want sponsorship from us for their education? That means they have to come back and serve with us. That is an indication of how happy they've been working with us for those two years. In Dr. Henry's time, there were a lot of people who did that."

- Johnny Oommen

Viru's ability and leadership as a doctor and mentor did not translate into receiving medical care for himself graciously. Johnny remembers one humorous story when Viru finally gave in and sought care at the hospital.

"Of all that can be said about Dr. Henry, I'd add that he's a good doctor, but a bad patient. He was sick and treating himself at home. He wasn't getting better so he packed up his pillow and came to the hospital. We started an IV line on him for fluids. He had a terrible reaction.

We wanted to give him a sedative to calm him down. Anil was worried and we told him the shot was something other than a sedative. We gave him something to calm him down. In the morning, he took his pillow and said, 'I don't want to be admitted. I'm going home.'"

- Johnny Oommen

The New Life English Medium School

The hospital's growth fostered another problem for the Henrys to overcome: the education of staff children. There was no primary school in Bissamcuttack for the children of staff. The only option for English medium training was to send their children off to boarding school, which was neither desired nor possible for all the staff.

"One reason we started the school was that Viru lost so many staff because their children were of school age. They didn't want them to be in a residence [at a boarding school.] They wanted to be in a city where they could be day scholars. We lost doctors and some nurses that way.
We also felt that not everybody can afford to send their children off to such. We needed a good English medium school right here, mainly for our staff. But you can't run it just for your staff. It won't be financially viable, so we said for the community as well. We had come to uplift the community so it would be open for the community."

- Nancy

An entry dated 1986 in the history of Christian Hospital Bissamcuttack reads: "The New Life English Medium School was started as part of the hospital in an old ward on campus. The goal was to bring quality education to the region, thereby contributing to the development of the people. It would also prepare young people who could be sent for professional training to be future staff of the hospital. Opportunity for education of their children would also enable professional staff from other areas to stay on long-term at Christian Hospital Bissamcuttack. The school, though initially planned only as a primary school, was later upgraded up to grade ten."[3]

"They started classes in 1986 in the old ward that had the private rooms. Viru built new private rooms: surgical private rooms in the surgical area and medical in medical side, and maternity in the maternity side. We had needed many more private rooms. Now we had 10 private rooms in each ward.

We didn't need the old private rooms because the building was far for our nurses to go. It wasn't convenient for the nurses to take care of patients that far away from the main hospital. So that emptied out the building and we had another use for it right away. That's where we started our school. That building was very useful for starting things.

It started up to 5th class because children can go into boarding by 6th. Dr. Sahu's own son came because she couldn't get the right place for him.[4] We realized we had to take the school to higher grades, but we didn't have a building for any more than 5th class. Then Viru went to get the funds. For each of these things, he had to look for the funds. He got them from different places. He was a very good salesman because they liked him and said they'd do it. He got very positive responses. Many agencies have helped build that hospital."

- Nancy

A building plan was proposed and the church, adjacent to the hospital complex, donated a portion of the land behind its building for the construction of the school. Viru once again worked with the Danish mission and soon raised funds for the school's construction. It was completed just in time, as the old ward overflowed with students and the 5th grade graduated into 6th. The classes occupied the first floor of the school and construction of a second level was quickly commenced so the school could accommodate classes through grade 10. The school also needed qualified leadership to teach through these grades.

"The church gave the land. The church owns the graveyard and the pastor's house is there too. In the middle is the school.

It wasn't very much land, but Viru built the first story to accommodate some classes. They had five full classes and by the time they finished the 5th grade, the lower level was ready. The 6th went there and I don't know if the 7th went there or not. We had to continue building the upper part so it could go up to up to 10th grade.

Mrs. Alvares was our first principal at the new school; she was from Goa, a Portuguese colony. She probably heard from the mission hospital and applied for the head of the school. She had been serving as vice principal at a recognized ICSE [Indian Certificate of Secondary Education Examination] English medium high school in Odisha. At that time, it was only a primary school so she was called the headmistress. We gave her the job of the headmistress and she did a very good job.

She was in the school for 1-2 years and she moved the school over to the new building. She stayed quite a few years. She was a widow and had a son and a daughter. Her son had gone to college right in Orissa. Her daughter, we sent to Vellore for a lab technician course and she became a technician in our lab."

- Nancy

Not uncommon for staff entrusted with important tasks by Viru and Nancy, Mrs. Alvarez pushed the New Life English Medium School to a higher standard, seeking the maximum certification for the school. In spite of doubts about the caliber of the student, the ability to attract and retain high-level teachers, and testing demands on the student, she forged ahead with her plan to give her students the very best education possible.

It's a very high standard of English education. They're very strict and have very advanced books in ICSE. What the other schools are using for fourth grade, we're using for 3rd. They are a year ahead. Now they've developed their own books. This is a national accreditation. If someone has graduated from a place like this, they very easily get seats in college and they very easily get jobs. The standard of English is very good.

She pushed for the certification So many people said it was too difficult. We're in tribal area. Some of the children's parents don't even know English. Some don't even know how to write their names. We got some criticisms. We had one doctor who had studied in both. He gave us some other guidance. He said, 'I first did ICSE and then I went into CBSE.' CBSE is the Central Board of School Education. He said that is definitely a lower level. He got excellent marks going into that and he didn't have to work very hard. He wished he had stayed in the other system.

That, in the end, had worked very well. We've had great principals that teach the teachers how to teach. To get qualified teachers there has been very difficult. They require that they must have their bachelor in education. We could get them with a degree but they didn't have the bachelor in education. We couldn't find places to send them to get it. Finally they found something that worked. Now they all have it. The board allowed us two years to get everything in order. We had to work up to the recognition.

Mrs. Alvares did a lot for the school to bring it up. When her daughter and son got married, she didn't want to stay there anymore. She said, 'I've got to go be near my children. I miss them so much.' She was also getting older. Suddenly, we were again going to be without a principal.

That was a real crisis for us. She was going to leave. She wasn't going to wait until somebody came. She finished that year and left. We had only a few months and we didn't get somebody in that time. We had to take the most senior teacher and make him acting principal. I was his mentor. I'm not a teacher of that kind. We end up doing everything out here. We do things we were not trained to do and you just kind of do it. I'd had enough teaching experience with nurses so I helped him to organize things and keep it regularized. "

- Nancy

The sudden absence of Mrs. Alvares was a shock to the school. She had singlehandedly nurtured the school into a state of recognized excellence, and she was gone. The school continued to attract more students, adding a bus, driven by Anu Oscar, to provide transport to students in the surrounding area. Johnny Oommen's sister came from Kerala and took charge of the effort to search for and recruit a new principal and head of the school.

"I sat down with Johnny's sister and said, 'We're in a crisis. We have to have a qualified person here. I have a dream that someone from Kerala will come here and take this post and you're the one who can make it come true. I know it. I just feel it.'

169

She was a very outgoing and capable person. She said, 'It's so hard. I don't know anyone who would come to Orissa. It's such a backward place.'

She was an exuberant type of person. I said, 'Somehow, I feel you are the one who's going to facilitate this.' I put it in her mind. I wrote to her again about it. I was after Johnny to tell her she had to do it. Johnny was already there working and I met her when she came to visit. I kept telling him, 'Please write to her. I don't have a lead. Nobody wants to come to Orissa.'

It's the hand of God. How did this girl come to visit and how was I convinced that she would do the job? I was convinced that she was going to do it. She did. She got Mr. P.O. and Mrs. Annie Matthews. They had just come back from Kenya and they were the heads of two different high schools. They already had jobs. Still, she went to them and asked.

'There's a place that is looking and I think you'd enjoy it,' she told them. 'It's very much like Kerala. It's all green with beautiful hills. The people are good. It's a Christian atmosphere. It's where you could do a lot to help poor people.'

They were good Christian people. I think they started thinking maybe we should do this. They were training more elite students in Kerala than they would do here.

Mr. Matthew came alone because Annie wrote to my husband with concerns. He wrote back, saying, 'Please come and see the place.' Mr. Matthews came and he saw the school that was nicely built by that time. He saw all the challenges. He saw this was a poor area.

The thing that convinced him is that he said, 'After I talked to Dr. Henry, I knew I had to go there.' Somehow, my husband convinced him. He saw enough positive things there. Johnny was there also to push it.

He said, 'I'm going home to talk to my wife and I'll give you a reply.' In those days, we didn't use phones that much. It was the 90s but we mostly used letters. Here comes the letter back, 'My wife and I are willing to come for one year as a trial.'

They came for one year as a trial in 2002. Now, in 2013; they've been there 11 years."

- Nancy

As with doctors and nurses, the success of the New Life English Medium School depended on the consistency of its staff. The 11-year tenure of the Matthews set a pattern for the school and for teachers to stay with and excel in the work of educating students in Bissamcuttack. Nancy says it was an important mission of the hospital to see the school succeed.

"They consider those children their own. Annie is a very motherly lady. They're very strict but very good with the children. They have organized it so beautifully. They taught the teachers to teach and they demanded they make a plan for their courses. When they got new teachers, they worked with them. She's very patient to work with others. She's the headmistress over the lower classes and he's the principal of the whole school. We wanted to give her more recognition and more salary instead of being just a teacher. We wanted to pay them well enough so they would stay.

The hospital heavily subsidized the school for years so they could keep it going and get good teachers. We strongly believed the school was essential so we kept it going."

- Nancy

Families, students, and even teachers recognized the excellence of the program and wanted to be a part of it. Like Dr. Henry's mentoring at the hospital, a positive environment and growth opportunities attracted people to the school, achieving financial sustainability in 2013 and a 500-student attendance goal in 2014.

In 2009, the school added a computer lab and hired a teacher to expand the curriculum into digital technologies. Once again, the Henrys' trust in a willing and energetic candidate paid great dividends.

"There's a young man, Malay, they depend very much on him. He is their computer teacher and also teaches other subjects. It's interesting how we got him. He was in Nabarangapur. They had a school in the mission hospital there. His father was a lab technician in the Nabarangapur hospital.

He wrote and said, 'I've learned some computer. Could you use a computer teacher? I would like to come and teach computer.' We didn't have any computers but we thought, 'He seems like a nice young man. Let's call him and talk to him.'

We called him and said, 'We don't have one computer yet, but we will get them. Are you willing to teach other subjects that are needed before that and wait until the computers come?' He said, 'Yes, I will.'

He waited at least two years. I was so worried he was going to run away. I said, 'Don't run away. I'm working on it.' We had to get the money. Finally, we got a lot of the money from Rebecca, a nurse friend of ours who comes out to help sometimes.[5] She paid for part of it and Avon Lake United Church of Christ paid for another part.

Between them, we could get enough computers to hold a class. There were two students on each computer, taking turns. Now they have even more. Malay was so happy. He said, 'You kept your promise.' He's such a sweet and sincere guy.

He said he would not leave Bissamcuttack. He's very loyal. He married one of the other teachers and they now have a child."

- Nancy

Reflecting on the 25th anniversary of the school in 2011, Dr. Johnny Oommen cited statistics from community health programs showing how an educated population is much healthier than one that has little or no access to schooling. "The issues of education, health, and development are not separate – they are all interlinked," he wrote. "But education is the key."

> "People ask us, 'Why is a hospital running a school?' We ask, 'Why not?' For education does more for health than healthcare itself. The Christian Hospital Bissamcuttack is therefore committed to giving the children of our region the best educational experience we can muster."[6]

Asked to look back and assess the success and progress of the school, Nancy has nothing but praise for the staff and teachers, along with the hospital staff's commitment to expand educational opportunities into the surrounding villages. The school and education initiatives are part of the ethos established by the Henrys. Invited back frequently to Bissamcuttack as honored guests, Nancy and Viru are received as the founders and mentors of the school that they believed in deeply.

> "When we went in April [2013], they showed the smartboard demonstration. There is so much new technology.
>
> Someone from the school always invites us and we talk to them and encourage them. We give them a little message in their morning assembly. We were there for two days and we went to the morning assembly. Then we went to the smartboard demonstration and met the children. They're all so affectionate with us.
>
> The atmosphere at the school is beautiful. It's just like a family.
>
> Even the hospital is just like a family. It's getting bigger and it's more of a challenge to keep it that way. When we were there, it was a close group. Now they're getting over 200 patients. They don't have enough doctors. They need a lot more, but they're carrying on somehow. It's still so very good

and we are so very proud of all the programs and how they are run."

- Nancy

---

[1] A gram panchayat is the cornerstone of a local self-government organization in India of the panchayati raj system at the village or small town level and has a sarpanch as its elected head. The failed attempts to deal with local matters at the national level caused, in 1992, the reintroduction of panchayats for their previously used purpose as an organization for local self-governance. There are about 250,000 gram panchayats in India. Definition retrieved from Wikipedia 17 March 2016.

[2] Christian Hospital Bissamcuttack, *Golden Jubilee Souvenir* publication, (1954-2004), pg 13.

[3] *Golden Jubilee Souvenir*, pg 14.

[4] Dr. Padmashree Sahubecame became Medical Superintendent of Christian Hospital Bissamcuttack in 1998.

[5] Rebecca Herr is a Registered Nurse and member of Bristol (New Hampshire) United Church of Christ. Since 1999, she has served as a short-term voluntary missionary representing Common Global Ministries, a collaborative effort between the United Church of Christ and the Disciples of Christ.

[6] Oommen, Johnny. *New Life English Medium School 25th Anniversary Program (BUDS)*, 2011.

Chapter 11: The Henry Children
Love and Loss

Brothers

By all accounts, Ajit was an outgoing and gregarious child filled with compassion and quick to share laughter with friends and strangers alike. Born in the United States after Viru and Nancy returned to care for Nancy's ailing father, he was just two years old when the Henrys returned to India.

In Bissamcuttack, Ajit had his own surgical gown and would often accompany Viru on morning rounds at the hospital, checking on patients and building rapport with the staff.

> "Ajit used to come over to me in the morning and say, 'What operation is there today?' Well, it was a 'GJ' – a gastrojejunostomy. They don't do it much anymore. It's rerouting the path of the food away from an ulcer.
>
> He would come in and say, 'Well, I've got two or three GJs to do. Oh, it's the same thing. That's boring.' Then he went home. He wasn't that interested. You have to do something exciting to catch his interest."
>
> - Viru

Nancy says Anil would say the same thing, but he stayed. He learned how to take blood pressure and lift patients from the trolley. Anil was most interested in the day-to-day work of the hospital. Ajit was not. At the time, the boys were nine and 10 years old, respectively.

> "Ajit asked a lot of questions. The anatomy when the abdomen was open, he would ask about that. 'Where's the spleen? And the liver?'
>
> This is when Viru was studying for his MS. He was sitting reading, studying a surgical book. Anil was standing over his

175

shoulder and said, 'I know you're reading about hernia.' Ajit asked, 'What is a hernia?'

'Protrusion of the intestine,' Anil would say, and asked, 'Papa, if I become a doctor, will you give me all these books?'"

- Nancy

The boys' education had been a challenge for the family. Though Anjali was doing well in classes at the blind school, the boys' access to quality schools was more limited. Nancy says the family couldn't afford to send all three children off to boarding while Viru was in graduate school. Leading up to that time, Anil attended local schools in Tilda, but had bad experiences and was withdrawn and Ajit was still too young. Nancy attempted to teach the children herself, providing them with grade-level equivalent studies, though not the classroom experience.

"Being an American, I didn't know much about the system so our kids had no early schooling at all. Anil was already six years old when we arrived in Ludhiana. In India, they start at four years old with lower kindergarten, upper kindergarten, and then first grade. By the time they get to first grade, they already know so many things: numbers to 100, simple addition, full alphabet. We went expecting to put him into first grade.

Viru decided to let him go to that village school that was cross the road. It was in a different language but he knew Hindi by that time. Everyone spoke Hindi to him."

- Nancy

"The nanny took care of the kids. We had both gone off to work so she was in charge of them. One day, she told me, 'Anil is scolding people with dirty words and he's learning it at that school where you're sending him.'

In the Hindi alphabet, 'ga' is like 'g' – they always teach by associating it with 'ganesh,' the elephant god. They have the words they use to teach the letters Anil said, 'What have you learned ga-ganesh? No, you have learned 'ga-gali.' Gali is a swear word in Hindi, in the local language. He would have understood what he was saying very well."

- Viru

Anil was withdrawn from the school in Tilda after this incident and a bout with measles he'd picked up from another student. Viru said, "I'm not going to send him there anymore," and Anil never asked to go back. Anil was six when the family moved to Ludhiana and should have been entering the first grade. A large private Catholic school, Sacred Heart, was outside the town and children from the Christian Medical College were bussed there for classes.

"That was the best school. I went out and talked to the nuns and said, 'Could you please give me the syllabus?' It wasn't yet time for school to start. We got there in April and school started in July. I took the syllabus, got the books, and taught him. That poor kid, we worked from morning to night. 'You have to finish this today,' I'd say. By evening, Anil would say, 'Mama, can I go out and play?'

We covered all the material so he was called to take a test. I took him over to the school and it was just about the beginning of school. They put him in a room and all these kids were running and shouting back and forth. Here's this little boy looking at these kids instead of paying attention to the test. He didn't pass the test.

His first test, and he failed. When they told me, I was upset.

'I know he knows everything in that syllabus,' I said. 'I taught him myself.'

'But Mrs. Henry,' they said. 'He didn't answer it on the paper so we cannot accept him."

I felt so sorry for Anil. I had worked so hard with him. He should have been in a separate room. That poor kid was taking the first test he ever took in front of all these [disruptive] kids. How can he pass?

It was very hard on him and I said, 'Don't worry, Anil.'

We had another Christian school that was not as good as [Sacred Heart] but it was okay, so we put him in that. It was Ewing Christian School, right across from where we lived. He had to go to school and didn't even have to take a test at Ewing; they put him right in the first grade.

He had a very good teacher, Mrs. Charles. She was very good in English and she was a very good teacher. It was a fairly new school and I think the first grade was the highest – it progressed to add a grade each year. They took her to the second grade and then the third grade, so he had the same teacher for those three years. Up to third grade, he was there and did quite well."

- Nancy

Nancy says Ajit was more rambunctious than Anil – defiant at times, and always mischievous. Busy and distracted, Ajit made many friends but was regularly in trouble for his antics.

"We put Ajit in lower kindergarten about the same time. He was such a naughty kid. He was so hyperactive; he couldn't sit still in the classes.

One day, he was running around chasing a girl with a dead crow in his hand out on the playground and the teacher was running after him. She couldn't catch him. I had to go to the school so many times as the principal beckoned us when issues like these came up.

'What should we do with Ajit?' the teacher asked. 'He's not able to sit still and learn.'

He was so young and had never been in a school before, and was an active kid. I was not as if they would expel him; however I had to see the principal several times to talk about

178

what to do about Ajit. Finally he went through the first grade in Ludhiana."

- Nancy

Both boys struggled in their early education experiences, having not attended pre-school in the languages in which they were now expected to learn proved to be a blessing and a curse. A curse in that their comprehension and perceived progress was slower than other students and a blessing in that it prepared them to work in a broader segment of Indian society, with its many regional Hindi dialects and professional expectations of English fluency.

> "Anil, although he found [early grades] very challenging, was a hard worker and determined he would pass. He changed schools to go to Kodaikanal International School and entered in the fourth grade. The fourth grade teacher was very good with him and gave him extra help. He passed okay. He wasn't the top student or anything, but he passed it.
>
> When he went into the fifth grade, his teacher was Mrs. King, the wife of the school principal. He also worked hard there, but he wasn't getting very good grades. I talked to the teacher about having him repeat a year, which Anil refused to do and worked harder to keep his grades up and do well."
>
> - Nancy

Ajit had been held back, repeating the first grade twice. Although he could read and speak English well, his Hindi reading comprehension was limited in spite of his excellent spoken Hindi. Teachers told Nancy that Ajit didn't know how to read. She couldn't believe it until she realized he was memorizing the words with the picture on each page and seeing the pictures and saying the correct words so Nancy believed he was reading. Nancy knew Ajit had great potential, yet she and Viru reluctantly agreed to have him repeat the first grade. It was reminiscent of Viru's need to repeat a grade as a child – he knew all too well the hardship and the necessity of the decision.

"When Ajit had trouble at the beginning of second grade they said, 'He's young enough and it would be better if he does first grade again.'

So we put him back in the first grade. I understood it was necessary. So I asked Mrs. King, 'These kids were in a school that wasn't up to this standard, even a different type of school. Should we put Anil back also?'

She said, 'No, Anil is working so hard. He will make it. I know he will make it. Gradually, he'll pick up and catch up with everybody else because he works very hard. Don't disappoint him by putting Anil back. It would be disappointing to be working hard and still be put back.'

Gradually, he pulled up his grade averages. In sixth grade, he did better, and in seventh grade even better. He finally caught up to the school curriculum.

From then on, he didn't have problems. Anil studied well. He was always a hard worker.

But Ajit wanted to play all the time, so he was a different kind of kid. After we put him back he started reading from the beginning. He used to bring home his books and I'd say, 'Let me see your homework for today.' He'd say, 'We already covered this.' I'd say, 'Okay, you read it for me.' He would read it perfectly so I thought he knew all these things, so I'd send him to play. What else is there to do?

He was actually memorizing. The teacher goes over it and over it and over it. He already knew English so he picked it up just like that. All he needed was the picture for reference, and he knew it."

- Nancy

Anil and Ajit were enrolled in the Kodaikanal International School in July, prior to Nancy and Viru assuming their roles in Bissamcuttack in the fall of 1975. Originally known as the Highclerc School and established under the leadership of American missionary Margaret

Eddy, Kodaikanal had been conceived as a "school at a hill-station would allow the children of missionaries to escape the tropical diseases that were claiming the lives of so many, and provide a cool and open atmosphere that stimulated learning."[1]

Ajit Transfers to a New School

Ajit, the youngest of the Henry children was, as Nancy described, "from a very young age protector of the underdog, whom he quickly identified and tried to help in whatever way he could. There were numerous times that he came to the rescue of others both at home and at boarding school."

> "It was not unusual for Ajit to notice poor persons, make friends, and try to help them. He often would relate to the person, tell us about it and discuss what could be done.
>
> For instance, one day when Ajit was in about the eighth grade, he came running home with an urgent request for 10 rupees. When I asked him why he needed 10 rupees, he explained that he had met the midget clown in the circus who was feeling ill, so he brought him from the circus ground to the hospital for treatment. He told me that the doctor ordered an injection costing 10 rupees, but the clown had no money. Ajit went and got his own 10 rupees, the treatment was given and the clown got well.
>
> At boarding school there were many times that he saved a frightened student from a bullying more powerful fellow. Ajit was strong and could use his strength to stop intimidation when he saw it. It was well known that if anyone was in trouble they could call Ajit.
>
> One time, at night, a group of students was walking back to the hostel along a narrow path on the edge of a steep hill in Musoorie. One of the boys slipped and fell about 20 metres down into the cud. Another boy was sent back to the hostel to call Ajit to come and help the boy. Ajit went down to the place where the boy was found unconscious. He lifted the boy

181

on his shoulders and carried him up the steep hill and back to the hostel.

The boy was airlifted to Delhi, where he received the best care. He not only lived through this experience, but also graduated with his class the next year. At their graduation the boy's parents came to meet us. They explained the whole incident and thanking us, said, 'We are so grateful to Ajit for saving our son's life.' During the graduation ceremony there was a huge applause when Ajit was called to receive his high school diploma."

- Nancy

Even as Anil continued his academic and interscholastic excellence, his beloved brother was not having the same success. Given the alternative of not advancing or repeating a grade to catch up to his peers, the Henrys made a difficult decision during Ajit's ninth grade progression.

"Ajit had passing grades but they weren't very good. By the time it came to eighth grade he wasn't failing, but they wouldn't let him go into ninth. They said he wouldn't be able to do it.

'If he's getting low grades now, it's better you take him home and teach him for one year,' his teacher said. I got a correspondence course, the Calvert Course. Those people go abroad and can continue to teach their own children. It was difficult, but I had to do this.

They said, 'If you can just repeat the eighth grade with him, he'll be ready. I'm sure your individual attention will make a lot of difference.' I took him home and taught him and he did quite well. He wanted to go back to school. He missed his friends.

But then, he had an incentive to learn. He repeated the eighth with me teaching him and when we finished that, he went and took a test. They said, 'He's done very well on the test and we have promised you that if he's done well on the test after you tutoring him, we will take him back.'

The admission officer was my friend. They were our neighbors actually. He said to me, 'As a friend I would like to tell you this. Ajit is known as a naughty kid. He doesn't study. It would be much better if you put him in Woodstock and let him get a fresh start.' He was going into the ninth grade. 'I think he could do it. He's grown up a lot from being home,' he told us."

- Nancy

Woodstock School is a 500-student Christian residential school in the hill station of Landour, 300 kilometers (185 miles) north of Delhi. Founded in 1854, the school was the northern counterpart to Kodaikanal in the south. Nancy says the decision to send Ajit to Woodstock and let him continue his education in a new environment was a turning point. He excelled in the new school and was accepted to college at the end of his secondary education.

"We put Ajit in boarding school too early, we realized. To go into first grade in boarding is not advisable at all. Anil was already in fourth grade, and there was a big difference in the way each of them adjusted to it. Ajit missed home and the individual attention. We learned it too late, and now I always advised it to everybody else. Don't put your kids in first grade into boarding school.

Now they don't take kids in the first grade. I think they won't take them before fourth grade now. They must have had more cases like this where they're too young to be in a hostel.

I remember we went to see the kids at school one time. Here comes Ajit out of the school. He had one shoe on with no sock and the other one with the shoelace dragging. It just hurt me like anything to see your child like that. Then I realized he was too young.

We continued up to eighth grade. We didn't bring him back to Bissamcuttack. We were working so many long hours and I wondered, 'How would I manage him at home?' I used to feel it when I went there that this poor kid is neglected there.

Anyway, we listened to the admission officer and we admitted him into Woodstock school. It's up in the hills, north of Delhi. Many of the missionaries from our mission went north and had their kids in Woodstock. It was the same type of school, slight difference, but not much.

He was so happy to get back to schooling. He was grown up by then. He did very well. He was not a straight-A student. Sometimes he got on the honor roll. He did well enough to get into St. Stephens College [in Delhi], which is one of the best arts colleges in India.

He appeared for the interview there. They knew of Woodstock. They had taken so many students from Woodstock already. They just looked at his grades. They said, 'He's gotten so many As in English. Why don't you put him in English?' He took up English there and he got his bachelors in English."

- Nancy

Viru had taken Ajit to his interview at St. Stephens and the selection committee was impressed. Not only were his grades good, but Ajit was handsome and muscular, just short of six feet tall and a candidate for the school's championship boxing team.

"Ajit was a boxing champion. They said, 'You're just the person we want. We want someone to represent our college in boxing.'

They trained him in it. He won the gold medal for boxing in his first year. He told both of us, 'Mom and Dad, I'm not going to do boxing again next year.'

'Why, Ajit? You won. You did very well,' we said.

'I don't like hitting anyone who I don't have anything against. I have nothing against that other guy. Why should I hit him?'

184

He never boxed after that. They wanted him again because he got the gold medal, but he refused. It wasn't fun hitting the nice guy over there."

- Nancy

"The second year Ajit was there Rahul Gandhi [son of Rajiv Gandhi – Prime Minister of India from 1984 to 1989] came to St. Stephens. He told Rahul, 'Don't worry. If anybody gives you trouble, I'll take care of it.' He was always the protector."

- Viru

Anil Pursues Medical Training

As displayed by his early interest in his father's work, Anil was drawn to pre-medicine in high school with the intention to be a doctor. Nancy saw it as a foregone conclusion that Anil would pursue this career.

"Anil knew what he was doing. He wanted to be a doctor and knew it was hard to get into medical college. He worked hard with his subjects. He was in sports, music – all the activities. They played basketball, soccer, and he was a long-distance runner.

I was in Kodaikanal for sports day. He had said, 'Papa, you have to come for my sports day'

'Don't worry,' Viru said. 'I'll be there, but won't be there until after it starts in the morning.'

Anil was in a long distance race, running up in the hills around the lake. Anil was getting very nervous. 'Papa hasn't come,' he said. He was very upset. His race was going to be next. I said, 'Don't worry. He'll come. Maybe his bus is late.' Viru did arrive, just as the race was about to start. Anil saw his father and took off, and he won.

Viru got there just in the nick of time. Most of the running, you don't see. Anil saw his dad before he started, and he was revived!"

- Nancy

Academically, Anil was head boy in his class. Continuing the same diligence in the classroom that he displayed in sporting competitions, he made application to Vellore and was accepted in 1984, the same year he graduated from Kodaikanal.

"Anil got an award at high school – a rotating trophy. Every year they give an award to the most outstanding all-around boy and the most outstanding all-around girl.

We were there during that whole week before Anil's graduation to attend baccalaureate and all the festivities. We were there for the last assembly before the school closed for graduation. This is a very big prize and they said, 'The winner of this is Anil Henry for the most outstanding, all-around boy in the class.' He knew that he was being nominated for it. There were other candidates, but he never told us. We were totally shocked when we heard his name. He got to keep it for a while.

All their names are on it. Then it stays in the school. That was 1984 – the same year he joined Vellore. They call it the joining batch. They don't get in it immediately. Some of them have to repeat some things so they're not leaving with their batch."

- Nancy

Anil, ever motivated, had made up his mind he would attend Vellore and did all that was necessary to gain entrance. Nancy says Anil's pursuit of the goal was unparalleled, and his hard work paid off.

"He finished high school in May and had to join Vellore very early in July. He didn't have much time in between. He did all his applications on his own, even seeking tutoring on his own. He was very independent from the beginning. He was the older boy in our family so he just tended to take things over on his own. He took the test and they called him for an interview. He got in and was the first student from Kodaikanal School to be accepted to Vellore.

We had some Indian friends in Vellore. Drs. Marcus and Saro Devanandan were the foster family of Anil there. They have a foster parents program in every batch – so many go to this family. Although Marcus has died, we're still friends and in contact with his wife and daughter. His younger daughter (Malini) works at Kodaikanal School as the school doctor. We always go to her house for dinner when we go there. Anil always sees her.

Marcus did a lot of mentoring with Anil. His elder daughter (Krishna) was also in Anil's class and was so sharp and intelligent. Anil would get so angry. 'That girl sits and reads some novel during class but she gets straight As. How do people do that when we have to work so hard for it?'

Krishna became an Indian professional dancer. She does South Indian dance."

- Nancy

"Marcus was a neurophysiologist and Saro, his wife, was an anesthesiologist. Anil got such love and affection from that family. It was just like home. All those kids were free to come in and out of that home. They could come and open the fridge if they wanted anything. Marcus mentored Anil because Anil said, 'I want to get into Vellore. So far, no one from Kodi has been able to get in there.'

He said, 'Anil, do you know what? You have just as much as everybody else, but your system is different. For instance, speed is important. Memorizing is important.'

He told him about this tutoring system and using questions banks. Because of Kodi, we knew him before he went to Vellore because he used to come see his girls in school. You have to study the Bible and know all about your organization. You have to get all these different books and start reading them. You do all that and you'll get in. That's what he did and he got in.

Since then, there have been others, as Malini got in two years later. They cracked the system and figured out what to do, so others have gotten in. But Anil was the first.

At first it was very first tough for them. They hardly have a summer holiday because of the system. They finish high school in May, and July 1 you're in medical school at another course. It's pretty quick. They graduate very young, these doctors. It's four and a half years, and then an internship of one year. So five and a half years altogether, and they're pretty young when they get out. That's why it's very good for them to go out and work in these mission hospitals and get experience before moving on to their post-graduate. The sponsored candidates have a two-year bond and they go out and work. The open candidates, anyone can apply for. They have thousands of applicants for two or three seats. They're all really wizards in this category. So many have stayed there and given their whole life's service to Vellore. They just love Vellore."

- Viru

The draw to Vellore – its prestige and environment – was unparalleled in the Indian Christian medical education system, even surpassing government medical education in Viru's assessment. "I don't think Anil could have gone to a better place," he said. "This incentive to work hard and do the best you can is unparalleled in Indian education."

"It's the whole group: the hospital, the school. It's the love and affection, their approach to medicine. They care about whether people really get well or not. You know, the extra things that come with the Christianity. They have a lot of Bible study and they have chapel.

They have a beautiful chapel there, built by missionaries. The people are very simple there. They're so intelligent and known all over India. Some of them have international recognition; they're so good in the medical field. They're humble people who dress simply. It's very different from Ludhiana, with the Punjab and ladies who wear makeup and dress up. It's a very different situation in the South.

Most of the students at Vellore are Christian, because of the sponsorships. The mission hospitals have to make a contribution to them and they are members of the council. When the council meetings come, a representative from each hospital attends. Viru attended for many years, and now Anil goes to it."

- Nancy

Anil and Teresa

Important to the history of Nancy and Viru is the conjoining of two families who were deeply involved in Christian medical mission in India. Teresa's father was the medical superintendent of the Christian Mission Hospital in Dhamtari, established by American Mennonite missionaries.

"We knew Teresa's parents when the children were very little. He was in Dhamtari as the medical superintendent, south of Raipur. We were in Tilda and we used to go to Dhamtari to meet there for mission hospital business. We were in the mission network with them."

- Viru

"Anil and Teresa were kids then, but we met them at various Christian affairs. They didn't know each other. They grew up separately. Anil was in Kodaikanal and she went to school in Dhamtari. They knew about our family. They saw each other once.

We were going to Orissa and stopped in to see them. That was the first time they met and they both knew they were going to Vellore. When they met there, it was totally their own arrangement. It wasn't an arranged marriage.

189

One CMAI secretary – the head executive – said of their engagement, 'The maharaja's son of Bissamcuttack is going to marry the maharaja's daughter of Dhamtari," on such and such a date. It was the way he announced it.

They got married when they finished their internship in 1990. Teresa had a two-year bond in Dhamtari and Anil had a two-year bond in Bissamcuttack. My husband laughed, 'Two coolies for two years.' A coolie is a laborer.[2]

They each served two years, but they did one year in each place – first to Dhamtari for one year and then they came to Bissamcuttack for one year."

- Nancy

"I was sure I wanted to do medicine and go to Vellore. That's when my schooling got more structured at Kodai, which is a 12-year school.

I went into 12th grade and had a fun time as a senior. I knew I had to take exams and take this entrance exam. When I got out, the plan was to write to Ludhiana and Vellore. Ludhiana could not take a batch that year because of terrorist attacks in Punjab. I graduated around the 15th of May in 1984.

I sat in the library every day studying for exams on the 28th. I went to Vellore and took the exam. We shifted our stuff back to Bissamcuttack and waited for results. My call for the entrance interview came in June. I was with an uncle and we were driving to Raipur. We stopped at Terri's place and dropped in to say hello. I found out she had gotten her call for the entrance interview already.

Our families knew each other, but I hadn't known her. They were in Dhamtari. From there, I went in for my interviews and got selected. Then it was a matter of medical school.

That was a fun experience, lots of activities: music competitions, I was on stage all the time. I would play my trumpet. Our class won the talent competition every single year, which is rare. We had a lot of fun with music. I was into soccer and basketball, going off for inter-college sports. I used to be on the school teams for soccer, basketball, and track for long-distance running at Vellore. It was totally fun. I made a lot of close friends.

Terry and I finished there, and did our internships together. We had our engagement during internship at Vellore, at the home of my foster parents, the Devanandan's.

After five-and-a-half years of school and a year of internship, we had our wedding. It was a grand occasion. Big receptions with 2000 people at each: one in Dhamtari and one at our place in Bissamcuttack. Then we worked in Bissamcuttack for a year. Then a year in Dhamtari."

- Anil

A Future Cut Short

The year was 1992 and Ajit had finished his education at St. Stephens and was considering a career in hospital administration. But first, he wanted to pursue further education in computer science and programming. Studying in Bangalore, Ajit completed his training and was ready for a new challenge. It was agreed that he should further his studies in the United States, and he made preparations to leave soon, following a visit home to Bissamcuttack.

"Ajit finished school in Bangalore and said, 'I want to do something more than this.'

We had been talking to a lot of people about a lot of these courses. They were quite expensive. They were trying to make money and not teaching them very much. Even Ajit was saying they had a limited number of classes. He got a job working in an office there. He learned more on the job than in the course. He said, 'You're wasting your money paying them these high fees.'

Then we decided to try sending him to America. He came back home and we were going to work on getting him to go abroad. He had gone back to get his luggage and got in an accident."

- Nancy

"By the time Ankita [Anil and Terry's first child] was born October 29, 1992, we were getting ready to take off for further studies in Vellore. During that time is when my brother had his tragic accident. Ankita was not even a month old. November 17, 1992 was the accident. I was still working with my parents. I was supposed to take the entrance exams in December, but my parents were heartbroken. They said I couldn't go."

- Anil

Ajit was making last-minute preparations for his planned trip to the United States. He had accompanied Anjali on the train from Bissamcuttack back to Miraj where she was working at the Christian Hospital in the department of psychiatry. The return train he was scheduled to take to Bangalore had been in an accident and was delayed.

"This was the ironic thing. He had been staying in someone's home as a paying guest in Bangalore. He left there and stopped along the way to call us to say the train he was supposed to catch had a very bad accident. We didn't know about it, but he called and said, 'I wasn't on that train. I went on another train and wanted to tell you.'

He called from a friend's house and left his motorcycle helmet in that house. He thought Mom and Dad would be worried so he told us he was safe after he arrived."

- Nancy

Ajit went to a dinner party after calling to assure his parents, leaving the party on his motorcycle to get a friend he'd known from Bissamcuttack, the son of the paper mill's chief executive. This friend was leaving Bangalore and Ajit wanted to include him in the dinner party's festivities.

> "He went out to pick up that friend because he was leaving. It was a farewell thing in this restaurant so he said, 'I've got to go get him also.' That's where the accident happened on the airport road, before he picked up the friend.
>
> A truck hit him from behind. He was thrown, I think, 20 feet away."
>
> - Viru

The impact from the truck, combined with head trauma when Ajit hit the ground, killed him instantly. It was as unexpected as any other accident, but remained an especially ominous tragedy as only hours earlier Ajit had called to assure his parents he had not been part of the fatal train wreck.

> "They caught the driver. It was a hit and run.
>
> The bystanders got the license plate number. This is in Bangalore. They're more aware of what's going on and know what to do. If that had happened around [Mungeli], nobody would have thought to get the license number. They did and gave it to the police.
>
> They found the driver some 40 km away, drunk as anything, sleeping in that truck. They took him to jail. Some lawyers wrote to us. I think they're trying to get business. They saw it in the paper, got our address and wrote to us.
>
> 'You have a very good case here,' they said. 'You could earn a lot of money. You'll definitely win. We won't take any fees if you don't win in the court.'
>
> That's the last thing we wanted to do was go to court. We were not there when it happened. We didn't know anything about it. We replied that we weren't interested in going to the court. That was the last thing we wanted to do.

A man made a mistake. The law will tell him what his punishment will be. Why should we go and try to get money out of him?

It's very painful to go through that."

- Nancy

"Money is not going to bring Ajit back.

The police got his address from his purse and they notified us. They returned his wallet with all the money he had. We had given him a certain amount of money and he'd hardly spent any of it when he left home. We got it all back. I was really impressed with the Bangalore police."

- Viru

Nancy received a call from a relative of the person boarding Ajit in Bangalore. At first, she didn't believe the caller was telling the truth or that it may be a practical joke.

"We had such wonderful friends in Bangalore. They just took care of everything. When we heard about it, the son-in-law of the woman he stayed with had called. Actually, Viru and Anil had gone out hunting, so I was in the house alone.

That young boy said, 'Ajit is no more.' I didn't know what he meant by that.

'What do you mean? What are you talking about?' I asked.

He said Ajit had an accident and I didn't believe him. I thought it was a prank. I said, 'Have you been to the police? Have you seen anything?' He said, 'No, I haven't. I just know about it.' He called back, after Anil came back. I just whispered in Anil's ear that this thing had come over the phone. He picked up the phone and talked to him.

Anil said, 'It seems that it is true.'"

- Nancy

With confirmation of Ajit's death, the Henrys sprang into action, getting to Bangalore as quickly as possible. Friends from southern India joined them to make arrangements for the return of Ajit's body to North India.

"We left in the morning to go to Visak [Visakhapatnam] to catch a plane to Hyderabad and then to Bangalore. Our friends were there. When we got there, we went to some very good friends' place. They all had gathered at the morgue where he was to pray with us and receive us. It was really very nice. Ajit had a girlfriend in Bangalore. She and her mother met us there.

So many people that we hadn't seen in a long time, but they knew us. One man, his son had been a doctor in our hospital, was now with the Bible Society. He had an executive job and was a good arranger. He had arranged a hearse and a pastor in the airport to come have a little service before the plane took off. We took that casket on the plane, below the luggage.

It was really very painful.

Anjali had to come from Miraj. She also had a boyfriend and he brought her to Bangalore. By the time she got there, she had missed us and had to fly to Bombay [Mumbai] to meet us up there. We had a long wait in Bombay and had to go to Nagpur. At that time, there was no airport in Raipur. We had a long wait to get a flight to Nagpur.

The time came for us to get on our flight and Anjali hadn't come. Anil was over there inquiring. He said, 'My sister is coming from Bangalore. We're taking our brother and she hasn't reached here. She was to be here.' The fellow said, 'We don't know anything about your sister, but we know that a blind girl is coming. That plane is late, but don't worry. The other plane will not take off until she comes.'

I mean, how people help, my goodness. They said, 'You go ahead and get on the plane. Anjali will be brought to you on the plane.' Viru wasn't going to let that plane take off – he stood down at the bottom of the steps and waited. She came directly from her flight to this flight. She never even went inside the airport. She was brought directly to that flight and up the stairs and then the plane took off. In such time, the airlines are very helpful, we've found.

There was a big politician, a Member of Parliament from Bihar – a state north of Orissa, near Nepal – sitting on the plane. He never made a noise. He was told the circumstances and he was quiet. We couldn't believe that he was just sitting there, waiting calmly. There was no commotion from anybody. They must have told everybody."

- Nancy

Ajit's body was transported north with Viru, Nancy, and Anjali. The extended family and many friends gathered in Raipur to prepare for the journey to Bhilai, the site of the funeral and burial.

"We were met by everyone at Raipur. Even Terry's brother came. He had arranged a van because we had to have a vehicle for the casket. They took us and we reached Virus's sister's (Vimla) house late at night, where the funeral was to be held. She had arranged the pastor.

We didn't live in that place, but they gave us graveyard space in Bhilai. Their church accepted these arrangements. He's buried not far from here. That was in 1992.

Ankita had just been born."

- Nancy

Ajit's death was a heartbreaking event for the family, especially given his youth, promise, and aspirations. Anil says there was a heaviness over Nancy and Viru, and all who knew Ajit, as they mourned. But gradually, their grief turned to memories and the family honored Ajit with a scholarship.

"After the accident, we stayed in Bissamcuttack and worked for a while. In February, my mother had a meeting in Raxaul on the Nepal border and so I forced my parents to take a family trip. We drove there and on up into Nepal. Ankita was only about four months old. Mom, as usual, was not so enthusiastic and remembered she'd forgotten her passport in Bissamcuttack just before we reached the border. That did not stop us and we smuggled her into Nepal and back again just as if she was an Indian citizen. That was the first time my parents went out after Ajit's death, so that was the breaking of the ice."

- Anil

"We established a scholarship fund in Ajit's name in Bissamcuttack. We started it for poor children. The children were always around him, following him. We said we wanted to make a tribute to Ajit that will live on. It was specially for our staff children that can't afford, but want to go to the English-speaking school, would receive help.

The hospital pays for most of the fees, but they still have to have uniforms, books, and other fees the parents have to pay. Those are the things we wanted to cover for the parents who couldn't pay. The Ajit Henry Scholarship Fund is there for our Bissamcuttack School. They go up to 10th grade in English medium.

We only have four people on scholarship at a time. We made an investment in fixed deposit. It's the interest on that to go on and on. Once a while, we'll put more in if the costs of fees goes up.

We're in the process of turning the scholarship fund over to the hospital and they will run it. They're setting up a committee to make decisions.

For instance, a little girl in second grade, her mother is a cleaning lady in the hospital and her father abandoned the family. She's been told to take the child out because she doesn't have enough money to pay for school. She will be getting the scholarship this year. We have others who have done it. One girl who had the scholarship is in Vellore studying to be a microbiologist. She's my cook's granddaughter.

Ajit was very popular, especially with the children. This is the right way to honor him."

- Nancy and Viru

Anil and Teresa Continue Training

Anil and Teresa had stayed in Bissamcuttack past their bond period to help at the hospital and be with family during their grief over the loss of Ajit. Their daughter Ankita was now a toddler and Anil and Teresa were eager to continue their studies.

"We went to Ludhianna in July or August of 1993 because my dad had done his studies there and I too had grown up there for a few years. We worked there. I was in general surgery and Terri [after beginning her OB/GYN studies] ended up in anesthesia.

That was a lot of fun and we made a lot of friends. Here too, I was involved in the musicals performed each year. That's when we did *Fiddler on the Roof, Starlight Express*, and *Joseph and the Technicolor Dreamcoat*. I was well respected by the candidates and teachers because I already had a lot of experience in surgery.

From there, having completed our post-graduate degrees respectfully in surgery and anesthesia, we came back and joined the staff at Bissamcuttack. The obligation was for three years, but we stayed for five. Our time in Bissamcuttack has always been fun. We know the community. We had a doctor's house in the back, where Johnny lives now. That's when the boys were born, on April 28, 1998.

In India, there is great festivity when a boy is born into a family. Dad always had fun with patients saying that all the babies he delivered were boys.

However, when Ankita was born, the joke was on him.

When found out the twins were expected, Dad was really sweating it out. 'Twins? What if they're both girls?' Of course, they were both boys. The kids slowly became toddlers. It was a lot of fun for them. They were about three so they would spend a lot of time with grandparents. Every evening, dinner would be at their place. That was standard.

Then, I sat with my uncle and I decided to make a change and go off to the States to take a change of pace in life. We decided to take off and my father was not happy at all."

- Anil

"Anil was very keen to the idea. He said, 'My father went to Ludhiana. I want to go there. I've had the Vellore experience. I want to go.' He knew it was a very good surgical department. They both went to Ludhiana, and had a bond for three years to repay the sponsorship. They both came back to Bissamcuttack, having a bond from the same place.

We initially asked Teresa to do OB/GYN training because we needed more help in Bissamcuttack. We had one doctor, but it was too busy for one person. Viru asked her to do that because those are the two things you need most: surgery and OB/GYN. You can run a mission hospital with those two."

- Nancy

Demands of the OB/GYN department were heavy, requiring Teresa to spend almost every waking hour on call. Teresa had delivered the oldest of she and Anil's children, Ankita, five months earlier and she felt the schedule would not let up.

"'I've never even seen my daughter awake,' Teresa told me.

They had a servant there who took care of Ankita the whole day. She couldn't leave to see her own daughter at all. She called and said, 'Papa, I want to change out of OB/GYN. Can I have your permission? Can you help me change?'

I was the chairman of the Ludhianna council at the time. She said, 'I can't live like this. I can never see my daughter. I can't do this profession.'

I was able to talk to the right people and she changed to go over to anesthesia. She wanted to do that. The department was very well organized. A man from the UK, Dr. Richard Pryor, had set up the department of anesthesia.

It's more structured: you have so many hours on duty and so many hours off. You're on call sometimes and get that time back. They didn't have to do all this overtime, except for emergencies. It was the opposite of OB/GYN department where you work anytime every day. She was very happy over in anesthesia. She's so well trained for the ICU."

- Viru

Following training in Ludhiana, Anil and Teresa completed three-year bonds in Bissamcuttack beginning in 1995, ultimately staying five years. Ever learning, Anil felt the urge to explore. Nancy's brother-in-law, Anil's uncle Herb, urged Anil to explore the medical profession in America. Because of different standards in education recognition, Herb felt it would be an opportunity to gain experience under a different medical system.

"Anil was trying to figure out what to do next. Then he comes up with, 'I want to go to America. I'm very curious to see what it's like.'

He had never met my family because we hardly went. They were always at school and Viru and I went without them. One time they went to America. I can only think of one time we took the kids to America. It happened to be their summer vacation and we took them with us. Most of the time they were in school and couldn't get away.

Anil wanted to study over there. He thought he would like to do another specialty, maybe orthopedics, over there. He was very upset because they wouldn't recognize the Indian Master of General Surgery. You have to do it again, they said. You have to be a registrar for so many years or they wouldn't recognize it. He's done all of that, so he wasn't interested. He was enjoying his time. He met a lot of my family that he didn't meet before."

- Nancy

Visa problems held up Anil's transition, but Nancy was able to resolve them.

"Anil had lost his American passport. He had to go report all that, and they were very slow to help him. I think they're very annoyed when someone loses their passport. He went to Calcutta and came back and said, 'Mom, you're going to have to go with me. They're not so eager to give me another one.'

So I went with him and there was no problem. I said, 'I'm very sorry he lost it. He's been registered since he was a baby.' I showed them he was on my passport. Then that got solved. I think they would have eventually. He had to have an American passport before he went. He got it immediately.

He was an American citizen from birth. He was both, actually. They're allowed to be both until the age of 18.

So Anil left in October 2000 and then in January/February, he was asking that the family come over because he was getting a job working at Baptist Hospital in Nashville with a group of vascular surgeons. They were glad to have him because he was a trained surgeon.

Herb helped him get that job because they lived in Tennessee and he had contact with the Baptist hospital in Nashville. They were happy to have him. He didn't need any registration for that job because he was always working with others.

When they finally came back, they were trying to convince him to stay on there. He decided not to get qualified over there at his level. It wasn't as exciting over there as it is here.

The life in the States was good, comfortable and lucrative, but he missed having a challenge in life. He also had colleagues around him who spent 30 to 40 years in medical practice and had nothing but money as the only satisfaction of their lives.

Therefore, the got in touch with the mission board and asked if they would want their services to go back with the board and serve. They both agreed to go back. They had small children, too."

- Nancy

Anil left for America in 2000 and then it took time for the children to get passports and visas that finally Teresa, eight-year-old Ankita, and the three-year-old twins joined him in Dubuque at the family base of Shashi, Terry's sister, and Dinesh, her husband, who became like a brother to Anil. The family later moved to Nashville in June of 2001.

"I had to go help get their visas also, for Teresa and the children. We went in the heat in the middle of May to Calcutta and got their passports. They left in June of 2001. The boys had just turned three in April. Ankita had been in our Bissamcuttack School up to second grade. She did third and fourth grade in America.

The kids went to a day care in Dubuque for a bit and Ankita went to the school there for a bit before moving to Nashville. Shashi and Dinesh's home along with Vishal and Praveen, their sons, graciously, has been and continues to be our home here here in the States.

In Nashville, the twins went to a nursery near the hospital. They used to call it their 'sleeping school' because you took a nap there. I couldn't get over the equipment they had there. They had computers at their level for them to sit and work on computers. They were just three and four years old. I was shocked they let kids work with computers like that at such a little age."

- Nancy

But life in America, and serving the hospital system there, was not challenging or exciting for Anil. As he'd expressed as a young person, being involved in peoples' lives was much more interesting than treating them as objects to be operated on. Anil says of the time, "I could have made a lot of money performing plastic surgery on people who didn't need it, but what would that mean?"

He and Terry were looking for something more, something fulfilling. And Viru had an idea of how that could happen.

"Viru knew they wanted to go back to India and he said, 'Have you consulted with the [United Church of Christ/Disciples of Christ] Global Ministries board whether they can use you out there?' I think, with that, they wrote to the board. They were moving back to India and asked if there was there anything they could do.

They grabbed them up. They were not getting visas for Americans to stay in India. The mission board was quite happy to have them. Anil and Terry are the only missionaries they have here in India.

They came back to India in 2003 – to the Christian Hospital Mungeli. Over there, they must have asked by communication if the board, the Church of North India, could use a doctor somewhere. Anil was interested to be in central India. Apparently, they asked him to come. There was a hospital that was about to close and the doctor there had never worked with a senior doctor.

Now he knows everything. He's learned so much from Anil. His name is Dr. Samuel. He was just a new doctor and they put him here. There were four patients in the hospital. The only thing that kept this hospital alive was donations from the Rambo Foundation [in the United States.] Every month they sent money. They paid the salaries with that. Otherwise, it would have closed. They kept it alive.

Dr. Samuel was doing what he could without much experience or guidance. What he's doing today is fantastic. He was ready to learn anything. He's always in [the operating] theater. He loves his work. He's now worked 10 years with Anil and can run the hospital when needed."

- Nancy

Anjali

Having completed primary school in India, Viru and Nancy made the difficult decision to send Anjali to the United States to receive specialized education for blind children. The family was fortunate to receive a full scholarship for Anjali to attend the Perkins School for the Blind in Watertown, Massachusetts. At just 10 years old, she left for the boarding school and a formative period in her life.

"I remember when I'd left for Perkins School, my parents were quite upset and my mother had given me a little purse that had all the things little girls would like. One of those things was a bag of cashew nuts. I just love cashew nuts.

So I was just happy to have that little purse with cashew nuts and other things in it. My other said, 'You didn't seem too upset by it.' But I said to my auntie Maggie, 'I don't want to be here.' She wasn't surprised.

My very first teacher became my very close friend, and later my matron of honor. She taught me a lot of things I didn't know. When I first got here my English was ok, but not great. It was heavily accented from what I understand. Her name was Roz Lannquist (later, Rowley) and she just passed away.

I remember all the things I learned, for instance, using a braille writer, which I love to this day. I learned typing and independent living skills; every day things that most people take for granted have to be taught. It's the only way.

Roz introduced me to many things for every day living. We had a class called community experience where they would take us out into the community and teach us about shopping and things people do every day. She was a teacher, but she was more like a friend. She always looked out for me because I was so far from home, living in the residential school.

I was there from 1975 to 1982 on full scholarship before the funding for it ran out. I had a choice to stay in the United Stated, in New Jersey, and I said, 'No, I want to go home.'

My years there were very influential. I am what I am today because of what I learned at Perkins. I give a lot of credit to my parents and brothers. First of all, in India they don't want girl children. On top of it, to have a female child and one who was disabled – they had a lot of strikes against them."

- Anjali

For the Henry family, Anjali's lack of sight was not to be seen as a disability. They insisted she was capable of the same achievements as their other children and instilled in them the values of caregiving, compassion, and innovation that enabled Anjali to find ways to overcome any obstacle presented by her lack of sight.

"My parents always taught my brothers that even though I couldn't do certain things, there were ways to work with it – to go around it.

I always wanted to go into medicine, but God had other plans. Anil and I had all sorts of plans for how I could be a doctor. He'd say, 'You do all the theory stuff and then when you have to see something, then I'll tell you.' He used to take me to the anatomy lab – when he was in Vellore and I was studying in Bangalore – and he would show me cadavers. He'd say, 'This is what you do with this, and this is how you cut that open.'"

"Understand, no one in my family every said, 'You can't see so you can't do that.' If I had a question, they showed me how it could be done.

I told my father, 'I want to see what a uterus feels like.' He said, 'OK, next time I operate on one, I'll let you see.'

Sure enough, he let me come into the operating room and he showed it to me and explained the various parts. I was quite fascinated by it. And he let me do the skin suturing, just the outside, and he said, 'From now on, you're going to do this. You do better stitching than I do.'"

- Anjali

Anjali says she feels some responsibility for Ajit's death, to this day. He insisted on accompanying her on the trip from Bangalore to Miraj, where Anjali was working at the time. Were it not for that train ride, she wonders, would he still be alive?

"My undergrad was in Bangalore, with my main focus on psychology. I was then working at the Christian Hospital in Miraj in the department of psychiatry when Ajit died. Then I went on to the Indore School of Social Work in north India and did my masters in medical psychiatric social work.

He dropped me off and we were lucky to get a seat because it was so crowded. I told him, 'Be careful,' because he was going back to Bangalore. He had just graduated and had to get his things together to go on to the next step of his life, but that didn't happen."

- Anjali

She returned to Bissamcuttack and hoped to work at the hospital with her parents, but Viru said there were no positions as mental health was not part of the hospital's service offerings at that time.

Viru's opinion changed after a patient arrived who, in Anjali's professional opinion, was "out of his mind." She prescribed a course of drug treatments and within days the patient had stabilized. "After that, mental health patients came out of the woodwork," Anjali remembers. She continued to serve as a staff psychiatrist in Bissamcuttack from 1997 to 1999.

"That was such satisfying work. The patients would say, 'You made me feel better.' Even when I was in Miraj working, many people would say they wanted to talk to me and no one else."

- Anjali

Anjali returned to the United States in 2000 and found jobs in Massachusetts doing crisis intervention work and braille transcriptions. At a summer camp for the blind in Spring Valley, New York in 2004, she became reacquainted with her former Perkins classmate John Gallagher. A romance blossomed and the couple decided to take the next step, relocating to the same town to continue their courtship.

"He's very cemented in this community; he's a very talented professional musician. Even though I loved what I was doing in Massachusetts, I knew that if we were going to see how things would work out I'd have to move to [Nutley] New Jersey."

- Anjali

Anjali moved to Nutley, New Jersey and the couple was soon engaged, marrying 21 October 2006 with Anil present at the wedding. John has served as cantor at St. Mary's Catholic Church in Nutley since 2000. Anjali continues her work as a counselor at a crisis call center.

---

[1] As of April 2016, Anil is the Chairman of the board of the school. Via https://en.wikipedia.org/wiki/Kodaikanal_International_School. Retrieved 25 March 2016.
[2] Coolie is a term used throughout areas of Asia and Africa to describe unskilled, or untrained, labor. Although it assumes racial connotations in certain locations, in India it most often refers to a person such as a baggage handler or porter without prejudice.

Chapter 12: Memories from Bissamcuttack
– Johnny Oommen –

As important as the Henrys were to the work in Bissamcuttack, the growth and reach of the hospital would not have been possible without many faithful staff members over the years. Viru and Nancy mentioned the constant struggle they had in attracting and retaining doctors, nurses, and staff members to Bissamcuttack. The hospital's remote and rural location was not an immediate draw for young and new medical professionals. Yet, those who did come were instantly struck by a dedication to the Henry's mission and how they invited others into the adventure of building a world-class facility in a largely tribal area of India.

One of those doctors, Johnny Oommen, now serves as the deputy medical superintendent at Christian Hospital Bissamcuttack and as team leader of the community health programs. Johnny describes the environment at Bissamcuttack as a family, with Viru as the head and "a terrific boss" who taught, mentored, and trusted those he hired.

> "I grew up at Vellore, on the campus where my father was the chaplain of the Christian Medical College. Therefore, I did all my schooling there. I did my 11th and 12th grades in Kerala. Then I went back to Vellore for my medical schooling. That was six years; I was 24 when I finished medical school.
>
> Here's how I landed [in Bissamcuttack]: Firstly, I was looking for something like this. This is the only reason I did medicine. To me, my choice of doing medicine was to work with people who did not get the opportunities that I got. That was my big philosophy at the age of 17.
>
> My big choices were between journalism and medicine. I applied for both and chose Vellore for medical school. In doing medicine, that was a tool for working with people who did not get opportunities. That was a big thing for a variety of reasons, coming from a faith basis.

By the end of my medical training, I was looking for a context where I could actually try and live out this thinking. In Vellore, with our training, we are asked to serve for two years after our training. Since I was from Vellore myself, my sponsorship was to serve for two years in Vellore. I actually asked to have it transferred to Tamil Nadu, with the Arcot Lutheran Church. My sister had worked with them and there was a little hospital that didn't have doctors, but my request was turned down.

The college wanted me to work in Vellore in community health, so I did that for a year. During that year, I had a chance conversation with Anil and Terri over coffee. I didn't know him well but I knew his parents ran a hospital. I asked him to tell me about the place. When he described it, it sounded good. He said they were desperate for doctors and asked if I would be willing to go. I said, 'I'm willing to go anywhere if the college will allow me to go.'

Anil got his dad to write a letter to CMC Vellore asking if I could be sent [to Bissamcuttack] for the second year of my service obligation period. I had a copy of the letter. The principal asked me, 'There's a letter asking you to go to a hospital in Orissa. Are you willing to go?' He didn't know that I already knew about it. I said, 'Yes, if you send me there.'

I got verbal permission, then written permission, to move the second year of my service period into Orissa. This was November 1987. I came out, planning to be here for a year, mainly to try it out and know what it's like. Also in the back of my head, I was asking what God would want me to do for the rest of my life or where He wanted me to go. It was part of that search as well."

- Johnny Oommen

First impressions are important and Johnny's initial thoughts about Bissamcuttack influenced his future return. He called the hospital "an oasis in a green desert." It was far from what he expected to see when he first arrived at the remote and isolated hospital in the hills. Staff relationships and camaraderie grew quickly after he arrived.

> "What struck me was: how on earth did this happen? You're driving down from the station in the middle of the night and everything was dark. There was no place with electricity for miles around here.
>
> Suddenly, there's this full campus with good buildings, electricity, water, support systems, and a good community, happy in what they are doing. It just didn't fit into the surroundings. It struck me like an oasis on an island.
>
> How did this happen? Who made this? What does it take? It was very interesting. It was very different from everything I had grown up with. The work was challenging. It was great fun. There was a lot to do and very few of us to do it.
>
> Boss [Viru] was very good at rallying the troops and being the life and soul of the party, keeping you laughing. He has a terrific sense of humor and ability to inspire you to go beyond the call of duty. It was really amazing; the work was very good.
>
> Everything just kind of matched."
>
> - Johnny Oommen

Christian Hospital Bissamcuttack offered Johnny the chance to explore his calling as a medical professional, motivated by faith and dedicated to serving those in greatest need. But he could have fulfilled that mission at any number of the Christian Hospitals affiliated with the Christian Medical Association of India. What made the experience at Bissamcuttack so compelling for Johnny was the relationships he developed in the context of medical mission, especially his relationships with Viru and Nancy Henry.

> "I joined the Bissamcuttack staff on the 30th of November, 1987. It was such a lovely place and there was so much to do. What I found here was somewhere I was really needed. My

being here, or not being here, was something that actually made a difference to people.

I realized that in a larger institution like Vellore, I would only be a cog in the wheel, possibly useful, possibly valued, but it would run without me. Here, it was a setting where there was so much to do and it fit very much into what I wanted to do.

A big part of this place was the Henrys. Dr. and Mrs. Henry were the absolute center of the place. It didn't occur to us to do anything without referring to them or speaking to Sir [Viru] and asking him. It was just part of how we lived. We were like a family and he was the head of the family, a patriarch. It made a lot of sense. It worked well for me.

I think there were five or six doctors for most of that year. Dr. Henry, Dr. [Padmashree] Sahu, and Dr. Hema Mohanty were there. They turned out to be the long-term people. There were 3 of us young men. The other two moved on to other hospitals. I think all of us were just training and finding our feet. Things just fell into place for me.

That's what I've seen with the way God works. The patterns just fall into place. He doesn't do these isolated flashes. It all kind of syncs. There were many things that matched: what I was looking for, what the hospital was looking for, the Henrys and the environment they created within the institution. It was a very unusual form of leadership.

Boss [Viru] always lead from the front. He was always ahead of everything. You could call it 'dominating' in a sense. Very fatherly. You were part of that team and you played for the boss. He had a lovely way of making everybody feel part of the team, valued, precious, at different levels of the team. He had ways of doing these things.

It was a happy place and they were good to me. Dr. Henry was a terrific boss to work with. He trusted me and allowed me to establish a pediatric department and build it up. Mrs. Henry was the one who took a lot of personal care. She knew

I was very interested in community health as so was she, so she went out of her way to follow up with me."

- Johnny Oommen

Johnny was inspired by his time in Bissamcuttack. The opportunity to learn, to grow programs, and especially to explore the possibilities for community health services in the region around the hospital, was, in his experience, without comparison. Still, he held his enthusiasm in check and pursued his post-graduate studies in community health without the sponsorship of the Christian Hospital Bissamcuttack – leaving his options open to work anywhere without the obligation of a service bond.

"Even after I left at the end of the year, [Nancy] continued to write letters, and send materials and Christmas gifts. Between the two of them, Sir was an extremely inspiring, unusual person. I've never met anyone like him; very different from anything I'd grown up with. Mrs. Henry was very good at focusing on people and letting them know they were appreciated.

Between the two of them, they asked if I would come back. They wanted to sponsor me for master's studies. I felt this was the place I wanted to come back to, but I wanted to come back on my own steam and not because I had a written obligation. I didn't take sponsorship. I went for my post-graduate studies as an open candidate, wanting to come back on my own.

In fact, about three-quarters through the first year in Bissamcuttack, I asked my parents to come visit me here because I thought this might be what I would be doing. I wanted them to come meet the Henrys and see the place.

My father told me that the decision to stay in Bissamcuttack was like a relationship between a boy and a girl. How do you figure out if it's love or infatuation? He said the best way to find out is to get out and look at it from a distance. If six months down the line you still believe this is the place you want to be, this is what you want to do, and this is what God wants of you, this is love.

I said, 'Okay. Let me leave to finish up my post-graduate training. If I still feel the same, then I'm coming back.' By the time I left here at the end of the year, I think I was about 60 percent sure I was coming back, but I left that open. Within a year of leaving, I was sure this was it.

A big part is my own search for what I need to do and be. The other part was the setting, and the Henrys, and the inspiration of who they were. All put together, a year after I left, this is where I was sure I was coming back to. Of course, Mrs. Henry always kept in touch. Finally, when Mercy and I decided to get married, the Henrys were among the first people we informed. They were witnesses to our wedding. We were married in Vellore."

- Johnny Oommen

Along with the excitement and opportunities presented by the mission hospital, the experience of Christian Hospital Bissamcuttack had made Johnny intimately familiar with the challenges of the environment. He wondered if it would be a good place to bring his wife Mercy, a nurse, to raise a family, and to have a career.

"Initially, I felt this kind of life wasn't compatible with marriage, so initially, I thought I wouldn't get married. But having been here for a year, I realized I probably needed to get married. It was too lonely and it wouldn't make sense to come back alone.

The challenge was to find somebody who was interested in the same thing. Good Indian culture says the wife follows the husband wherever he goes, but that wasn't enough for me. I hoped to find the person who also takes this as a calling and not as a duty to her husband.

Mercy and I had known each other long before from the Student Christian Union, so we had similar thinking and philosophy. It just kind of fell into place. We were both looking for the same things. We met over dinner and, before the end of it, we had more or less decided that this was it.

I brought her to Bissamcuttack because I wanted her to see the place and meet the Henrys before she made her final decision. She loved the setting, so we got engaged. By the middle of 1991, we were married.

Dr. and Mrs. Henry offered to sponsor Mercy for her higher education through the hospital, so that she would train and we would come back together. That's what they did. She got her Masters in nursing and then we came back together in 1993."

- Johnny Oommen

Leadership and the Draw of Bissamcuttack

Viru's leadership is a main feature of Johnny's memories. Unorthodox in many ways from other management styles he had encountered, Johnny believes Viru's direct and all-knowing presence was exactly what the hospital needed, especially during the period of rapid growth. A manager with innate knowledge of the people and projects underway, who also showed deep care for those working for him, Viru gained the trust and loyalty of those around him, working side by side for the common goals of the hospital.

Unique as it was, Viru's leadership was the key to providing continuity at the hospital and in gaining support from sponsoring organizations, community leaders, tribal alliances, and staff.

"You could write a separate book on his management styles because he didn't fit any of the books. On the one hand, he was in total control. He made the decisions. There was no question. On the other hand, you had a dinner and he would be the last person to eat. He would be carrying the babies. A person could be way down on the pecking order, but he respected them. Anybody could go to him. It's a very different, patriarchal model. A good one.

In a way, he didn't give a damn what people thought. He did what he wanted to do. He enjoyed himself. People have these ideas of mission hospitals where everybody's singing hymns and clapping their hands and going to heaven.

He broke all the rules that he needed to. He wasn't going to pretend to be something he wasn't. You have to enjoy what you're doing and not get carried away with the idea of sacrifice a lot of missions suffer from. You just plunge into the battlefield, pitch your tent, and do what needs doing – and have fun while you're at it. Those [virtues] were very infectious.

At parties in a churchy environment, smoking and drinking are looked down upon. Boss didn't have a problem with that at all. No evening was complete without a drink for him. I don't drink, but I saw the happiness of his ability to vibe with all sorts of people because he was open and people were comfortable with him.

He would be up any time of the night if there were a need in the hospital. He'd go hunting on the weekends. All things that people said were taboo, but he just went ahead. We all got a share of the meat. It was a different world. I came from a very different society. The Henry home was always open; we were constantly invited over to eat."

Dr. and Mrs. Henry are the perfect combination for leadership. They had differing and yet complementary perspectives on many issues. He saw the forest. She saw the trees. He couldn't see the trees. And she couldn't see the forest. And they'd sort it out over the dinner table, and by morning, we'd have a solution.

Dr. Henry would say, 'Everybody, we must take up the challenge!' And Mrs. Henry would add, 'Oh yes, Dr. Henry takes up the challenge, and the rest of us pick up the pieces!' And we would all have a good laugh and get to work at whatever was Boss' latest project.

All this would go on with them calling each other Papa and Mama and teasing each other endlessly; an unusual style of leadership and management where two were always better than one, and the two were actually one.

- Johnny Oommen

Another tactic, or more precisely an approach to staff relations, employed by Viru was the staff outing. Johnny remembers the power of these retreat days in strengthening relationships, providing relaxation, and making sure a certain level of integration happened within the ranks of the staff.

"He had this thing for taking staff out for picnics. That, in itself, is not a strategy, but you have to understand why he does the things he does. He would get rich patients to donate money to the picnic fund and when there was enough money, he'd take all the staff out for a picnic. We'd all go out and eat together.

He had his reasons for doing this. He said, 'The staff are not rich enough to eat meat at home, so maybe if we have a picnic, we can eat meat together.' It sounds very simplistic, but if you analyze the impact of those picnics, those were huge team-building exercises. I remember doing this and I took it back to Vellore with me.

I remember playing dog-and-the-bone with his footwear at the hospital picnics. The first time I saw him get the staff to do this my reaction was, 'Hey! I gave up playing this when I was ten years old.' Then I watched what he was doing. All the staff lined up in these two rows and counted to 50 on each side, with his shoe in the middle. He'd call out 'twenty-three!' and two staff would go running.

On one hand, it was ludicrous. On the other hand, you could see the medical superintendent and a gardener fighting to pick up a shoe. That, I think, is what they would call in management books: 'non-hierarchal group dynamics.'

He got this by gut instinct. Some of the things he did, if you asked him 'Why?' he had very simplistic answers. If you analyzed the depth of what he was doing, not even realizing the value of what he was doing, he sensed it. You can't teach somebody to do that. If you look at a cross between benign dictatorship models and servant leadership models, it seems like opposite paradigms, but he had one foot in each model. It was a brand of leadership of his own making."

- Johnny Oommen

Both Johnny and Viru had strong ideas about the future of programming at Christian Hospital Bissamcuttack. But Johnny believes the strength of the Henrys' leadership allowed them to trust others, relying more on the "servant leadership" qualities than the "benign dictator" model, especially when the values and goals of others aligned with the hospital's vision.

"We worked together for 11 years. We didn't always agree on everything, which is fair enough, we're very different kinds of people. We do things differently. I think that's okay. I respect him for what he is and what he has done. Really, both of them. When you talk about Dr. Henry you mean Mrs. Henry as well. It's a package deal.

No, we did not always agree on everything. But he allowed me that space.

When I came back wanting to do community health, I told him I wanted the space to develop community health and that I didn't want to get tied down in the hospital. I told him, 'There will always be patients in the hospital. There will always be need and I'll never get out to the field.'

He said, 'I have two conditions as well for you. Don't ever ask me how to do community health because I don't know how to do it. I'm a surgeon. You've got to do it yourself. You can ask me for help only if you need money and you don't have enough so you need me to help you raise resources. Or if you need somebody to cut a ribbon to inaugurate a program and you don't have anybody, I will come. Besides that, it's all you.'

I got the total space. He was able to allow you to do that even if you had different thoughts at different times. He allowed me to develop it the way I thought it needed to go and he was always available to support me. You always knew he was behind you. You knew he'd always pick up the tab if you got into a crisis. You could depend on him and confidently go forward. I think we created our spaces. There were areas that were his kind of thing and not my kind of thing. There were areas that were my kind of thing and not his kind of thing. I think a lot of that is because that's the kind of person he was. He was willing to let you grow even if you had a slightly different idea from his.

On the other hand, we have had disagreements and I think that's okay. It was within the family. Viru and Nancy were like parents for us. You do have disagreements, but they can be sorted out within the context of that relationship. Some things, you just agree to disagree. It's not the end of the world.

For organizations like ours, we need to be able to do that. If each of us gets onto our high horses and says, 'It's my way or the highway,' you either destroy organization or you keep rolling from place to place. There is no place that is 100 percent yours. That's part of the give and take that comes into any long-term commitment."

- Johnny Oommen

Integrating Johnny's wife Mercy into the fold of Christian Hospital Bissamcuttack came in the form of helping Nancy build the capabilities at the school of nursing. With an eye toward offering the more comprehensive three-year GNM [General Nurse Midwife] degree, Mercy brought the necessary skills with her in 1993 to move the program to the next level by 1996.

"Mrs. Henry's method was that any new person first has to work in the hospital to get a feel of the services. Mercy came back specifically for building the school of nursing site.

The school of nursing, at that time, had only one course, the simpler, two-year ANM [Auxiliary Nurse Midwife] course. The idea was to start the three-year GNM course, which Mercy had the training required. Mrs. Henry started working with her and Mercy started going over primarily into nursing education, while Mrs. Henry continued at the hospital.

With the hospital being the main part of this place, you could say that the spin-offs would be the school of nursing, the English-medium school, and the community health department. Mercy was dealing with one and I was dealing with another. We had our spaces, which I think was very important. I think that helped us to grow and give us space to develop things differently, which is probably important for the long-term retention."

- Johnny Oommen

Evolution of the Community Health Programming

In December 1998, just after Johnny completed his initial one-year commitment at Christian Hospital Bissamcuttack, Dr. Madsen had become too ill to continue her village clinic work in Bandhaguda. Viru returned with her to Denmark, helping her settle in a retirement home. "Dr. Ma" lived in the retirement community for three years, studying theology and remembering "her beloved India."[1] She died 22 December 1991, at the age of 78.

Dr. Madsen had grown deep connections within the local community, and especially in regard to the reach and esteem of the community health programs. Though in her last years in India she didn't work directly for Christian Hospital Bissamcuttack, her ties between the village and the hospital were integral to outreach programs.

After Dr. Madsen left Christian Hospital Bissamcuttack in the care of the Henrys, the hospital's community health programs began by sending nurses into villages to meet residents' preventative, ongoing, and diagnostic health needs. Although located in fewer locations than Dr. Madsen, the hospital's community health programs provided a greater level of services.

Johnny arrived in 1993 and assumed the charge of community health programs, inheriting and reinterpreting the needs these programs previously offered.

> "There were two programs before I took over. One was Dr. Madsen's program, which was a community health, literacy, and development program. She had primary healthcare and literacy across a 90-village stretch, which is almost twice the range I'm doing. A bigger range, but probably less depth. That's the trade-off.
>
> [Dr. Madsen] would get to a village maybe once or twice a year. While she was there, she would do a lot of work. She'd stay out there for 20 days. I don't. Her village workers were all men. Mine are all women. These were choices we made for the model.
>
> Dr. Madsen's program between 1978 and 1988 was, in some ways, different from what we were doing. I think she was doing it 100 percent. Our program deals with other things. Also, it was in a time when everything had to be free. It was charity-driven. That was right for that time. What we do cannot be that way. There has to be some kind of involvement through contribution.
>
> The other program we had when I joined was the nursing school community health program, which was headed up by Mrs. Henry. The Dakalguda program. She managed that as part of the nursing school in order to educate the nurses, they had to have a community health program.
>
> Mrs. Henry didn't want them to just go out for a day of field experience. She wanted a functioning program. This was built

around a nursing education and therefore focused primarily on maternal and child health.

These two programs were in geographically separate areas.

By the time I came back from my master's degree, Dr. Madsen's program had stopped. There was some sort of rudimentary stuff going on.

But the nursing school program was going well. In that sense, I inherited the legacy of two different kinds of work, each reflective of the personality of the leaders. I tried to pick up those two strands and develop them into a program. We started with the nursing program and parts of what was left of Dr. Ma's program and put them together.

The work we do now is less disciplined than the nursing school program. When nurses do work, they are very methodical, very precise. When doctors do work, we take shortcuts on everything. I don't think we're as clearly clean-cut as the nursing school program and not as spread out as Dr. Madsen's program. We've drawn those two strengths together.

What is different is that we've turned it around from being agency-centered program for the people out there to a community program where we are the facilitators. Now, we've reached a point where most of the staff are from the community itself so we've blurred the lines between who is community and who is staff. We did that on purpose. We're also much more into formal education. We've done a lot of work with that."

- Johnny Oommen

Johnny is reflective about what could be considered "success." Asked to place a monetary valuation on educating a student through primary school, account for live births or a decrease in infant mortality, he says the cultural expectations of regions like Bissamcuttack are very different than other areas of India.

"Can you place value on a child getting primary education? Our partners asked us to do this. We had some management friends come this year to try this. They did an analysis of our numbers and they felt there was value for the money, return on rupees invested. You can do it by monetizing benefits or creating unit of benefits. They tried to monetize the whole thing. They came out with a healthy looking statement, but I'm not sure it was worth the paper it was written on.

I'm not really convinced. The cultural setting we're in is very different. Using urban numbers doesn't work. I don't think it really matters. I think it is necessary for us as a team to ask ourselves those questions so we don't fool ourselves into complacency. It's easy to become complacent; to pat yourself on the back, but it doesn't really answer the question.

In the philosophy of Christian involvement in healthcare and community health, is it the journey or the destination? You're caught between various issues. We use impact indicators, outcome indicators to ask ourselves, 'Did mortality change? Are lives better off? Are more children educated?' It's important to ask those questions.

Sometimes our calling is only to be obedient. Our calling is not necessarily to success. How do you define success? I find that in my professional and spiritual thinking, my professional thinking says that the destination is more important than the journey. Spiritual thinking says the journey is more important. It's probably good to look at both. Much of truth is a balance between seemingly opposite forces, a dynamic equilibrium. We have to keep a constructive tension."

- Johnny Oommen

Still, intrinsic values guided the mission of the hospital throughout. Johnny says a patient-focused mentality built on delivering the best care for the lowest cost, and caring for the whole person, were always top of mind for caregivers and administrators at Bissamcuttack.

Beyond the efficient, effective and patient-centered running of the hospital, the Henrys' approach to staff development is a value embedded in the ethos of the organization. Although staff were expected to continually seek training, they were encouraged to do so not only for the good of the hospital, but for their own advancement and achievement.

> "Dr. Henry held this place together with wit and humor. He'd get up at the end of chapel and make these jokes or speeches that were both funny and inspiring at the same time. One of the things he ask periodically is, 'Who is the most important person on this campus?' He reminded us that the patient is why we're here. Without that, this doesn't make sense. The hospital is here for the patients, not that the patients are here to finance our salaries. It seems like a very simple thing, but that was very clear. Similarly, the school is here for the children.
>
> I think that was a very non-negotiable value.
>
> To me, another non-negotiable value is the way we've looked at money. I feel that the way we've looked at money has always been that money is a necessary tool but not the goal of the exercise. We need money and need to be sensible in the way we use our money, but the purpose was not money.
>
> This needs to permeate not only the large macro-decisions, but also the micro-decisions. If we can be honest and true, the money will come. The confidence that one can do something and it will turn out okay. It is true that with the micro-decisions: for each patient you choose not to do a test just for the money or a surgery for the income.
>
> You're saying clearly, 'That's not the way we work.' You need to guard yourself against that because that's the way the world works. That will constantly come to you. I think the way the institution has looked at money has always been this end result. We need to safeguard that because it's not a value that has a life of its own. It's easily ruined.

I think a third value that this institution has held very strongly is a concept of a family. We're a team. It's a word that's been used and abused and over-used, yet there's no word to replace that. It's necessary to see everybody as a part of the job: big jobs, small jobs.

In India, we're very feudalistic, caste-ist in our thinking. Hospitals can be like a caste system. I'm afraid salary scales have a way of hardening that hierarchy. Sometimes, we don't put our money where our mouth is. Fundamentally, this is a team and you need all kinds of roles to be played.

I think another value Sir [Viru] and Ma'am [Nancy] brought here is situational excellence. You need to do things well. Being in a backwards area is not an excuse for mediocrity. There's no reason why we can't do as well or better than somebody else. We shouldn't settle for doing things poorly, hiding behind the fact that we're on a small case. The standards can be set high.

Excellence will be situational. It will be different in different locations. We shouldn't settle for mediocrity. I think in every building and every position, the ways they've built up systems were meant to be good systems.

I think another value we were taught to believe in was that in everything we do, we should focus on building up good people. The natural expression of this value is investment in in education and training because these are ways of capacities; of building individuals into stronger people. I think that is intrinsic to the way the Henrys worked and what this institution stands for."

- Johnny Oommen

As a mission hospital, the approach to faith expression, evangelism, and outreach has been very different from other religious organizations. The above values guided the operations and interactions with patients who, for the most part, are not Christian. Johnny says the hospital kept religion "behind us - helping us to stand up and to help people."

"You have to consider the way we look at religion. There is religion and there is spirituality and those are two different things. It depends on how you define them. I would define religion as being more on the outside. Spirituality is more on the inside. This hospital is unapologetically called the Christian hospital and we're not ashamed to say that. We're not hiding it. The large majority of staff are from the Christian community and our processes are built around prayer.

The way we have used religion is to build the capacity of our staff and students to be able to serve others, but not at the point of contact with patients or the community.

Our religion, in this institution, is kept behind us. If I take that as a figurative analogy, it is behind us, helping us to stand up and to help people. We're not into converting people or preaching to the non-Christians. We're not trying to push religion.

It's an interesting position on religion for a faith-based organization. How did this happen? Probably due to the idiosyncrasies of the various people who have led this institution. I resonate with that. Therefore, in a world where most of the religious expression is becoming fundamentalist and the lines are being drawn, that's a very important feature of this hospital.

There is no doubt that we are a Christian hospital, in the sense of that's where we get our logic, direction, and dedication from. We don't wear it on our sleeves and we're not trying to push it. The morning prayer is for the staff and students to get the energy and direction we need to serve.

We're not trying to convert anyone."

- Johnny Oommen

Still, reflecting on the history of Christian mission activity in Orissa, Johnny feels the hospital, through its care for all people and community involvement, has raised the profile of Christians in the region. Whether or not that converts people, Johnny says, is not his concern; patients and the community have recognized the hospital and its staff living into a Christian ideal.

"For a person who doesn't know anything about Christianity, what is their introduction to Christianity in this region?

It could be some evangelist standing on the street, condemning all other religions.

Or it could be the Christian hospital where you went for treatment without worrying about being looked down upon. You went for service at a hospital that is clean and has a work ethic that is very different from the community around, a hospital that doesn't steal money. That's a huge witness.

There's a need for us to live out the gospel. If our lives don't speak, then words are counterproductive. If your life speaks, then words are superfluous. This is the way I read the institution. I don't know if all the staff would agree with me on this and that's fair enough. What I'm describing now is an observation of what we practice.

The chaplain has a very circumscribed role here. He's a chaplain to the staff and students, not so much to the patients. He's available if a patient wants to talk to him, but he does not go and pray for a patient unless the patient has requested it. His primary role is to service the spiritual needs of the staff and students.

All this has evolved without it ever being written down. I once made a job description for the chaplain. Our elderly pastor of many yers was retiring, and a young man was to take his place. The role of the chaplain in our hospital is critical and strategic, it was important that they get the philosophy right. If you see this in terms of a case study in mission, it's very fascinating.

I describe the way we do community health as 'kingdom values in secular mode.'"

- Johnny Oommen

How Christian Hospital Bissamcuttack – and the mission established by the Henrys and carried to this day – fit into formal ideas of "mission" has been debated and studied by theological students from many countries. Why, they ask, has the hospital thrived and grown, and continued to attract faith-motivated staff as a mission hospital, when its primary objective has not been to spread the Christian faith by conversion?

> "There are certain theological problems in this whole mission debate, one is this thing called 'The Great Commission.' Jesus didn't call it that. We did.
>
> Now, if you ask what are his operative commands, the evangelical side has made The Great Commission the operative imperative. To me, it is 'If anyone would follow me, let him deny himself, pick up his cross and follow me.' Why can't that be the Great Commission? The last thing [Jesus] says before his ascension is 'Be my witnesses unto the ends of the world.' Why can't that be the Great Commission?
>
> I think we've had a theological trick played on us. I think that the evangelical churches have taken Paul as their role model instead of Jesus. Paul's church-planting methodology has become the concept of mission. Jesus's methodology was to go and get crucified in three years. I would place us closer to the Jesus scale."
>
> - Johnny Oommen

Far from being crucified, the sacrifices of the staff and supporters of Christian Hospital Bissamcuttack and its associated ministries, has sustained a mission for over 60 years and spanning several generations of leaders. No leaders, however, match the longevity of the Henrys; none can claim facilities and program growth on the scale the Henrys initiated and oversaw.

---

[1] Christian Hospital Bissamcuttack, *Golden Jubilee Souvenir* publication, (1954-2004), pg 13.

Chapter 13: Retirement Planning

By the mid-1990s, Christian Hospital Bissamcuttack was a very different institution than it had been when the Henrys arrived in 1975. Two decades of detailed management, strategic recruitment, and facilities growth positioned the hospital as the model for mission hospitals in India. The successes borne out by the Henrys' hard work were recognized around the country, and internationally, as a model of sustainable heath care delivery.

As the Henrys aged and approached retirement age, the question arose of what would happen to the hospital once they were no longer at the helm. It is fair to say that most of the innovation, expansion, and program management fell under the watchful eyes of Viru and Nancy. Although team leaders had been given authority to manage their areas, oversight and advice from the Henrys was always close at hand.

Their guidance and care of Christian Hospital Bissamcuttack and its patients, staff, and students was central to its existence. The Henrys, ever aware of their role, were ready to hand over management tasks, even as personal loss was felt at each transition. The development of Christian Hospital Bissamcuttack had been the culmination of their life's work, and letting go was a slow and difficult process.

> "Boss and Ma'am were like parents or grandparents for all the staff. That wouldn't be challenged. Nobody would have asked the question, why aren't they moving on [retiring]? I don't think that question would have been raised in the minds of staff. They were like parents to the institution and to us as individuals.
>
> I don't sense that as a problem for staff so much as it was in [the Henrys'] minds. I think it was more a question for them, and institutionally, what the system was going to be. We were moving from a personality-based institution into what was now going to be system-based. Then, rules and precedents would become important over time.

It wasn't easy for them to let go, move out, and hand over. This was a baby they built.

Dr. Henry said he'd always admired Dr. Madsen. When her time came, she was able to hand things over. Though she only moved seven kilometers away, she never interfered again with the management. He specifically told her not to and she didn't.

When [the Henrys'] time came, it was more than the natural pains of letting go and wondering what's next for the hospital. Would it last or would it go down? All those confusions of growing older, those were very much a part of the problem for many years.

I don't think the staff struggled like that. The staff would say, 'As long as they're alive, we'd like for them to be in charge.' They were sensing that was not a healthy arrangement, yet it was not easy to let go.

Once you've lived in this place, it's not easy to leave. They were also sensing that stretching out their departure would be unhealthy as a precedent. It wasn't easy. There were a couple of years of lots of confusion where they found that difficult to let go. They did that in phases. I think the question entered their minds of how long should we be here? How long can we be in charge? Would it be fair on the next person? The question was also of what's Anil going to be doing?"

- Johnny Oommen

Anil had grown up seeing his parents transform Christian Hospital Bissamcuttack, working alongside them in most areas of hospital administration. He and Teresa returned to Bissamcuttack in 1995, following their masters training in Ludhiana, and worked there for five years. Viru and Anil discussed the transition of the hospital at the same time Anil was considering relocation to the United States. Anil and Teresa would ultimately leave for Nashville, Tennessee, in 2000, and the hospital in Bissamcuttack would transition to one of the Henry's most trusted doctors.

"In 1997, they made the next person, Dr. Sahu, a deputy medical superintendent. She had joined the hospital in 1987 and [the Henrys] gave her the position in hopes of preparing her for leadership. In 1998, Dr. Henry handed over the medical superintendent post to her. At this point, he was 65. That became the rule – at 58 you retire, but you can get extensions up to 65. He continued as a consultant for another 5 years.

He was still here and available, yet not in charge. That wasn't easy for him either, to see it run differently, worrying that it would go down. It'll happen again and again with each leader. I think they went through a lot of these questions.

They had not yet built a house for their retirement. They bit the bullet at one point when they said it was time to move on. Dr. Henry needed a new challenge. By then, he was in the new challenge of trying to revive another hospital. He was spending time there. That gave him a new moral lease on life, even at the age of 70.

He needed to go and get his teeth into something. He needed to feel valued. In a place like this… he was sensing, am I overstaying? We discussed this many times.

For him, his doing – his work – was his self-definition. He always used to say, 'The day my hands stop working as a surgeon, I need to get out.' We would say, 'We love you regardless and it's nothing to do with whether you're doing or not. Your being continues even if your doing stops.'

Retirement wasn't going to be easy for him because he was a person who was always active and things kept happening around him. Yes, they struggled with that. They took the decision and said, 'We need to get out. It's time for the new leadership.'"

- Johnny Oommen

The Henrys had decided it was time to transition leadership in Bissamcuttack; time "to get out" according to Viru. But their

231

commitment, and what many say is their love for the work at Christian Hospital Bissamcuttack, kept them from leaving for more than five years after the leadership transition and official retirement announcement.

> "Dr. Henry was operating, but staying out of administration as much as he could. Then they moved to Tilda. Their hearts are still here. They are always welcome here, because so many of our staff owe them so much. "
>
> - Johnny Oommen

The retirement of Viru and Nancy followed their illustrious careers of building, nurturing and directing a sustainable mission outpost hospital. Far from the confines of established Christian educational and medical institutions, the Henrys forged a methodology and managerial concept that benefitted Christian mission hospitals throughout India.

> "The impact of their lives is never adequately measured in terms of the hospitals they ran. The hospital has a lot of significance, which is way beyond just this. For many people, Dr. Henry was the only Christian they knew. What that means today, nobody knows. You can't measure these things."
>
> - Johnny Oommen

Measurement had been at the root of much of the mission work in India. How many baptisms? How many attendees in church? How many confessions? How many Sunday school students? The hospital, although staffed and operated mostly by Christians, did not use these measures. Rather, they focused on increasing the quality of care the hospital provided, and increasing the number of patients they could treat annually. It was the unapologetic mission of the hospital to offer care to all, especially those with little or no financial means, and to practice and proclaim faith through this type of service.

Mission efforts in Bissamcuttack began at the turn of the 20th century, but until the hospital model arrived with Dr. Madsen in 1954, the impact of Christianity in the area had been minimal. Johnny

Oommen believes the hospital gained more prominence than the church – as a model of Christian practice instead of conversion under the leadership of Dr. Madsen and the Henrys – and was a turning point for the recognition of Christianity in the area. Still, the association of the church and the hospital continued to be a complex relationship.

"The mission came here in 1905. Then in the almost-50 year period between 1905 and 1954, when the hospital started, nothing happened. It was shutting down and opening, depending on world wars. The business was in the construction of buildings and preaching, which was not backed up by any action. It's not fair to criticize today, but that was the understanding of mission at that time.

In India, there are graves of missionaries and their children that have died. There's a guy here, a Danish doctor and his wife who worked here in 1970-1972. They came here for one or two years. He's written a book in Danish, called 'A Day in the Sun.' He starts off very critically. He says, 'I look out of my window and I see the grave of some Danish child or some German child who came and died here of malaria at the age of two. What is this mission? Was it worth it?'

If you look at the mission here between 1905 and 1954, it's a story of world wars, of changed lines, Europe changing the lines here, of British rule, of buildings, with maybe 10 Christians.

Then, you see Dr. Ma starting in 1954. The hospital becomes more than the church. Dr. Henry always said, 'Remember, the church came first. The hospital came second.'

The pastor here keeps quoting him on that. The hospital came second. In that period of time, the hospital eclipsed the church. The church became the smaller body, but because there was a mission hospital here, that fueled the church. A lot of staff are in the church. You can't separate the two adequately. That presents some problems: the people who are members of the church are members of the hospital staff and so on.

The hospital became the front-line of Christianity here. If you said 'Christian' in Bissamcuttack, the next word is 'hospital.'

Most people would think of our hospital as the most Christian thing here. Fair enough. Even when Orissa had anti-Christian riots in 2008, in Bissamcuttack, barely anything happened. I think it is, primarily, because here when you say 'Christian,' it's service that comes to mind: hospital and school. People do not see it as a threat.

What has happened in the past 10 years is there has been a huge church movement occurring in the hills around Bissamcuttack. When this church is imploding with fighting and politics, in the villages something we never would have anticipated is underway. There is a huge movement happening and lots of people are becoming Christian.

We try to stay far away from that sort of evangelism. In our work, we believe that God is love and we do not try to convert anybody. Things are happening, whether we like it or not."

- Johnny Oommen

Sharing Knowledge and Experience

As Viru and Nancy transitioned from leading the hospital and nursing programs in Bissamcuttack, their work with other organizations increased. Viru's work as chairman of the Church of North India-affiliated Eastern Regional Board of Health Services (ERBHS) led him to a consultative role with restarting the shuttered mission hospital in Diptipur, Orissa, a three hours drive north of Bissamcuttack.

"When he decided to go to Diptipur, he got help from the old British Baptist missionaries. They sent some help for renovating the hospital and getting equipment.

For a couple years, he went 15 days every month, almost every month. If we had to go out or something, he didn't go. This started in 2002.

It's a needy place that needs a hospital in a rural place. The board wanted to keep it going, but we couldn't get anybody to go there. So he said, 'Until we can find somebody to go there, I will go there.'"

- Nancy

Re-opening the hospital involved the repair and cleaning of most of the facilities. Along with purchasing equipment for the operation of the hospital, Viru ensured the primary functions of the hospital were in good condition, but his limited time there – just 15 days per month – could not sustain the ongoing operations.

"In Orissa I have served 34 years; four at Khariar and 30 at Bissamcuttack, however in my native state of Chhattisgarh only four years. We have felt a love and affinity for the people of Orissa, so that after retiring, I have reopened a dormant hospital, the Christian Hospital, Diptipur, Bargarh District, which is also located in Western Orissa.

Seeing the extreme poverty of this area, I am doing honorary service as a surgeon. In my 45 years of service I must have performed thousands of surgeries and am continuing to help by operating in struggling rural mission hospitals."[1]

- Viru

In May 2004, Dr. Rajnish Samal arrived and was installed as director of the hospital at Diptipur. A newly minted graduate of CMC Vellore, his OB/Gyn specialty was in great need at the remote hospital, far from other medical facilities.

In the period between 2000 and 2009, Viru and Nancy served as consultants to several mission hospitals and provided development advice in addition to conducting evaluations for the ERBHS. During this time, Viru was also invited to be chairman of the board for the

Christian Medical College in Ludhiana, where he had completed his doctoral specialty in surgery.

A special invitation for the retirees arrived in late 2006. The Evangelical Hospital Tilda asked the Henrys to return to the hospital they had served from 1968 to 1972, to base themselves there and to assist with the nursing school and hospital. Nancy detailed their transition in a 6 October 2005 letter to the Global Ministries of the United Church of Christ and Christian Church (Disciples of Christ), for whom she was serving as a long-term volunteer and nursing consultant.

"Dear Friends,

Greetings from Tilda and Diptipur, India.

Yes, the Henry's have finally moved out of their home of 30 years in Bissamcuttack. Thirty years which saw Christian Hospital Bissamcuttack develop from a small rural hospital of 40 beds to a multi-specialty center of 150 beds; a nursing school with ANM and later GNM training totaling 80 seats; a community health project with school for tribal children; and English Medium School up to High School level, while the CHB family grew from 30 to 250 members. The community also developed including the establishment of the Community College. Over these years the blessings of God have met need after need increasing the facilities and conveniences, and bringing unending challenges and joys. This has been a home we take with us in our hearts.

December 3rd and 4th was the celebration of the hospital's Golden Jubilee. It provided a mountain-top experience for the CHB family who carried out every detail including a Thanksgiving service, cultural program, reunion with former colleagues and students who came back for the occasion, fellowship meals, and a public meeting with honored guests, Dr. George Chandy, Director of CMC Vellore and Dr. Pramod Meherda, Rayagada District Collector, adding their meaningful participation. It has been a wonderful opportunity for all not only to share in the preparations and activities, but also to reflect on the past and the present, and together go into future with the Jubilee theme, 'A Common Hope for Tomorrow.'

After almost a month of sorting, discarding and packing, on 10 March our departure came with much affection and tears, preceded by farewell dinners, gifts to help remember, a Christian Hospital Bissamcuttack family photo album, etc. We will never forget on that last day, our walk from the bungalow down to the main entrance of the hospital complex, both sides of the road lined with the CHB family, including staff and their families, student nurses, friends from the community, patients, and particularly the children of our New Life School waving goodbye.

It simply was time, though very difficult, for the Henrys to move on to new challenges. But we left with the satisfaction that our next generation of leadership, chosen from above, will carry on the torch and bring this hospital to even greater heights.

Of course the real joke of the matter was our April Fool's Day return to Bissamcuttack!

After our tearful departure, we were back in Bissamcuttack on 1 April, at the request of the Collector whose wife was having a 2 April Caesarian section delivery of their second son to be born at CHB! At least our CHB family knows that we are not so far away.

In the meantime we are having opportunities as consultants and mentors in our Church of North India group of hospitals where we had met, married, and worked before leaving for further studies in surgery at CMC Ludhiana.

Viru, with the help and support of Global Ministries and ERBHS/C.N.I. Synodical Board, re-opened Christian Hospital, Diptipur, bringing light back to the 'village of light' after almost three years of silence and darkness. The grace of God has brought Dr. Rajneesh Samal, M.D. in OB/Gyn to be the new leader followed by Dr. Diptiman James, M.B.B.S., both from CMC Vellore and then Dr. Ipsita Dip who later who we found out that this was the time that both met and later on Deeptiman and Ipsita got married.. Dr. V. K. Henry will also be available as honorary surgeon consultant to round off the team. It is a matter of joy that the people of this area can again look to this hospital for help in time of suffering and need.

Evangelical Hospital Tilda has invited us to make our base there. The School of Nursing can use our services as well as the hospital. We look back on our almost four years of service in this hospital before going to Ludhiana and will work with the children of our staff of those days! We are of course pleased that Mungeli (with Anil, Teresa, and children) is only one and a half hours away!

Finding ourselves at a crossroad, we look forward to new opportunities of sharing our experience of more than 40 years building up the mission hospital in the spirit of Christian love and fellowship. Please keep in touch as we are eager to have news of you also.

God bless and keep you in His peace,

Virendra and Nancy Henry"[2]

For the Henrys, the return to Tilda felt like life had come full circle. It had been a formative time for their ministry and learning, with Viru's first assignment as medical superintendent and Nancy's first call to supervise the School of Nursing. The skills and experience honed in Tilda had served them throughout the successes of their careers, and now they were returning to be experts-in-residence and continue to share their love for medical mission and serving the people of India with other struggling and developing hospitals.

"Tilda is part of the same board where Viru was still the chairman. They knew he was planning to leave Bissamcuttack so the board suggested he would come to Tilda. Dr. Suna who was there invited him to come. He said, 'We can give you the bungalow to stay in if you can. Your wife can come with us, because we would be glad to have you working with us.' We were there on a volunteer basis.

Dr. Suna was also sitting in on these board meetings of the ERBHS, so he got all the news of our planning to leave Bissamcuttack.

We came to Tilda after it had gone through a period of decline. They needed a new maternity. Equipment-wise, it didn't have much. He used to keep it painted. It looked clean. It didn't look poorly maintained. But a lot of the bungalows were not maintained at all.

Somebody suddenly left Tilda prior to our arrival. Dr. Suna was the only doctor and his wife was expecting a baby. They didn't have anybody else, so he had to do it all.

Dr. Suna didn't want to be the medical superintendent. I think he wanted Dr. Henry to come as a consultant to take on that role. He felt a lot better with him there. A lot of things came up and he wasn't able to cope with them. He was a trained surgeon, but he said he wanted to be a doctor.

His wife did more running of the place than he did and that wasn't always positive. There were a lot of staff problems. He wanted Dr. Henry to come so we went there. He did help in the decision-making.

One time a patient was referred to the city hospital and they said our hospital had removed the kidney, which wasn't true. The media were there to find out. A lot of people started coming there. We were in Diptipur when that happened. We came back and he helped him. He felt very good when Dr. Henry was around. When we were in Diptipur, he wasn't that happy. It was a security feeling when he was around.

Finally, Dr. Suna left and the hospital called Dr. Satyajit Jiwanmall. It's so hard to get a doctor. This family with all these doctors, he immediately thought of this place. His wife had just finished her studies. They were thinking of going abroad at this point. When they got this offer, they scrapped that idea. He's the son of Dr. Kiran Jiwanmal – the third generation to be in charge of Evangelical Hospital Tilda.

I was teaching in the school of nursing. The young principal there at the time didn't ask me anything. I didn't feel like a very good consultant. Anytime I would offer something, she'd say, 'No, we don't need your help.' I wasn't able to do so much, but I was teaching. When the young principal left, Mrs. Gideon took over again.

She was always consulting me because we were there together in the earlier days. We had a great respect for one another. The first time we were there, she became my tutor.

I was the nursing superintendent [1968 to 1972] and she was my ward-in-charge. It was natural that she felt free to consult on a lot of things. Then I did get involved in the management of the nursing school. I didn't run it, but we talked about various problems and how it could be solved. She did what she wanted to do. It wasn't the kind of consulting where she had to do what I said. She had someone to talk to when there were problems."

- Nancy

With Nancy's guidance the nursing school at Tilda grew, adding an internship to the standard three-year nursing course. Viru's skills in building management and hospital expansion were also called upon as Dr. Jiwanmall sought help for construction projects.

"There were 60 students in the Tilda School of Nursing. They would take 20 students in each year for the three-year course. Later, they added an internship program so we had to make an extension to the hostel.

We were there until my accident in 2009. This young doctor, Satyajit had to build this building and he had never done any construction before. He was very grateful for my husband. He guided him in what to do. They got in touch with the right people to be a contractor and do all those things. It was not complete when I had my accident and had to leave. He completed it. By that time, he had more confidence and had more people helping him. He called my husband for the opening of the extended wing."

- Nancy

By all accounts, the Henrys were enjoying their retirement by continuing to assist the growth and operations of mission hospitals affiliated with the Church of North India. Their years of experience were an asset to new doctors and those facing the trials associated with restoring mission hospitals that had fallen into disrepair, were failing because of mismanagement, or had been abandoned when western funding ran out.

Anil and Teresa were nearby in Mungeli, having returned from America in 2003 to take on the challenge of rehabilitating a barely functioning mission hospital, what Nancy called a "family tradition." The Christian Hospital Mungeli would play a vital role in the next chapter of Nancy and Viru's lives, to which Nancy alluded, the accident that forced her to leave her work in Tilda.

> "That was the first time he was in charge of a hospital. It didn't take him long to pick up everything and now he wants to do it on his own. I'm the consultant for the nursing, but Anil is pretty independent.
>
> Teresa and Anil were already in Mungeli when we moved to Tilda in 2005.
>
> It was 4 April 2009, when we were coming back from Orissa, when the accident happened.
>
> Anil wanted us in Mungeli. As an Indian son, it's his responsibility to do that."
>
> - Nancy

---

[1] From "Biodata of Dr. V. K. Henry", written by Viru Henry as a reference for the Christian Hospital Bissamcuttack, *Golden Jubilee Souvenir* publication, (1954-2004).
[2] http://www.globalministries.org/sasia/overseasstaff/new-opportunities.html, retrieved April 7, 2016. Edited for clarity.

Chapter 14: Double Tragedy

Using Tilda as their base beginning in 2005, the Henrys stayed active with consulting activities; work at the Evangelical Hospital Tilda; service on hospital, school board and advisory committees; and visiting Anil and Teresa and their children in nearby Mungeli. They were productive, contributing wisdom from their lifelong experience in mission hospitals and nurturing the culture of sustainability they had fostered in these institutions.

Although the Henrys made infrequent trips back to Bissamcuttack, their home of 34 years, they were invited to attend the annual corporate recognition at the J.K. Paper Company in Rayagada, 45 kilometers (28 miles) south of Bissamcuttack. J.K. Paper is a major employer in the region and Viru and Nancy had become friends with the managers of the company and the Henrys were often invited to their special events.

> "J.K. Paper Mill invited Viru to be the chief guest during their Orissa Day [April 1] celebration in 2009. They asked me to be on the stage to give honor to Dr. Henry for doing so much work in the area. We also spent a little time in Bissamcuttack at the hospital. Then we came back to Tilda. My accident was coming back from that."
>
> - Nancy

As the Henrys were departing the train in Tilda on 4 April 2009, Nancy fell between the train platform and the train when the cars lurched forward as she was stepping out of the car with her baggage. Nancy's leg became entangled in the step and the moving train dragged her down the line until and emergency stop could be called.

> "I flew below the train, getting off. The train started to move. Viru got out and stepped down. I was ready to step right down and the train started moving. I must have lost my balance. I didn't even feel myself go down. I just knew where I was when I got there.

I don't know how I fell. It was starting off so gently and I was putting my foot down. There was no bell to sound that the train was going to move. The guard had given the signal. The guard was in the guard carriage, just behind us, and he saw me fall. They have an emergency button connected with the engine room. They immediately called to stop it, but it took a little time before it stopped. Johnny told me it must have gone about the length of one of those cars before it stopped. I had a lot of broken ribs and an injured spleen. I was bleeding inside. That's why I had to have a tube in my chest for a long time to drain that out."

- Nancy

Viru watched horrified as the accident unfolded before his eyes. "Get yourself against the platform, put distance between you and the train," he pleaded from above, helpless to assist because of the distance from the top of the platform to where Nancy was trapped.

"I tried to press myself flat against the platform so I was hoping the train would pass me, but I was pulled out. I remember my legs going up in the air, so I think it did pull me, my leg was caught.

I remember calling out, talking to my husband, 'I love you. I'm going to Jesus now.' I really thought I was gone. Then I went unconscious.'"

- Nancy

Accounts of how far Nancy was dragged under the train vary anywhere from 30 to 100 meters (100 to 325 feet.)

Nancy's memories of her rescue are foggy. She had sustained several broken bones, broken ribs, internal injuries, a concussion, and lacerations. Her journey under the train involved being dragged over rail ties, bedrock, and other debris. That she was alive, let alone in and out of consciousness, was miraculous for the 74-year-old.

"Some policeman – some angel – got under the train, picked me up, and brought me out. The Tilda hospital van was there to pick us up anyway, so they brought it on the platform right next to the train. I remember that, when I was being taken up on that stretcher.

I remember them lifting the stretcher up. There was not a long enough place so they put it along the seat and one part was out this door and the other was out the other door. One person sat there with the doors open. I remember it was bumpy."

- Nancy

The Tilda staff rushed Nancy to the hospital where Dr. Satyajit Jiwanmall was waiting to provide triage.

"I called Anil immediately. We were in the day of mobile phone so he called him and he came from Mungeli as quickly as he could. [Nancy] had all the right emergency treatment in Tilda hospital."

- Viru

"I heard that we stayed in Tilda one night. Anil and Viru didn't want to take me to Mungeli until they were sure I was stabilized."

- Nancy

Anil's memories of the accident are mixed with emotion. On the one hand, his mother had been gravely injured and Viru needed his support. On the other hand, Anil was one of the most accomplished surgeons in the region, able to provide critical care to Nancy's needs as a patient. He sprung into action, calling on the resources of Christian Hospital Mungeli and friends and colleagues in the area.

"Dad gave me a call and said mom had been in an accident. He didn't say anything more. We had our blood bank opening going on at the same time. We had just finished morning prayers and people had started to congregate at the blood bank for the commissioning.

Immediately, I got the call. I said, 'I've got to go, guys.'

I remember calling Satyajit and asking him, 'Should I come by car or bring the ambulance?' He told me to bring the ambulance. I grabbed the same ambulance we have today and I was off.

There was nothing else they could tell me at that point.

When I got to Tilda two hours later, they were in the ICU. I remember all three doctors – Satyajit, his wife (Rani), and dad – looking at my mom. She was out in shock, with blood pressure too low to record, a thread pulse, pale as anything. They were all in shock too.

I quickly examined her. I said, 'Give me a needle and a syringe.' I aspirated her left side lung. Blood came out and I put in a chest tube. There were about three liters (3.2 quarts) of blood and I did it on the other side.

I shifted her to the minor operating room and immediately started calling for blood. She's A- and we're all A+. People started coming from everywhere to give her blood. We had to give her almost eight bottles of blood to stabilize her. I called up to Mungeli for a monitor and ventilator. Tilda didn't have this stuff. They loaded up a vehicle with equipment and blood, as two people in Mungeli had given blood as well.

It took me until two in the morning before she was a little stable. I was continuously working with her. I talked to a friend in hematology who told me not to give my blood to her because it was A+.
I had people telling me to take her to Apollo and other corporate hospitals, but I knew that she was in no state to be shifted and this was the job that I did everyday in my own setting and knew I could do as well as anyone else with the right kind of support.

I finally went to put my head down. It was one of the most intense days of my life. I closed the door and let loose in a good cry."

- Anil

For Anil, the visitors presented a challenge as he used all his training and expertise to care for his mother within the cacophony of voices giving advice. Nancy stayed in Tilda another day, but the next morning Nancy was prepared for transport to Mungeli. Anil had more sophisticated equipment there and could attend to his mother in the familiarity of his own hospital.

> "The next day, Johnny and about 15 people had come from Bissamcuttack. Then I felt I had to bring her to Mungeli where I had everything at my fingertips.
>
> The next morning, we put the things in the ambulance. Luckily, she didn't need a ventilator but we had it on standby. We shifted her here. She had what we call a 'flail chest.' She had seven or eight rib fractures on the right and five on the left. Her rib cage was no support at all and the weight pressed against her lungs. I strapped her chest and prepared her for journey."
>
> - Anil

> "I only remember bits and pieces. So many people came from Orissa to see us. They knew it was a very serious accident so they all came running. They said I talked to them all, but I don't remember seeing any of them."
>
> - Nancy

Over the next two weeks Anil and his team of doctors and nurses – plus a host of staff from Christian Hospital Bissamcuttack – maintained careful watch over Nancy, keeping her stable and free from infections or secondary ailments. It was a stressful time for Viru, who was now in the position of watching his wife come close to death and slowly recover. He'd overseen the recovery of thousands of accident victims in his time as a doctor, but seeing his wife in peril took an emotional toll.

"When Mrs. Henry had her accident and she was in Mungeli; at that time Dr. Henry was still well. Many of our staff wanted to go and spend a week, each in turn, to look after her.

They said some things had to be done by family members and all of them considered themselves family members. A number of our senior nurses took turns to go and stay with her in Mungeli.

Mungeli was a new place for them. Although Anil and Terri were there for [Nancy and Viru] as family, the rest of the staff in Mungeli had other important duties and were not there in that sense.

At every point in time, even when [Viru and Nancy] were in Vellore for treatment, staff from Bissamcuttak was with them. Some of them were assigned, some went on their own. They went to help them. The loyalties are very deep."

- Johnny Oommen

"A little more than two weeks later I had a board meeting at the Kodiakanal International School where I was the Vice Chair and where Ankita, my daughter and both my twin boys were studying. Mom was stable and so I decided that I could sneak a trip and attend the meetings. We had imaged mom's spine and I'd sent it to my friends. They'd said the spine looked fine and I was confident in that. I got her out of bed and started mobilizing her. It was important for her to get out of bed and start lung excersizes as soon as possible to get better. I went for this meeting and then dad called and said she was developing weakness on one side.

That's when we thought the spinal cord was getting pinched. She had walked a few steps a day or two before I left I got back from Kodiakanal and rushed her to Bilaspur for an MRI. It showed there was a collapse of the T5/T6 vertebrae."

- Anil

The collapse of Nancy's T5/T6 vertebrae was a serious situation. Not only was the collapse pinching the spinal chord, and causing Nancy's temporary leg paralysis, further movement or agitation of the area could sever the spinal chord, rendering her irreparably paraplegic.

> "Once [the vertebrae collapse] was diagnosed by the MRI, they said, 'We've got to get her to Vellore fast.'
>
> From Bilaspur, we briefly returned to Mungeli, then from Raipur we went to Vellore by flight. They carried me up in a wheelchair. They just kept me there in the wheelchair. I thought it was kind of strange. It wasn't even fastened down. I was just there sitting on a wheelchair, but I never said anything. I was afraid to eat anything because I'd been so sick."
>
> - Nancy

> "We brought mom back to Mungeli that night after the MRI, booked our tickets, and the next day we were on a flight to Vellore. I arranged someone to pick us up and she got to the hospital. She went into severe electrolyte imbalances because of the heat and the travel. She became very sick and disoriented."
>
> - Anil

> "When we got to Madras [Chennai[1]], she was unconscious again, so they took her off the plane on a stretcher. The CMC Vellore ambulance came and picked us up. She didn't revive the entire 140 kilometer (87 mile) trip to Vellore."
>
> - Viru

Travel took its toll on Nancy's already weak and injured body. Attempts to stabilize Nancy and build her strength to withstand the arduous surgery that would enable her legs to work again, and avoid paralysis, took more time than anticipated. Frustration grew. But a decision had to be made. Everyone knew it.

"When mom arrived in Vellore we shifted her to the ICU. Meanwhile they were doing further tests on her.

Her wish was to undergo surgery if it was an option, rather than being in bed her whole life. She was in and out during this time, and wasn't in her full mind.

They kept scheduling her for surgery and cancelled four times, because they were afraid she wouldn't make it through. They wanted to do a anterior and posterior stabilization of the spine which would take a minimum of six hours. Ari Chacko, a friend of mine from college was the surgeon. He was worried and I could see that.

In the end, the top cardiologist came and evaluated her. He wanted to do an angiogram for prognostic value. I called the then Director and the others in the team and we had a meeting. I said she wanted surgery rather than being in bed for the rest of her life.

'She's already given permission. We've given you permission,' we said.
The rest is in God's and you have our faith, prayers and support.

Dad had been a council member at CMC Vellore for years and highly respected in the community and a good friend to many of the seniors there. I was a graduate. Mom had done training there and also was highly respected. They knew Bissamcuttack. They'd respected them for years. I understand it was traumatic for them to have mom there.

Then they finally agreed to operate.

She was supposed to go for surgery the next morning, May 3. She came completely out [woke up] and yanked her feeding tube out on May 2. Surgery was going to happen the next day. She came to and asked why she was being fed through a tube." Since she was very weak, we were giving her both NG feeds as well as try and feed her orally. This was very

250

important for her to regain her strength and for the body to heal. As she had been semi conscious she did not realize the tube till that morning when dad and myself came to see her at 8:00am in the morning. That is when things got bad for dad.

- Anil

For nearly a month, Viru had watched over the ailing Nancy, his beloved wife and partner. The once preeminent surgeon and healing professional now felt powerless and emotionally drained as he surveyed the extent of Nancy's injuries and the many people who attempted to provide care. Devoting his mental energy to caring for Nancy's needs as others looked after her medical condition, Viru neglected his own health and cumulative stress took its toll.

> "They had a feeding tube in me trying to get more food into me. I didn't like that tube at all. I used to fiddle around and I pulled it out. He was with me in the ICU and came and sat down.
>
> I said, 'I finally got that tube out.' That's when he had a stroke. I think it went through his mind, 'Oh no, how will this happen? How will she get surgery?' I think it was too much.
>
> Here, I was saying it as a happy person. I kept saying, 'I can eat. Take this tube out.'
>
> They kept trying to get more food into me than I could eat. They had a tube plus giving me food. I took the tube out and poor Viru... right in front of us. Anil was standing just a few away. I called him over and I could see the reaction on his face."

- Nancy

Viru's stroke wasn't his first cerebrovascular incident. While the Henrys were in the United States in 2005, he had a TIA (transient ischemic attack), often described as a mini-stroke. Viru was prescribed medication following this attack and by the time of Nancy's accident had transitioned to maintenance medications.

"Dad was supposed to have been taking his medicine for hypertension [high blood pressure.] I don't know how many days he hadn't taken it.

He looked at mom [after she pulled her tube out] and that was it. He literally keeled over on her bed.

We had friends right there. One of the junior doctors had just seen mom and was doing rounds. We called for him and they got him right out. He would have been in the MRI in not even 5 minutes. He remembers the MRI as it is a VERY noisy machine as it takes pictures of the brain.

He calls it, 'Somebody put me in a coffin and I was still alive.'"

- Anil

Though he was taken for treatment quickly, the effects of the stroke were still progressing. Thanks to the advanced diagnostic capabilities at CMC Vellore, the analysis was relatively quick, though the full extent of the blood restriction to the brain during the stroke manifested itself over the next day, even as Nancy struggled to regain strength for her own needed surgery.

"They had a trolley right there and they lifted him onto it and went a few places down. He got immediate treatment in one of the best institutions in India. I heard that it was a very massive attack. They gave him an injection that immediately stopped it. Whatever damage was done before that was done, but they got it stopped.

By God's grace, if he had to have a stroke, it was in the best place. He never had high blood pressure. At that point, his blood pressure shot up due to stress.

We used to call dad 'chintamani,' which means a person who worries about everything. He always worried about most anything and this got worse as he got older..

- Nancy

"They started treating him immediately. We moved him to the neuro-ICU and his treatment started.

Then his stroke evolved the next day. That's when we realized how much he had been hit. We couldn't do anything about it.

Dad had his stroke on May second. Mom was operated on May third and was kept in the HDU [high dependency unit] overnight.

On May 4 is when they shifted her to the neuro-ICU. While Mom was being brought into the Neuro-ICU, dad was being shifted to the ward. That is when they crossed each other and said, 'Happy Anniversary.' That was May 4, their 45th anniversary."

- Anil

"She had surgery on the third. I had my stroke on the second. Then, on the fourth is when we saw each other for our anniversary. The next day, Nancy was shifted to semi private ward and we were in the same room and we stayed in this ward for two weeks. We got comfortable with the routine, with the regular interruption of the physical therapist."

- Viru

"This is the thing, when we arrived in Vellore, [Viru] was very fit.

He could operate and drive. I went into crisis again and they had to delay the operation. My electrolytes were imbalanced. I had to have treatment. My lungs were not... I had fractured ribs so I wasn't breathing very well.

The anesthesiologist said she would not give me anesthesia until my lungs expanded so I had various treatments for that. I had to blow on things and they put that CPAP on me. They got me in shape by the third of May. He was getting very impatient because they kept putting it off. It was a full month after the accident. A day before our wedding anniversary, I had my surgery."

- Nancy

During Nancy and Viru's rehabilitation, Anil was still in charge at Christian Hospital Mungeli. Fortunately, two cousins were able to be in Vellore helping his parents. It was an arduous few months while Nancy and Viru recovered to the point at which they were able to relocate to Mungeli for their long-term care.

"I could have done nothing without the support of my cousins and close family. My cousin, Annoo, Antu and Ladoo (Anil Paul) came in shifts along with my uncle Guloo. We had the support of Archana my cousin who was then in Vellore to help. We also has staff from the hospital that were part of the shifts to help Mom and dad, some of them were Sumitra and Nilima and of course Avinash who dad was very fond of. I was still running a hospital. I would go back and forth. I would come to Mungeli and manage things. I was sending emails all around the world. I had meetings and stuff going on, but they were there to help.

At one point, I sent an email with a picture of a sign and it said, 'HDU, No visitors for Nancy Henry.' She was so popular that it was hard to keep people out.

They were so involved with the physio in the ward that when the team advised them to go to rehab for physio and get admitted there, both Mom and dad refused.

We bought wheelchairs in Vellore for them and that was how we got to physio and around the place. Finally I was able to convince them to see rehab. So we loaded wheelchairs and all and took the 30-minute drive.

I had a friend and classmate Ashish Macaden from medical school and he was their doctor for therapy. They would listen to him so he was the one to say that they would shift rehab. We had to wait for an air-conditioned room. Finally, they agreed to move there and stayed about two months. That's

254

when we got our house to be handicap accessible and had the bathroom setup and the ramp for the wheelchairs installed in Mungeli."

- Anil

Despite Anil's insistence, the transition to Mungeli was not without issue. Nancy believed she and Viru were well situated for long-term physical therapy and recovery in Vellore. They did not want to leave until they were actually walking but Anil's friend Ashish convinced them to transition to Mungeli. Anil felt he and his staff could dedicate the resources needed for his parents to restore a resemblance of living to which they were accustomed.

"We went to Vellore in the middle of April and stayed there until July. We came back [to Mungeli] in the first week of July. We didn't want to leave Vellore and I was very upset."

- Nancy

In addition to ensuring the facilities in Mungeli were established for the arrival of Viru and Nancy, staff accommodation for long-term rehabilitation needed to be in place. Anil made sure those involved in the care of his parents were ready to receive them.

"The helper, Nilima, at therapy spent almost a month with them there. Our maid, Sumitra also spent time. A lot of the issues were with mom, so we had to have a female there to help with changing and bathroom. For my Dad, the cousins were there.

Eventually, the doctor had to tell them there was no benefit to them staying in Vellore. They didn't believe that, but they ultimately agreed to leave. Dad's younger brother was there. All four of us were going to fly back here.

I had driven the ambulance back to Mungeli and now had brought dad's car to help with mobility in Vellore. Dad was very worried about how I would get all the stuff in the car. I brought belts and belted four suitcases on top of the car. The wheelchairs were in the back of the car, with the trunk open.

We left at 4 a.m. for Chennai and a friend picked up the car and took it to his home.

We flew from Chennai to Mumbai and had a 45-minute layover in Mumbai, and both of them had to use the toilet. That was my uncle's first flight experience. He stayed with one and I took them one by one to the toilet. The airport staff were not happy and told me to hurry as boarding was getting over. I could only do so much.

Once that was over, we caught our flight and the ambulance picked us up in Raipur with all the family to help.

That is when we started the therapy and work in Mungeli. Mom slowly improved, even though she came here with supports on."

- Anil

"It was a very hard journey for us. We had to go by car up to Madras [Chennai] and then we had to wait. The hardest thing was that it was an entire day of traveling. Finally we got to Raipur and then we had to wait there to do some things. By the time we got to Mungeli it had been very difficult.

Anil put us in the ambulance because there was a place to lie down. There were so many people on there that wanted to go back to Mungeli, there was hardly place for us to sit. I was so worried about Viru. It was a hard journey back."

- Nancy

By the spring of 2013 Nancy was moving around Christian Hospital Mungeli with ease, sometimes with a cane and other times with a walker. Her rehabilitation had progressed well, despite unexpected complications, and she was instructing at the School of Nursing and helping with Viru's physical therapy.

"My surgery was on the vertebrae. They put metal rods and screws in it; you can see it on the x-ray. It had a cage, but I don't know what that meant. It was to stabilize it. You have to live with it because it's there. I was talking to the neurosurgeon and he said, 'It's done its job.'

In a recent x-ray, one of the screws has come out. It doesn't matter because the bone has taken over.

My surgery – the rod – is four years old. I asked the physical therapist about my activity. I'm doing everything: picking up things from the floor, going on bumpy rides.

I said, 'Is that okay?' He said, 'Well, you had the surgery to have a normal life again, so I guess it's okay.' It is wonderful what they can do these days."

- Nancy

Nancy remains incredulous about her recovery. Many had dismissed the possibility of her being able to walk again. She credits therapy, persistence, and "the grace of God" for the incredible progress of her recovery.

"I was in a wheelchair for quite some time. I put on calipers that they used to put on polio victims. My knees would buckle. They didn't know if it would come back or not, but it did, by the grace of God.

I still have a foot drop on the right foot. This one I can only go down on, not up. The nerve that controls the muscle in your foot is irreparable. When I walk a lot, I wear this plastic thing, ankle-foot orthotic. It keeps my foot flexed so it won't drop down when I pick it up. When I'm not wearing it, I have to be careful. I'm very blessed that's the only thing I have left. I also have this tingly feeling in my legs so I don't know if that will go away."

- Nancy

Viru's recovery from the stroke was slow but steady. Although he moved around the hospital complex in Mungeli using an electric scooter, he was able to walk between the scooter and nearby locations by 2013. Rehabilitation efforts include physical therapy to enable motor functions in his hands along with speech pathology.

Though Viru's speech was heavily slurred, he was witty, often telling jokes and stories, looking to Nancy or Anil to interpret what others misunderstood. Viru and Nancy rarely missed the hospital's daily chapel services and enjoyed interacting with hospital staff at these and other gatherings. The Henrys remain a patriarch and matriarch to the broader Christian Mission Hospital community and, according got Johnny Oommen, the consummate example of Christian care providers.

> "If you ask me, I see the hand of God. Just watching them through this accident, their reactions have been very different. Their internal strengths are different and how they handle it is different.
>
> Yet it's all part of their journey. He's going to be 80 soon.[2] It's going to be 50 years since they got married – 1964 to 2014.
>
> It's not a fairy tale. There have been tough times: Ajit's death, Mrs. Henry's accident, Dr. Henry's stroke. Those are probably the toughest personal parts of the journey.
>
> They're hard-working people. They respond to work. Work challenges are a different story, but personal tragedies are a different ballgame altogether. They've come through all of it. I think Mrs. Henry's personal strength has been a big part of how they came through personal tragedies. She's made of very strong stuff.
>
> We, as family, have watched this. We've been part of it. You can share pain to some extent, but some things, you can't take. We've had our own burdens to carry so it's all mixed up in there. I always thought they'd come back [to Bissamcuttack] to live in their old age, but they are well cared for by Anil and Teresa, and that's what matter most."
>
> - Johnny Oommen

At 11:00 a.m. on 21 December 2015, Dr. Virendra Kumar Henry passed away. A series of cardiac events in the days prior to his death combined with health issues following the stroke had taken their toll. Members of the Christian Hospital Mungeli family said goodbye at a 22 December service before Viru's body was transported to Bissamcuttack for the 23 December funeral and burial, surrounded by staff and friends of the hospital and community to which he and Nancy dedicated so many years of service.

---

[1] The city of Madras, the capital of the Indian state of Tamil Nadu, was renamed Chennai in 1996. Common usage among Indians regularly interchanges these names.
[2] Viru turned 80 on 29 June 2013. The interview was conducted 23 May 2013.

Chapter 15: A Heritage of Caregiving

A Legacy of Mission in India

On a macro level – within the Christian Medical Association of India (CMAI), the Christian Medical Colleges at Ludhiana and Vellore, and at the hospitals where they worked and established programs – the Henrys' legacy is known throughout India and around the world. Taking a closer look at each facet of their ministry – to include hospital rehabilitation and growth, educational programming, and investments in their family and individual staff members – it is clear the Henrys' impact has influenced, and will continue to shape, the success of mission hospitals in India.

The following article, "A Legacy of Mission in India," appeared in the Spring 2011 issue of *Still Speaking Magazine*, a periodical of the United Church of Christ's Publishing, Identity and Communications Ministry, and is included here with permission. It was published following the author's initial trip to India in early 2011 to commemorate the 50th anniversary of Nancy's commissioning as a medical missionary nurse.

Definitions of a family legacy in ministry can be elusive, but as with many things – you know it when you see it.

Continuing nearly 50 years of medical ministry in India, Drs. Anil and Teresa Henry are heirs to a lasting mission to provide medical care for the least, the last and the lost of rural India. Along the way they are building community, establishing educational opportunities for young people and for those in medical vocations and, in tangible ways, spreading God's love.

The First Spark

Nancy Lott was commissioned as a medical missionary nurse by the Board of World Mission in 1960. Her home church, Avon Lake (Ohio) UCC, was proud to have one of its own heading to the mission field.

India was a world away, but Nancy went with the congregation's blessing and support.

A few years into her overseas service Nancy met and married Dr. V. K. (Viru) Henry. Though the Board of World Mission didn't have a protocol for continuing support to missionary nurses who married indigenous personnel, Anil says his mother and father stayed true to their mission. Undeterred by organizational policies, Avon Lake UCC continued direct support of Nancy and Viru.

The Henrys ultimately were assigned to the Christian Hospital in Bissamcuttack, in the northeastern Indian state of Orissa. The hospital had suffered years of decline due to the changing landscape of mission support from Europe and the United States. Beginning in 1976, Viru and Nancy restored the hospital into a thriving complex of health care, education and community outreach.

Informally known as "Dadi" and "Dada" to the staff in Bissamcuttack, Nancy and Viru's 30-year ministry there was one of nurturing parenthood. Facilities for patients' families were established so intermediate care could be provided – such as cooking and washing – greatly reducing the hospital's costs while meeting patient needs more directly.

A primary school and nursing school soon followed, founded with the help of local Christian congregations and international partners. As the hospital grew, Nancy saw the next frontier of their ministry as community outreach to the surrounding villages.

Nestled in the deep valleys around Bissamcuttack, villages had been isolated from one another and the medical care that was nearby: so isolated in fact, that as education efforts began, the outreach staff not only had to learn a new spoken dialect that didn't resemble Hindi or Oriya, but they had to establish a written script using Hindi characters.

A network of remote nursing outposts, along with traveling medical teams, began forming relationships in these villages that would lead to what is now a thriving ministry of preventive and emergency care.

While these ministries were developing, one of the Henrys' sons, Anil, was watching and learning alongside his parents. As a young boy he would help his father – observing hospital rounds, pushing gurneys and assisting with surgery. "He even had his own theater dress (i.e., surgical scrubs) in his own size," says Nancy, remembering Anil's declaration at a young age that he wanted to be a doctor.

Perhaps most importantly, Anil saw the energy and passion his mother put into the programs she established in Bissamcuttack. Intentional or not, Anil's youth was a training ground for the future.

Educated at boarding school and then medical school in south India, Anil met Teresa at medical school in Vellore, India. Each went on to complete a post-graduate specialty, Anil in surgery and Teresa in anesthesiology. After working for a time in Bissamcuttack, Anil and Teresa moved to the United States in 2000, where Anil was employed by Baptist Hospital in Nashville.

Anil found his hard work and training had paid off. Living a comfortable suburban life in the United States was a dream come true. He and Teresa lived in a nice house, their children attended good schools, Teresa had the freedom to be home for the children, and Anil had a great paying job at a prestigious hospital outfitted with the best technology medical science could provide.

To Mungeli, With Love

But something was missing. The purpose and drive he had experienced with his parents wasn't present in his day-to-day work. The American life in medicine was lucrative and comfortable but according to Anil there was clearly something lacking.

"It was comfortable to think that I could be doing this for the rest of my life like my other colleagues at Baptist. However, looking at one elderly surgeon who was a friend was an eye opener. He was a General Surgeon who had worked at Baptist for about 35 years. He was very hard working. At one time I remember he had a hairline fracture of his forearm and was in a plaster. He still came to work and attempted to work. The staff told him to take rest and he would keep saying that he could not afford it.

Meanwhile, he was maintaining his mansion in the best part of town, his boat docked in the lake. Then one day he was retiring and we had a big party.

Two weeks later, someone came into the operating room looking for him. People turned around and asked, 'Who are you looking for?' That was it, there was another surgeon doing exactly the same thing that this person did for all these years. Meanwhile, my retired friend was looking at downsizing his house, as he could not afford to live and maintain the mansion. He also did not feel he could keep the boat much longer. This hit me the hardest and I realized that his life was getting over and what had he done. What had he left behind in his life that would show his years of hard work?"

Anil remembers. "I had definitely seen what my parents had done; it was difficult and a challenge. After about four years of staying in one place and building up finances, we decided there was more to life."

Teresa agrees. "We both thought we were not doing all we could in the United States," she says. "We thought we could do much more by serving the people of India rather than staying abroad."

Together they decided to inquire if returning to India as medical missionaries would be possible. Contacts with Global Ministries, the combined international mission organization of the United Church of Christ and Christian Church (Disciples of Christ), led to a request for the Henrys to administer a lagging ministry at Christian Hospital Mungeli, a hospital started in 1896 but at the verge of closure for the past 40 years and being supported by the Rambo Committee who were clearly fatigued at supporting a losing battle.

"I first told dad (Viru) that the Board had asked me to go to Mungeli. I had no idea about the place and so asked dad to look at the facility." Anil says. "He called me back and said, 'You wanted a challenge, you got it.'" That was it, and we decided to take up the job.

Anil and Teresa settled their affairs in the United States and were commissioned as Global Ministries missionaries by the Alabama-Tennessee Association of the UCC with a service at Fisk and then later on again at Avon Lake UCC, the same church from which his mother was commissioned and had supported his parents.

The Henrys arrived in Mungeli during the monsoon season of 2003. The facility and the director's home had fallen into disrepair. It took about three months for the house to be repaired. During this time, Terry and the kids went to stay with Nancy and Viru, and Ankita was prepared and packed up to go to Kodaikanal International School (boarding school) to join the fifth grade.

There were only four patients in one fourth of the wards that were in use. There was even a dead monkey on the upper floor, and it had been abandoned for years.

Anil and Teresa began restoring sections of the hospital. The main wards were reorganized and cleaned. The operating theater was remodeled. An intensive care unit and recovery room were established. Roofs were repaired, doors installed, walkways paved.

The twins joined the first grade at the Rambo Memorial English Medium School, which had 80 children in it and was struggling to stay open. At that time, they were the only two children who exclusively knew English. By 2004 the Church of North India, who was running the school, asked Anil to take it over or they would close it due to lack of funds.
The school was taken over by the hospital with the vision to bring about change in this "backward" part of Chhattisgarh through low cost English Medium Education, mainly focusing on the village children. Today this school educates almost 1000 students K-12. About 650 of these being village children, bussed from all the surrounding 30 kilometers (22 miles) around Mungeli. It was work fit for a general contractor, but a surgeon and an anesthesiologist — along with their dedicated staff — began to turn the tide on years of decay.

In the 12 years since the Henrys arrived, the Christian Hospital in Mungeli has seen a complete transformation that continues to evolve.

Facilities were built patients' families staying at the hospital to care for their ailing or recovering relatives. And more building projects are underway – a burn care unit, a cancer center, a nursing school, staff apartments, more housing for nurses, and a new school facility to replace the aging buildings at that site.

A Mission Within a Mission

Boundless energy, creativity, administration and an entrepreneurial spirit may not be prerequisites for success in missionary service, but these traits and more exist in Anil and Teresa.

"My feeling is that I should be the initiator of projects and then we should find people to take up responsibility," says Anil. "We do so well because we do one project – then we open it up and off you go, on to the next one.

"I have critics on my staff who tell me, 'Sir it's not possible.' I tell them, yes it is, and we start. That's the way we do it, one project after another."

Within the community, the Henrys are known beyond their work with the hospital and school. Wandering the shops of Mungeli, American and European visitors from the hospital are easily identified and the townspeople are friendly and quick to engage in conversation.

"My son, he is in third grade at Rambo English School," says a local bicycle shop owner. "Dr. Henry saved my life," a man announces at another shop, lifting his shirt to reveal a foot-long scar across his abdomen. "They are good people, good Christians," says the Jainist patriarch of a fine clothier in Mungeli.

A reputation for quality medical care, a growing school, and exemplary character found at the Christian Hospital in Mungeli are all part of the legacy of ministry. Whether at the daily chapel service attended by staff of the hospital and school, on morning hospital rounds where each patient receives individual attention, in the administration of the hospital complex and its many new projects, in the multiple surgeries performed each day, or extending hospitality to visiting guests and volunteers – Anil and Teresa exemplify commitment to ministry in the face of undeniable challenges.

Anil's parents, Nancy and Viry, after a serious train accident and stroke, respectively, are now living with Anil and Teresa, taking advantage of the physical therapy facilities at the Christian Hospital in Mungeli as they recover. Seeing what Anil and Teresa have accomplished in such a short time, Nancy says, "There are similarities to what we achieved in Bissamcuttack, but the situation here is different – they began with nothing."

Anil is wistful about how God has provided for the mission. "Resources are the least challenging part of this job," he says, noting the struggle to retain trained doctors, nurses and technicians in Mungeli. "We've been here eight years – the hardest thing is that we struggle to get human resources. If we had them, we'd be flying much faster."

Tenacity Transferred

In further interviews, Anil detailed his and Teresa's transition to Mungeli from the United States. The desire to contribute to Indian society, and serve as medical mission personnel, was inherited trait from their parents. Not only were they up to addressing the challenges of the struggling mission hospital in Mungeli, but they were encouraged by the model set out by Viru and Nancy in their work in Bissamcuttack.

> "I was used to working many hours and in Nashville I worked a lot less.
>
> By American standards, I worked too hard. We used to travel all over the place – we'd drive somewhere and I'd leave the kids and Terri at someone's place, then fly back to Nashville, then fly back the next weekend to pick them up and drive back. They got to see a lot of the States that way.
>
> Terri's sister was in Des Moines [Iowa]; their home was and still is our home in the States. The children all grew up together and were very attached. Many a times, we would take all four boys out shopping and people thought that we had quadruplets as all four boys had their ages all within two years. Ankita was the big sister for all of them but many a

267

times had her hands full. We then got ourselves settled in Nashville, about 110 miles from my aunt and uncle [Nancy's brother and sister-in-law.] We used to visit Herb and Peg every month and a half or so at Uplands in Pleasant Hill.

But the work I was doing was monotonous and I realized I would hate doing it for the rest of my life. Though it was good money.

That's when I got in touch with Global Ministries and told them I was interested in taking a position.

What changed my thought completely was this senior consultant who had worked at Baptist for many years and was working away even after he broke his arm. I asked why he didn't just take a break and he said he couldn't afford it. It was hard to believe he couldn't afford it. He worked all the way through a broken arm. He joined in, worked as hard as anything. His thought was that he needed to have a good house and a second house on the beach, with a boat. One day he had to retire and he retired. That was it. They couldn't maintain the boat or the house. He realized he hadn't done much for himself for all those years. That's the cycle of life there – I didn't see any meaning of life in that."

- Anil

Global Ministries initially asked Anil and Teresa to go to Tilda to help revive the facilities and the faltering nursing school. But the doctor in charge of Tilda at the time did not want to move out. Anil had made contact with Raleigh and Joanne Birch, long-time supporters of Global Ministries and the Rambo Committee – the U.S.-based support agency of Christian Hospital Mungeli – who told Global Ministries' leaders, ""He has to go to Mungali because we've been sending money and they have no leader there."[1]

With commissioning services at Brookmeade UCC in Nashville, Tennessee and Avon Lake (Ohio) UCC – the church that had commissioned Nancy in 1960 – the Henrys were ready for their return to India and the challenge awaiting them at Christian Hospital Mungeli.

"Avon Lake said they wanted to honor us as well, so we had a second ceremony with them. That was when our ties with Avon Lake grew.

We packed up our things and came to Mungeli, stopping in Europe for about a month of traveling. When we arrived here it was a shock.

I had never seen the hospital. When they asked if we would go to Mungeli, I called my father on the phone. He said he'd been there 40 years ago. At that time, it was a famous place but he thought it was really in trouble. He said he would take a drive by Mungeli and tell me what it was like.

After his visit he told me, 'You wanted a challenge. Well, you've got one.'

There was no way to explain what this place was. It was a mess. There was nothing here. It was like a graveyard. W

But we never looked back, just forward. I had to go to Bilaspur for internet and send all my communication through a dial up connection. The electricity over here runs on 240 volts, but the actual supply was only 90 volts, so you could physically see the filament of a bulb as there was not enough voltage to actually have any light. They built a substation around the second year we were here.

We had a microwave that wouldn't work on the voltage. Air conditioner, forget it. The operating room had two or three air conditioners but they could never run. Most of our machinery couldn't run. It was disheartening.

One of the first things we bought in 2004 was a generator. They had a generator that is usually used in the fields to pump water. That is what they used to run the lights on the operating room.

If the lights went off, they would push the jeep and go out with a 5-liter can to buy diesel to pour into generators so they could operate. When we arrived, the hospital could not afford to keep diesel on hand. The place ran hand-to-mouth."

- Anil

Bissamcuttack's Education Legacy

Viru's belief that education would do more to alleviate poverty and improve the health of rural people in India was displayed in the educational initiatives instituted in Bissamcuttack and other mission hospital locations. In addition to nursing and vocational training schools, Johnny Oommen detailed the primary and secondary schools established to fulfill Viru's convictions.

"This commitment finds its expression in the service of about 1500 children at present (2011), through the following:

- The New Life English Medium School in Bissamcuttack – the only English Medium ICSE School in the block, serving the children of Bissamcuttack and Muniguda since 1986.
- The Christian Hospital Bissamcuttack Creche – providing preschool education and daycare for toddlers in Bissamcuttack since 1988.
- The Mitra Residential School in Kachapaju – a Kuvi-cum-Oriya Medium School run in partnership with an association of 16 hill-tribe villages since 1998.
- The Mitra AQTE [Add Quality to Education] program – helping parents in 25 villages Add Quality to the Education their children get in the local government primary school through support of volunteer teachers since 2005.
- The Mitra ECCNE program – for preschool children in six villages.

The flagship in the education mission of Christian Hospital Bissamcuttack is the New Life English Medium School. It has broken new ground, set standards and changes the lives for 25 years now [as of 2011.] What would life have been like for the children of Bissamcuttack without NLEM? And after many years of hard work and sacrifice, the fruits of NLEM are beginning to show. The first few batches have produced some engineers, a doctor, nurses, laboratory technicians, teachers, businessmen and good citizens for our country.

We can only thank God for those visionaries who saw what others couldn't see way back in 1986. They put their hand to the plough and did not turn back. Others followed. And together, we as a community, have done something we can be justifiably proud of; something for which future generations will remember us with gratitude as a generation that made the difference in the history of Bissamcuttack."[2]

- Johnny Oommen

Anil and Teresa have continued this tradition as well, reinvigorating the Rambo Memorial English Medium School associated with Christian Hospital Mungeli and starting a residential school of nursing as well as the Springer Community College for drop out school children.[3]

Bissamcuttack Staff Memory : Prabhasini Margaret Khosla

Prabhasini Margaret Khosla came to Bissamcuttack in 1996 as a candidate for the General Nurse Midwife (GNM) program. She had passed the 12th grade exams and was qualified for entry to the program even though her English language skills were poor. Viru and Nancy saw great promise in Prabhasini during the interview process and she has remained a dedicated nurse at Christian Hospital Bissamcuttack since her graduation, now also teaching sociology in the School of Nursing.

Her emotional testimony speaks to the tenderness she felt from the Henrys, and the love she shares for them.[4]

"Here are some thoughts and feelings regarding Dr. and Mrs. Henry.

The first thing is, I'm not a worthy person to talk about them. It is because of their love and care that I am still here and able to come up and sit in front of them when they visit.

Their name itself is so high. They are my second parents. Our worldly parents have given us birth and guided us in some way. The Henrys professionally guided us.

I was unable to say a full sentence in English when I arrived here. In my interview, Dr. Henry said, 'Tell me why you came here – in English.' I was so afraid.

After that, they encouraged us to speak in English and to do our further studies. During that time, my father was earning about 1,000 to 2,000 rupees ($22 to $44 USD in 2006) in a month. He was an ordinary pastor at that time.

The hospital gave us so much support and an opportunity to get this education at low cost. I was able to do my BSc. Nursing because of this institution and because of this husband and wife. They encouraged us to do these things and to come back and serve in this institution.

October 1 was our joining day. They would call all the first years in front of the chapel to introduce ourselves. Dr. Henry would tease us and he would say things in an opposite way. If we were not listening, we would say the wrong thing. Even after the Capping Ceremony, he would joke, 'In my uniform, I will sleep. In my cap, I will keep money.'

Even for the guesthouse and our hostel, Sister Henry's garden was so beautiful that the town people would come to take photos. I didn't have a camera but it is still in my mind. By thinking of it, we can delight. She was planting trees and guiding others to do it.

The second thing I can say is that they are both the king and queen of Bissamcuttack. I've never seen any king and queen. I've only seen pictures. In reality, they both were king and queen of this place.

About Dr. Henry, his name is and of itself. There's no need to explain about him. His name says that everything about him is great. Everybody knows about him, even in remote villages, because of his beautiful care. He was a famous surgeon in this region. Everybody respects him. We have fear and respect together. Nobody used to come and talk like he did. He was a very good leader.

He used to come in the front after morning prayers and guide us. Most of the time, he used his nature of humor to introduce, welcome, and give farewell to everybody, just like a family.

When we came here, everyone was saying, 'CHB family. CHB family. Christian Hospital Bissamcuttack is a family.' To me, it really felt like a family. Most of the time, I used to forget my own family members because we were getting that family here, love and care.

During Christmas time, when everybody was going on vacations, we were staying at the hostel. Dr. and Mrs. Henry used to invite us to their house for lunch. It was so happy, this feeling. We felt like such negligible people, but we were special in their eyes.

Sir, about him, you might have heard from everybody, he's a very good singer. He's a very good comforter. He used to sing two songs I like very much: 'Thy Kingdom Come' (an Oriya song) and Mahua pedu tole (the famous Mahua song.) Every special occasion, all the staff used to sing these two songs together.

There were so many times we would get to spend time with Dr Henry. On Founder's Day, September 5, the whole staff, we used to play games.

There's a picnic and Sir is the leading person to make us play. He would teach us tug-of-war and a ball game, and an Indian game with a handkerchief in the middle. I have heard that he used to go hunting.

During Christmas, he was always Santa Claus. He used to make us all laugh.

On his birthday, June 29, and Sister Henry's birthday, January 27, they used to send sweets to the hostel for us. We were so delighted that they were thinking of us.
As a doctor, we would see Sir go and sit with patients and touch them. The patients then heal very well. He was so great. By touching his hand, patients would think they were good inside.

All the collectors [government officials] knew him well like a friend. He was caring in nature. He would visit staff family members, especially those who are low-income people. He would even go to the marketplace and find the cost of food. He would know the price is going up and he would quietly increase the staff salaries. That's his good quality. He would collect the information and increase the staff benefits.

Sister Henry was a good administrator. She was like five people in one. In her personal life, she took good care of her family. Dr. Henry was so dependent on her. She used to take care of the hospital side, maintenance side, and the school. Now, four people are taking care of this one person's job. The hospital was busy at that time. She was taking so much workload. She was my teacher also. I have learned a lot. She has respect for every culture.

On my first visit, she was speaking pure Oriya to us and I was so impressed that a foreigner could speak our language. In any function, I've seen her in Indian dress, never jeans. She respects this culture. Sister Henry told us a story of her going to different marriages and seeing the bride cry. She asked Dr. Henry and he said that is the culture. She joked with him, 'You should have told me before we got married so I could cry like a good Indian bride.'

Before I came here, I heard that Sister Henry is very strict. I saw her strictness, but it is because she wants to take care of everything. We were afraid to make mistakes because we'd have to face her. She was so caring for the patients. She was so perfect and that's why we were afraid. She was punctual to come to duty, but not to go back home. She was a very busy person.

She used to get newspapers and talk about culture. For every example, she would use these. She used to take us to the movies. She took us to a Hindi movie about when the husband's status is lower than the wife's status.

I am the sociology teacher now so I am showing the students these movies so they can understand.

When she was teaching us ward management, she used equipment and problem-solving examples in the hospital. She guided us nicely. Moments like that have formed us.

During my third year, she used to tell us, 'Before going to provide patient care, you should study and make sure your equipment in is order.' She used to encourage us to think one step ahead. She taught us problem-solving methods. It is very useful for personal and professional life.

When I was a third year nursing student, four of us had an epidemic of chicken pox and were admitted to this hospital. Nobody was allowed to come because we were isolated. Sister Henry used to come with sweets and a sweet smile and visit us.

Sister had a good attitude. She knows everyone by name and she called everybody by name, even when we were first year students. She remembers us by name now. I felt delighted that she knew my name and thought I should know everyone by their name.

Because of their love, I am telling this thing. I am not worthy to speak of their name. My heart fills with pleasure and tears come. It is very difficult to see them in this situation [post-accident and stroke.] They need support and care because they supported everyone with care.

At the time of Sister Henry's accident, Sir had a stroke. I can think of them separately. I ask God that if he would take their soul, that he would take both their souls together, not individually. They are separate bodies, but mind and soul are one. I would ask God to use them until their last breath and take them together."

- Prabhasini

Reflecting on the Henrys' transition from Bissamcuttack to Tilda after their retirement, Prabhasini still remembers the sadness and loss felt by the absence of the Henrys' presence. A loss only accentuated following Nancy's accident and Viru's stroke.

"It was so difficult for us to let them go. Sir definitely thought about the new generation to grow up and take care of this institution.
The new leadership is very good but we were still asking for our parents' presence. We were so sad. When Sister underwent her surgery, we thought we were losing our parents. When we got the news that they were all right, we thought of our parents. They visited us after their recovery, and seeing them is a blessing.

I'm on the staff now, and we're organizing retreats. We've taken a three-year project and we're doing a nurse education in this area, teaching low-education girls. Also, for better education, we are teaching the tutors and service site staff in the nursing education resource unit.

I am the coordinator of Roshni [light/illumination] program with the girls from the villages. We have a one-week program teaching conception, menstrual hygiene, sexual health, family health, and pregnancy care and delivery and nutrition. This time, we thought we were missing out on HIV/AIDS so we included this in the last program.

We're getting [HIV infected] patients, so we're teaching prevention and causes. In the outpatient department, they are testing HIV, STD, blood grouping, hepatitis, and things that can transmit to the baby."

- Prabhasini

While Viru shunned the term "missionary," and Nancy preferred to let her life be a witness to her Christian faith, Prabhasini says the influence of the Henrys' lives were testimony enough to their purpose and calling.

"There's no need to say that we are Christians. The Henrys' activity was such that they definitely feared God. Sister Henry used to guide us spiritually and Sir would invite us to join the prayer. It shows through their lives, and how they are dedicated.

[You can see it in] their daughter, Anjali. She is a good singer. She was treating psychiatric patients. When I heard that she was a psychologist in the U.S., I had no idea about this thing. I was of a low educational level. I passed with 31 percent in 12th grade. I had no idea that even blind people could do this.

I said, 'God has given me everything, but I'm not able to do what this honorable person can do better than us.' It was inspiring us to help others and also to help us to grow. Their family was telling us that we have to grow."

- Prabhasini

The Legacy Condensed : Johnny Oommen

The accomplishments, and the heritage Viru and Nancy created, are unprecedented in the history of mission hospital, community building, education, and outreach initiatives, says Johnny Oommen. His assessment is the measure of their impact on medical mission and the provision of care from Christian institutions would not have the excellence, impact, or reach it does today without the Henrys.

"It's not something that could have been planned. The story is not something that could have been imaginable. You can't separate out the story of the Henrys and the story of

277

Bissamcuttack. If you put all those strands together, it's such an improbable story. I think what comes through, for me, is the grace of God. Nobody else could have thought up such a story.

They were totally different strands: Dr. Henry, born in a family in Bilaspur. Mrs. Henry, who took a leap of faith to come to India as a missionary nurse. What has happened out of this is amazing.

God works using people. When I step back and look at these stories, what strikes me is a phenomenal picture. It's amazing that this happened and how it worked. The hospital, their work, and how Anil came back at the right time, just when they needed him. All this put together is a story being played by a hand way above us.

Our own lives have also been part of that strand. We've been very lucky to be part of this. Looking back, we've had a good time. We've enjoyed ourselves.

Much has happened and much more has happened than what we've done. If I look at what Dr. Henry and Mrs. Henry did, it's a lot, but what has happened is much more than that. It's as if two plus two has become five, six, or seven. Those little things have added up. God's wisdom has been very much present here, sometimes in spite of us.

Without half these chapters, it would still be a story, but there's so much more to the story. Mrs. Henry, in all her humility, would never accept that the story is bigger than that. Dr. Henry would never agree either.

But when I step back and I see the impact of their lives in this place, it's much more."

- Johnny Oommen

[1] Joanne and Raleigh Birch died within days of one another, 26 August and 30 August 2012 respectively. Described as "devoted supporters of the Christian Hospital in Mungeli, India," they continued the mission of the hospital to "provide sight to the curable blind," through over 50 years of involvement with the Rambo Committee.

[2] Oommen, Johnny. *New Life English Medium School 25th Anniversary Program (BUDS)*, 2011.

[3] More information on Christian Hospital and the Rambo Memorial English Medium School can be found at http://chmungeli.org/.

[4] Prabhasini Margaret Khosla's 55-minute interview, recorded 28 May 2013 in Bissamcuttack, is edited for length and clarity.

Postlude: Saying Goodbye to Dr. V. K. Henry

by Dr. Johnny Oommen

Dr. V. K. Henry – Viru, Dada, Boss, Sir – passed away at his son Anil's home in Mungeli, Chattisgarh on 21 December 2016. He was 82.

The last few months had seen him weaken after repeated strokes and restricted mobility. The end came quietly. As word went out, there were hundreds of people calling up to express their condolences and respect for him.

The family had a difficult decision to take. Should he be buried in Mungeli where he had lived for a few years now, or Bhilai where Ajit had been buried, or Bissamcuttack where he had lived and worked for the longest period? It was finally decided to go with what he had wanted – Bissamcuttack as his last resting place.

The family gathered in Christian Hospital Mungeli for a Thanksgiving Service with the staff and students there. They then travelled with his body in a motorcade to Christian Hospital Bissamcuttack. Word had spread through the region of his passing. By the time the body arrived around midnight, there was crowd of friends and fans gathered at the Hospital Chapel. There were large printed banners all over the place put up by people who had benefited so much from his work and love.

The people of Bissamcuttack shut down the whole town as a sign of respect for Dr. Henry who had put its name on the map through his selfless work and service. All shops were closed. Traffic came to a standstill as an open van with his body was taken on a final drive around the town. The first stop was at the Maa Markama College, which he had helped establish and run as Founder President. Then through the town, with people laying flowers on the body every few meters. The town has never seen such a spontaneous outpouring of love and affection.

Over a thousand people gathered for the final service at the Hospital Chapel where the body was laid for public viewing. A grateful people bid a tearful goodbye as he was buried in the local church cemetery.

It had been 17 years since Dr. Henry handed over leadership of Christian Hospital Bissamcuttack, and 11 years since Viru and Nancy left for Tilda. Such was the charisma and magnetism of the man that all these years later a whole town would stop and stand still to say goodbye to him. They said thank you to Nancy, Anil, and the family for bringing him home, and giving them the privilege of organizing the funeral.

Bissamcuttack, Odisha, India
August 2016

Appendix: A Brief History of Christian Mission in India

An exhaustive history of Christianity in India would be a long and detailed volume that won't be presented here, especially as some very good ones have already been written.[1] Still, it is important to understand the context of Christianity and other religions as a setting for the work of Dr. Viru and Nancy Henry in the Christian mission hospitals of India. The purpose here is not to rewrite this history, but rather to look at the cultural and religious environment in which Christianity spread throughout India, especially as it relates to missionary activity in the 19th and 20th century. The Christian mission hospitals that exist today, and the mission drive that led to their formation, are possible because of many things: this long and complex history, the growth of Indian Christianity, and the mission influences that originated primarily in Europe and America.

Parts of that story have come under scrutiny as Western interference, or as an all-too complicit sibling of colonialism. There can be no doubt that some of those who came to India as missionaries were motivated by a sense of Western superiority and its unfortunately subtle, and sometimes not so subtle, implication of Indian backwardness. But a fairer reading of this history is seen in the lives of men and women who felt compelled to know and live and work alongside the Indian people. Many Western missionaries were motivated by their faith and often propelled by an evangelical zeal to gain conversions to Christianity. Yet missionaries who were exclusively dedicated to the purpose of conversion are not well represented in the literature of the past two centuries. Rather, mission activity focused on the helping professions, health care, economic development, agriculture, and education are the norm rather than the exception. Within this context churches were established, ministries of outreach occurred, and conversions surely happened.

Leading up to what we now know as Western Christian mission activity in the colonial era is the development of an indigenous Christianity that began shortly after the time of Jesus of Nazareth. Jesus' disciple Thomas, of "doubting Thomas" fame, is said to have arrived on the western shores of India in 52 CE. The churches he established, and subsequent waves and movements of Christian expansion within India, were the foundation of a distinctly Indian Christianity. It can also be said that Indian Christianity has been a cultural influence that produced an evolution within other Indian religions.

As with most pre-modern histories, the early history of Christianity in India and the development of religion in India in general, is best understood as part factual history, part embellishment, and part legend. Although historians who are authorities on religion in India may argue over the nature of these stories and legends, they are nonetheless helpful as markers to the understanding of religion in India. The truth of this history, which includes the stories and legends, exists in the events they commemorate. The proverbial saying of storytellers around the world, "I'm going to tell you a true story, and some of it actually happened," applies here as it does to any second-hand retelling of events.

Still, it is clear that Christianity came to India shortly after the end of Jesus' earthly ministry. The most common source cited is the Acts of Thomas that tells the story of the somewhat reluctant apostle's selection as the evangelist for the Indian subcontinent. Arriving in 52 CE, this story tells us that Thomas established seven churches in the southern portions of India – Kerala and Tamil Nadu. Early references indicate Thomas found success in spreading Christianity among the Malabar (Cochin) Jews who found refuge in India following the destruction of the First Temple in 587 BCE. Other Jews may have also arrived into this community after the destruction of Jerusalem by the Romans in 70 CE.

The period from the 12th to the 19th century can be characterized as a time of religious expansion on many fronts. Hinduism maintained its position as the dominant religion of culture and government, Islam gained its foothold in commerce and trade and Christianity held its place as the religion of education and social mobility. Many argue the spread of Christianity is in part due to its appeal to people from the lower castes and to those considered outsiders. Although many prominent Brahmans converted, historic records show the majority of conversions to Christianity were from the Dalit caste. Dalits, and the largely animistic outcasts and untouchables, saw in the Christian message a promise of freedom from the hierarchy of caste. In some ways this liberation made sense – at least within the Christian community. A Dalit could rise to the status of pastor or deacon through education and training, though in Hindu culture they would continue to be considered Dalit. In contrast, those from higher castes like the Brahmans would often lose societal standing upon conversion to Christianity, even if he or she assumed a leadership role in the Christian community.

Although a true partitioning of mission areas did not occur in India as happened in Africa and Southeast Asia, particular groups gravitated toward and were given entrée into specific areas. Far southern India remained largely Roman Catholic, as did the far east coast. Western India, in large part due to proximity, remained aligned with the Syrian Orthodox church. What is considered north India – from Delhi to the south and east – came under the influence of Northern European, and later North American, missionaries.

This ecclesial region, which became the Church of North India (CNI), was host to many waves of missionaries from Holland, Scandinavia and the United States during the mid 18th until the late 20th century. All the while this region held to its original inspiration from the St. Thomas Christian community. Ultimately, the foreign mission influences – American congregational, Dutch and Scandinavian Protestant – based their efforts in the north and east. The conglomeration of Dutch, German, Scandinavian and American Protestants that found their way into the regions of the north was the major source of western missionary activity in this period.

A united Church of North India had been proposed as early as 1929 and was ultimately established in 1970 through the merger of the Church of India, Pakistan, Burma and Ceylon (Anglican); the Church of Northern India (Congregationalist and Presbyterian); the Baptist Churches of Northern India (British Baptists); the Church of the Brethren in India; the Methodist Church (British and Australian Conferences) and the Disciples of Christ denominations. Geographically the CNI covers the whole of India except for the four southern states, and accounts for nearly two-thirds of the entire country. It is spread over varied areas, ranging from hills to deserts and to coastal regions, covering both rural as well as urban populations. A 2009 census of the Church of North India by the

World Council of Churches showed its membership at 1.5 million persons in 4,500 congregations served by 2,000 ministers. Many Christian institutions are partnered with the CNI including 65 hospitals, nine nursing schools, approximately 250 primary and secondary schools and three technical schools.

Important to the story that follows is the location of Dutch, German and American missionaries in the late 19th and early 20th centuries in the states of Madhya Pradesh and Odisha. The Rev. Oscar Lohr was the first American missionary to be sent to India (BY THE UCC) and specially to this region.[2] In 1867 he sailed from Boston to Mumbai, then called Bombay. Lohr met other missionaries who convinced him to work with people in the Sadh sect of Hinduism in central India. Ascetic in practice, adherents call themselves the Satmani and worship of a monotheistic God named Satnam, a Sanskrit-derived word meaning "the true name."

Although the state of Madhya Pradesh was divided into two states in 2000 to include both Madhya Pradesh in the north and Chhattisgarh to the southeast, the Christian community maintained a strong presence through the region as it expanded its reach, establishing schools, churches, and more hospitals in the region.

It is into this context that Nancy Henry – a missionary nurse from Ohio in the United States serving with the United Church Board for World Mission (UCBWM) – and Dr. Viru Henry – who hailed from Bilaspur and whose grandparents had converted to Christianity – enter the story that would transform the expression of Christian mission hospitals in the Church of North India.

There are four mission hospitals in the Chattisgarh-Odisha region that have been greatly influenced by Nancy and V. K. Henry. It may be useful to add some background information on each of them:

A. Evangelical Hospital, Khariar, Odisha

    The hospital was founded by the late Rev. Herman and Marie Feierabend, a trained nurse, on 2 January 1930 on behalf of the American Evangelical Mission of the Evangelical Synod of North America (now the United Church of Christ.) The hospital had to fight serious problems in staffing, due to the remoteness of the place. It was initially run as a dispensary, but developed into a hospital in 1930. Over the last eight decades, it has grown to be a 150-bed hospital with multiple specialties. It is part of the healing ministry of the Church of North India.

B. Evangelical Mission Hospital, Tilda, Chattisgarh

Dr. Milton C. Lang established the first mission hospital and medical station in 1927 on a 12.5-acre plot near the railway station in Tilda, in the state of Madhya Pradesh. Lang's house was built first so he could oversee the hospital's construction and he provided basic medical needs from his home, using the garage as a dispensary.

Dr. Lang soon became ill and had to leave India in 1928, although the Tilda hospital construction was not yet complete. Another American missionary, Dr. Elmer Whitcomb, arrived with his family in 1929 to resume the oversight of the Tilda hospital. An accomplished physician and surgeon, he had completed a course at the Tropical School of Medicine in London. Prior to his departure for India, he and Dr. Lang met in Switzerland to discuss the plans for Tilda.

Whitcomb served in Tilda until 1953, assisted by Nursing Superintendent and nursing school founder Sister Minnie Gadt, from the Deaconess Hospital in St. Louis, Missouri, who also arrived in 1929. Dr. Lawrence Jiwanmall joined the Tilda staff in 1934 and would serve with Whitcomb and Gadt for 10 years before leaving the mission hospital for private practice.

C. Christian Hospital, Bissamcuttack, Odisha

Lutheran Missionaries from Breklum in northern Germany came to Orissa in 1882, and established a mission station in Bissamcuttack in 1905. Their work grew into what is now the Jeypore Evangelical Lutheran Church, Odisha. The hospital was started by Dr. Lis Madsen from Denmark in 1954. Dr. V. K. Henry and Mrs. Nancy Henry built it into a viable, flourishing, multi-sevctoral institution between 1976 and 1998. Today, it is a 200-bed hospital with work in patient care, community health, nursing education and schools for children.

D. Christian Hospital, Mungeli :

Christian Hospital Mungeli was founded in 1897 by the Foreign Christian Missionary Society's Rev. E.M. Gordon and Dr. Anna Gordon. Mr. G.W. Jackson opened the Mission Station at Mungeli in 1887.

In 1925, Dr. Victor Rambo took charge of Christian Hospital Mungeli. Under Dr. Rambo's leadership, CHM became known for its work in saving and restoring sight. Because many of the blind could not travel to the hospital, Dr. Rambo pioneered the use of "eye camps," where surgical teams from the hospital travelled to villages to perform cataract removal and other eye surgeries.

Today, Christian Hospital Mungeli is a busy 120-bedded hospital led by Drs. Anil and Teresa Henry.

---

[1] The two-volume "A History of Christianity in India" by Stephen Neill; vol. 1, 1984, "The Beginnings to 1707" and vol. 2, 1985, "1707 to 1858", Cambridge University Press; is used as the source for much of the historic discourse that follows. Another valuable source of information is "East of the Euphrates: Early Christianity in Asia" by T.V. Philip, 1998, CSS & ISPCK, India. Original documents are cited where available.
[2] Hilsley, Brian C., "Miss Marion Conacher, MBE – Wardie Mission Partner 1981-1993", http://www.wardie.org.uk/wp-content/uploads/2014/03/TILDA.pdf

"To God be the glory!"

- Nancy Henry, August 2016

Made in the USA
Middletown, DE
19 October 2016